A DICTIONARY

of

MUSICAL THEMES

A DICTIONARY

of

MUSICAL THEMES

by

HAROLD BARLOW and SAM MORGENSTERN

Introduction by

JOHN ERSKINE

CROWN PUBLISHERS, INC. NEW YORK

CONTENTS

INTRODUCTION

By John Erskine

This dictionary of musical themes, by Harold Barlow and Sam Morgenstern, supplies an aid which students of music have long needed. When the authors showed me the plan of it a year ago, or somewhat earlier, I applauded at once, and agreed to write a word of preface. We should now have something in musical literature to parallel Bartlett's *Familiar Quotations*. Whenever a musical theme haunted us, but refused to identify itself no matter how much we scraped our memory, all we should have to do would be to look up the tune in Barlow and Morgenstern, where those ingenious dictionary-makers would assemble some ten thousand musical themes, with a notation-index or theme-finder, to locate the name of the composition from which the haunting fragment came, and the name of the composer.

After a brief but exciting conversation, Mr. Barlow and Mr. Morgenstern went off with my promise of a preface, as it were, in their pocket, leaving me very thoughtful — and inclined to become more thoughtful with each passing hour. I knew there had already been attempts to index music, and I was fairly familiar with the difficulties which had in the past tripped up bold experimenters. A dictionary such as Bartlett's can classify quotations according to the subject with which they deal, and can arrange them in the usual index method by the letter-order of the opening words. But no method has been hit on to index musical sounds, nor the variations in pitch by which a theme is articulated. No method, that is, which permits the musical material of a theme to remain strictly musical.

I understood what Mr. Barlow and Mr. Morgenstern would try to do; since letters can easily be indexed, and musical notes cannot be, they would try to translate the notes into letters. After much thought I feared this would prove a task far beyond even their enthusiasm, and the result might be less useful than they hoped. But they put an end to my doubts by bringing to my study one day a section of the theme index, and challenging me to give them a theme they couldn't speedily locate. My conversion was prompt. I am glad to record here my confidence in the theory of this book, and my admiration for the manner in which the theory has been worked out.

As the authors are more than ready to admit, the ten thousand themes, more or less, which can be identified quickly and easily with the help of this book, do not encompass the entire literature of music, but they do include practically all the themes which can be found in compositions that have been recorded. It is hardly likely that a music student will be haunted by a theme from a composition not yet considered worthy of recording.

The authors believe, and I agree with them, that their dictionary of musical themes will be useful to the trained musician, even to the professional performer, who is more likely than the beginner or the amateur to have a firm grasp of the musical material which has gone into well-known masterpieces.

The book is divided into two parts. The first part contains ten thousand or more musical themes arranged by composers. The second part is the notation-index or theme-finder. If we consult the dictionary in order to locate a theme, we shall begin with the second part of the book, and conclude with the passage in the first part which gives the answer we have been looking for. But there are many occasions when a musician needs to refresh his memory about the themes in a given composition. Though he knows the name of the composition and of the composer, he may need to remind himself of the theme in the first movement, or the second, or the third. Of course he can go to his music shelves and consult his copy of the complete work. That is, if his music shelves are large enough to contain the scores of ten thousand sonatas or symphonies. I suspect that the convenience of the Barlow-Morgenstern dictionary will soon be recognized by serious students of musical literature.

How enormous that body of literature is, and how rapidly it increases, we sometimes forget. It is well within the truth to say that no pianist, no violinist, and no singer, pretends to have in his repertoire all the important compositions for piano, violin, or voice. Each musician has probably read over hundreds of pieces he would gladly include in his repertoire if life were long enough. A pianist who keeps in his repertoire, and in condition for performance, a thousand pieces of respectable length and difficulty, is an unusual artist. If his repertoire were three times as large, he would still be something of a specialist; the piano repertory has long since grown beyond human capacity to master completely. If recital programs do not seem more repetitious than they sometimes are, it is because of the helpful capacity of audiences to forget music which they themselves do not play. Sometimes they wish to recall at least a theme or two of what they have forgotten. From now on they will probably consult the Barlow and Morgenstern dictionary of themes.

The present volume does not contain themes from vocal music. To cover vocal as well as instrumental compositions, another volume would be needed as large as this.*

I have been speaking of trained musicians as well as of the average music lover. Both can use this dictionary without difficulty. The theme index is ingenious and, as I now believe, simple. If a theme or a tune is running through your head, and if your musical ear is good enough, you will be able to play it in the key of C major or C minor. Then if you write down the letters by which the notes are named, and find the resulting letter sequence in the index, you will be directed at once to the name of the original work and the name of its composer.

It is this process of identifying the theme when it is played by ear that seemed to me at first complicated and likely to discourage those who consult the dictionary. But I am confident now that once we have tried the method for ourselves, we shall find it extraordinarily simple.

Like any other dictionary of quotations, this book will perhaps be most useful to the young. Music is now a well-established subject in American education. Though many children in our schools are fortunately taught to play and sing, all of them — and this is equally their good fortune — are put in the way of listening to recorded music, to great masterpieces performed by great artists of yesterday and today. Not so long ago school children

---

* Publisher's note: The editors are working on a companion volume of vocal music.

used to go along the street humming a snatch of ragtime or jazz. Nowadays the youngsters are just as likely to hum a passage from Schubert or Tschaikovsky, or whoever was the composer who last spoke to them from the disc in the music class.

"What is that you are humming?"

Sometimes the children remember, but more often, like the elders, they forget. But when they have learned to consult this dictionary, they will place the passage at once.

I believe this book is destined to a wide and increasing usefulness, both to mature music lovers now and to the army of children whom our schools are training to be the music lovers of tomorrow.

PREFACE

WHEN we began the research for this book, we both felt like the Sorcerer's Apprentice, for each theme that we found seemed to loose a crowd of others waiting for us. It looked as if this one book might stretch into volumes. However, the limits we set ourselves made the completion of the work seem possible within a lifetime.

This work contains about 10,000 themes. They have been chosen primarily from recorded, instrumental pieces. No vocal works, excepting those which in instrumental arrangement have become better known than their originals, have been included. We feel that the book contains almost all the themes the average and even the more erudite listener might want to look up.

Certain works we omitted because the scores were unavailable in libraries, and publishers who were more than helpful could not supply them. A few other works we left out because we could not, after great effort, secure copyrights. Though the book does not exhaust the subject, by far, we feel that we have compiled a fairly complete index of themes, not only first themes, but every important theme, introduction, and salient rememberable phrase of the works included. In certain modern works where a number of varied phrases could be construed as thematic, we tried to present them all. Naturally, in the development of a work certain phrases occur which are as rememberable as the themes themselves. To include these would amount to reprinting the pieces in their entirety. A few ultra-modern works we left out. We felt that anyone likely to remember their themes, or more aptly their combinations of notes, would in all probability know their source. Consequently, these works would hardly fit into the scope of this volume.

Careful search through so many hundreds of works by different composers living in different eras in divers countries leads the research student to rather interesting generalizations. Permeating the work of many of the great and prolific composers we find certain combinations of notes, a certain "melos." This "melos" or melodic line seems to be a strong ingredient of their style. Schubert, Beethoven, Mozart, each has his ever-recurring theme song, but so disguised that it makes for artistic variety rather than monotony.

Many themes in compositions of the same period seem to possess similar melodic lines. In our notation key we had to carry some themes to seven or eight letters before their lines began to diverge. It is not that the composers were necessarily imitative. Melodic thinking of the period simply took on certain characteristics, rhythm and harmonic background giving these almost identical lines their variety.

Since the folk tune plays such an integral part in serious composition, one finds special national characteristics in the melodic lines of composers of various lands. Certain interval as well as rhythmic combinations make for Spanish, Russian, German, and French themes, and those of other countries too, of course. Identical motives are used again and again by composers, both consciously and unconsciously. The famous Mannheim motive (G C Eb G C Eb D C B C) as found in Beethoven's First Piano Sonata, Mozart's G Minor Symphony, and Mendelssohn's E Minor String Quartet, is probably the most obvious example of this. We found a rather wry footnote to the first page of one of Clementi's Bb Major Piano Sonatas, stating that when he played this piece for Kaiser Franz Joseph, Mozart was in the audience. The theme of the Sonata is identical with the overture of The Magic Flute, which appeared a few years later. Mozart was famous for his phenomenal memory.

Parody quotations of themes, such as the Tristan Prelude in Debussy's Golliwogg's Cake Walk, are both plentiful and amusing. The Lullaby in Strauss's Domestic Symphony is a steal from a Venetian Boat Song by Mendelssohn, and whether Prokofieff knows it or not, the last half of the second theme in the second movement of his Sixth Piano Sonata bears more than a sneaking resemblance to Mendelssohn's Spring Song.

And so the research student becomes a tone sleuth.

The book should prove useful not only to those who are bothered

by a theme and can't remember its source, but also to those who
know the source but can't remember the theme. We ourselves
shall certainly use it in both capacities.

A book of these dimensions could never have appeared without
the aid and encouragement of a great many interested people. We
owe a debt of deep and sincere gratitude first to Miss Gladys
Chamberlain, Director of the 58th St. Music Library of New
York City, who turned over the entire resources of that splendid
organization to us, and gave us unreservedly of her time and
advice. We want to thank the members of her staff, Miss Mary
Lee Daniels, Miss Eleanor Chasan, Miss Lilly Goldberg, Mrs.
Hilda Stolov, Mrs. Leah Silton, Mrs. Elsa Hollister, who were
more than helpful.

In the music division of the main library of New York City,
we wish to thank Mr. Philip Miller, and two of his indefatigable
pages, George Klinger and Noel Schwartz.

Our thanks for the special kindness of James Blish, Mrs. Rose
Gandal, Alex. M. Kramer, Robert Lowndes, Ben Meiselman,
Dr. Rudolf Nissim, Herbert Weinstock, and the many music
publishers and copyright owners who gave us assistance. We are
indebted to Robert Simon, of Crown Publishers, for his constant
encouragement in the undertaking; and to Miss Elizabeth Galvin,
his assistant, without whom this book would probably never have
appeared.

S. M.

New York, N. Y.
April, 1948

ADAM, Adolphe (1803-1856)

La Poupée de Nuremberg (The Nuremberg Doll) Overture — 1st Theme — A1

2nd Theme — A2

3rd Theme — A3

4th Theme — A4

Si J'Étais Roi Overture — 1st Theme — A5

2nd Theme — A6

3rd Theme — A7

4th Theme — A8

ALBÉNIZ, Isaac M. F. (1860-1909)

Suite Española, Pft.
Cadiz (Saeta)
By permission of Associated Music Publishers, Inc. — 1st Theme — A9

2nd Theme — A10

Cuba — A11

Seguidillas — 1st Theme — A12

2nd Theme — A13

Sevillanas — A14

Iberia I, Pft.
Evocación
By permission of Associated Music Publishers, Inc. — A15

Fête Dieu à Seville — 1st Theme — A16

2nd Theme — A17

Iberia II, Pft.
Triana
By permission of Associated Music Publishers, Inc. — 1st Theme — A18

2nd Theme — A19

Iberia III, Pft.
El Albaicin (El Polo)
By permission of Associated
Music Publishers, Inc. — A20

Iberia IV, Pft.
Jerez
By permission of Associated
Music Publishers, Inc. — A21

Malaga — A22

Cordoba (Nocturne), Pft.
By permission of Associated
Music Publishers, Inc. **1st Theme** — A23

2nd Theme — A24

Pavana-Capricho, Op. 12,
Pft.
By permission of Associated
Music Publishers, Inc. **1st Theme** — A25

2nd Theme — A26

Sous Le Palmier, in E Flat
(Tango Flamenco), Pft.
By permission of Associated
Music Publishers, Inc. **1st Theme** — A27

2nd Theme — A28

Tango in D, Pft.
By permission of Associated
Music Publishers, Inc. — A29

ALFVÉN, Hugo (1872-   )

Midsommarvarka
(Swedish Rhapsody), Op. 19,
Orch.
By permission of Associated
Music Publishers, Inc. **1st Theme** — A30

2nd Theme — A31

3rd Theme — A32

4th Theme — A33

ARENSKY, Anton (1861-1906)

Suite No. 1, Op. 15,
2 Pfts.
Copyright by the Oxford
University Press
Reproduced by permission. **I. Romance 1st Theme** — A34

2nd Theme — A35

II. Valse 1st Theme — A36

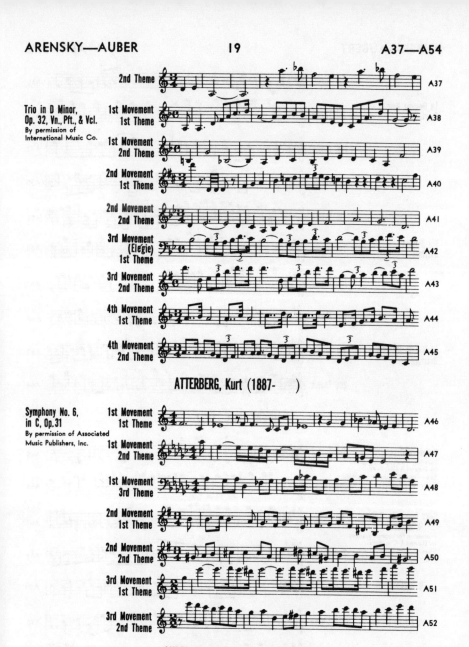

ATTERBERG, Kurt (1887-   )

AUBER, Daniel François (1782-1871)

3rd Theme — A55

Le Domino Noir
Overture — 1st Theme — A56

2nd Theme — A57

3rd Theme — A58

4th Theme — A59

Fra Diavolo
Overture — 1st Theme — A60

2nd Theme — A61

3rd Theme — A62

La Muette De Portici
Overture — 1st Theme — A63

2nd Theme — A64

AUBERT, Louis (1877-)

Habañera, Orch.
Permission for reprint granted
by Durand & Cie, Paris.
Elkan-Vogel Co.,Inc.Philadelphia,
Copyright Owners — 1st Theme — A65

2nd Theme — A66

Suite Breve, Op. 6, Orch.
I. Menuet
Permission for reprint granted
by Durand & Cie, Paris.
Elkan-Vogel Co.,Inc.
Philadelphia,Copyright Owners, — 1st Theme — A67

2nd Theme — A68

II. Berceuse — A69

III. Air de Ballet — 1st Theme — A70

2nd Theme — A71

3rd Theme — A72

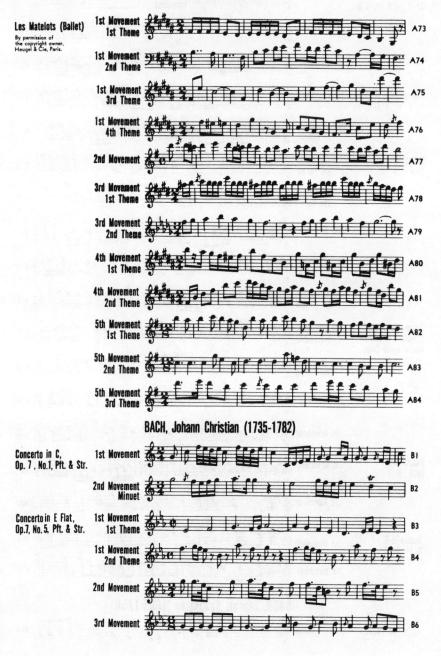

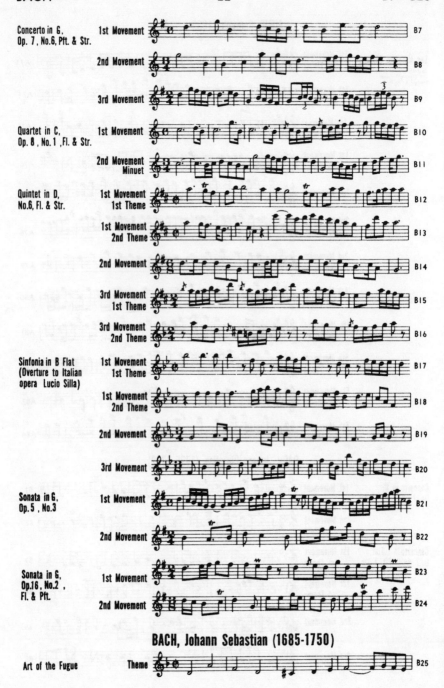

Concerto in G, Op. 7, No.6, Pft. & Str. — 1st Movement — B7

2nd Movement — B8

3rd Movement — B9

Quartet in C, Op. 8, No.1, Fl. & Str. — 1st Movement — B10

2nd Movement Minuet — B11

Quintet in D, No.6, Fl. & Str. — 1st Movement 1st Theme — B12

1st Movement 2nd Theme — B13

2nd Movement — B14

3rd Movement 1st Theme — B15

3rd Movement 2nd Theme — B16

Sinfonia in B Flat (Overture to Italian opera Lucio Silla) — 1st Movement 1st Theme — B17

1st Movement 2nd Theme — B18

2nd Movement — B19

3rd Movement — B20

Sonata in G, Op.5, No.3 — 1st Movement — B21

2nd Movement — B22

Sonata in G, Op.16, No.2, Fl. & Pft. — 1st Movement — B23

2nd Movement — B24

BACH, Johann Sebastian (1685-1750)

Art of the Fugue — Theme — B25

Christ Lag in Todesbunden (Church Cantata, No. 4) — B26

Jesu, Joy of Man's Desiring (from Cantata 147) — 1st Movement 1st Theme — B27

1st Movement 2nd Theme — B28

Ein Feste Burg Ist Unser Gott — B29

Komm Süsser Tod (Schemelli No. 42) — B29a

Wachet Auf Organ Chorale — B29b

Brandenberg Concerto No. 1, in F, 2 Hns., 3 Oboes, Fg., Vn., Str. & Cembalo — 1st Movement — B30

2nd Movement — B31

3rd Movement — B32

4th Movement Minuetto, 1st Theme — B33

4th Movement 2nd Theme Trio — B34

5th Movement — B35

Brandenberg Concerto No. 2, in F, Tpt., Vn., Fl., Ob., Str. & Cembalo — 1st Movement 1st Theme — B36

1st Movement 2nd Theme — B37

2nd Movement — B38

3rd Movement — B39

Brandenberg Concerto No. 3, in G (2nd Movement is only a bridge) — 1st Movement — B40

3rd Movement — B41

Brandenberg Concerto No. 4, in G, 2 Fl., Vn., Str. & Cembalo — 1st Movement — B42

2nd Movement — B43

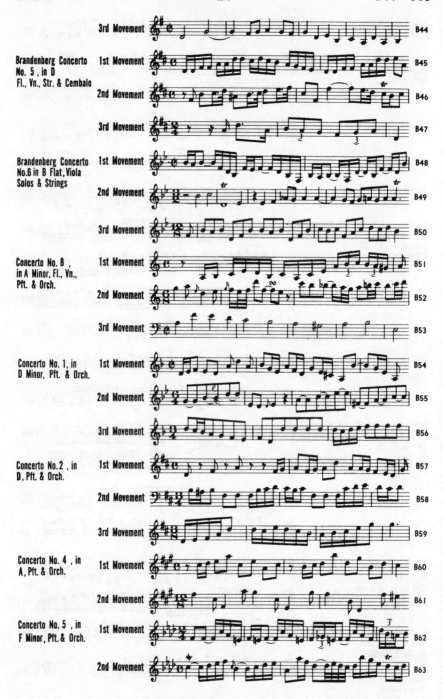

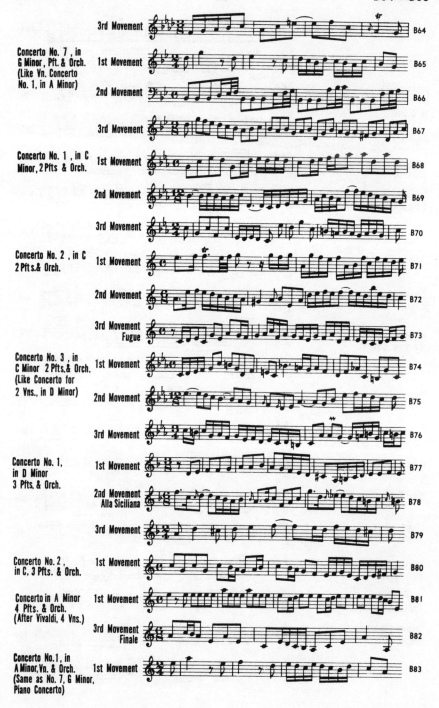

2nd Movement — B84

3rd Movement — B85

Concerto No. 2 in E
Vn. & Orch.
1st Movement — B86

2nd Movement — B87

3rd Movement — B88

Concerto in D Minor, 2 Vns. & Orch.
1st Movement — B89

2nd Movement — B90

3rd Movement — B91

Chromatic Fantasie & Fugue
Fugue Theme — B92

Prelude & Fugue, in A Minor, Organ
Prelude — B93

Fugue — B94

Prelude & Fugue, in G Minor, Organ
Prelude — B95

"Little Fugue" — B96

Organ Fugue, No. 9, in D Minor — B97

Organ Fugue, No. 12, in G Minor — B98

Fugue in D Organ — B99

Fugue in A Minor, Pft. — B100

Aria for Goldberg Variations, Pft. — B101

Two-part Inventions Pft.
No. 1, in C — B102

No. 2, in C Minor — B103

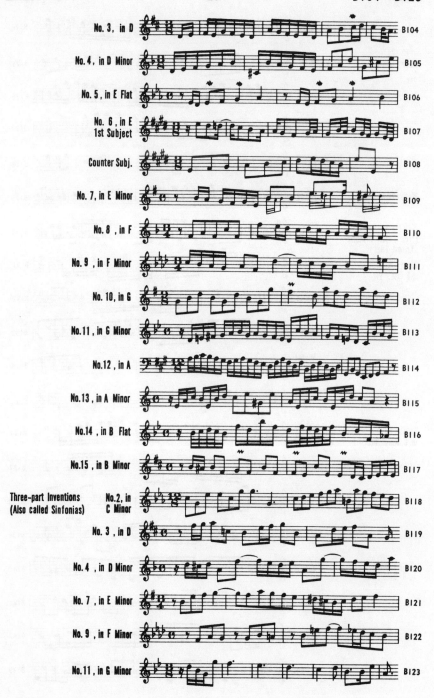

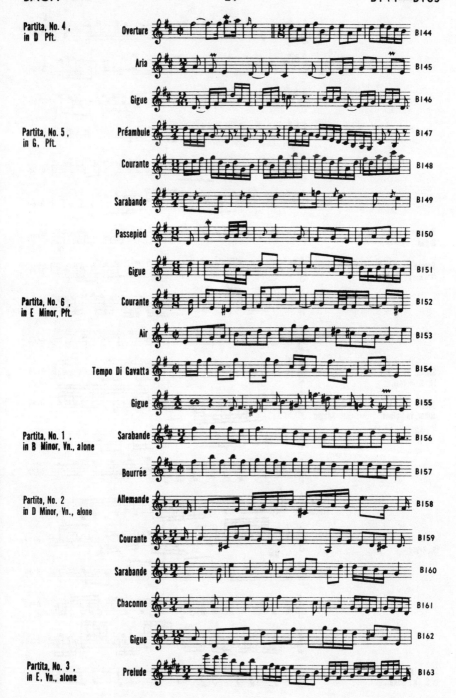

Partita, No. 4, in D Pft. — Overture — B144

Aria — B145

Gigue — B146

Partita, No. 5, in G, Pft. — Préambule — B147

Courante — B148

Sarabande — B149

Passepied — B150

Gigue — B151

Partita, No. 6, in E Minor, Pft. — Courante — B152

Air — B153

Tempo Di Gavatta — B154

Gigue — B155

Partita, No. 1, in B Minor, Vn., alone — Sarabande — B156

Bourrée — B157

Partita, No. 2 in D Minor, Vn., alone — Allemande — B158

Courante — B159

Sarabande — B160

Chaconne — B161

Gigue — B162

Partita, No. 3, in E, Vn., alone — Prelude — B163

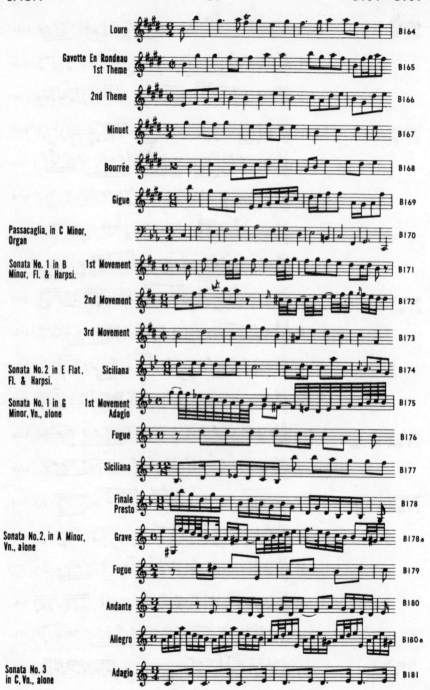

Loure — B164

Gavotte En Rondeau 1st Theme — B165

2nd Theme — B166

Minuet — B167

Bourrée — B168

Gigue — B169

Passacaglia, in C Minor, Organ — B170

Sonata No. 1 in B Minor, Fl. & Harpsi. 1st Movement — B171

2nd Movement — B172

3rd Movement — B173

Sonata No. 2 in E Flat, Fl. & Harpsi. Siciliana — B174

Sonata No. 1 in G Minor, Vn., alone 1st Movement Adagio — B175

Fugue — B176

Siciliana — B177

Finale Presto — B178

Sonata No.2, in A Minor, Vn., alone Grave — B178a

Fugue — B179

Andante — B180

Allegro — B180a

Sonata No. 3 in C, Vn., alone Adagio — B181

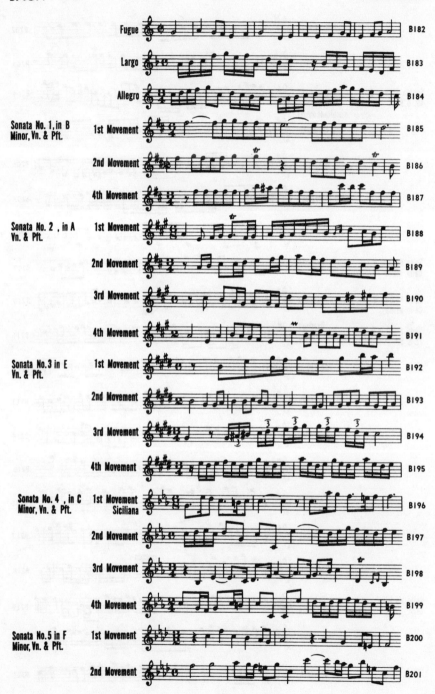

3rd Movement — B202

4th Movement — B203

Sonata No. 6 in G,
Vn. & Pft.

1st Movement
(both themes
simultaneously) — B204

2nd Movement — B205

3rd Movement — B206

4th Movement — B207

5th Movement — B208

Suite No. 3 in C,
Cello, alone

Bourrée — B209

Suite No. 6 in D,
Cello, alone

Gavotte — B210

Suite No. 2 in B Minor,
Fl. & Str.

Overture
1st Theme — B211

2nd Theme — B212

Rondeau — B213

Sarabande — B214

Bourrée — B215

Polonaise — B216

Minuet — B217

Badinerie — B218

Suite No. 1 in C,
Orch.

Overture
1st Theme — B219

2nd Theme — B220

Courante — B221

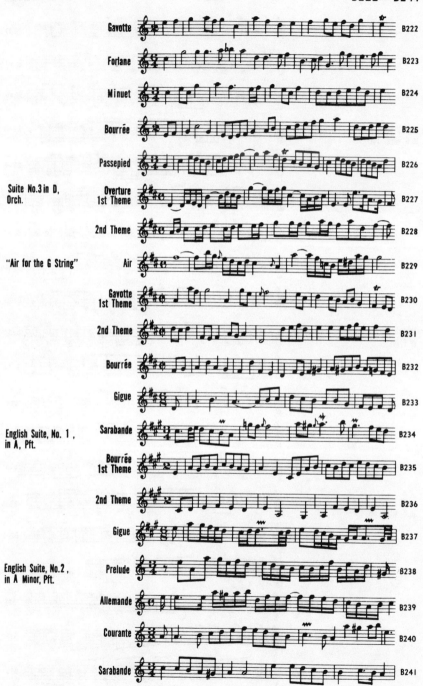

Gavotte — B222

Forlane — B223

Minuet — B224

Bourrée — B225

Passepied — B226

Suite No.3 in D, Orch. — Overture 1st Theme — B227

2nd Theme — B228

"Air for the G String" — Air — B229

Gavotte 1st Theme — B230

2nd Theme — B231

Bourrée — B232

Gigue — B233

English Suite, No. 1, in A, Pft. — Sarabande — B234

Bourrée 1st Theme — B235

2nd Theme — B236

Gigue — B237

English Suite, No. 2, in A Minor, Pft. — Prelude — B238

Allemande — B239

Courante — B240

Sarabande — B241

English Suite, No. 6, in D Minor, Pft. — Courante — B262

Sarabande — B263

Gavotte I — B264

Gavotte II — B265

Gigue — B266

French Suite, No.1, in D Minor, Pft. — Courante — B267

Sarabande — B268

Minuet I — B269

Minuet II — B270

Gigue — B271

French Suite, No. 2, in C Minor, Pft. — Courante — B272

Sarabande — B273

Air — B274

Minuet — B275

Gigue — B276

French Suite, No. 3, in B Minor, Pft. — Allemande — B277

Sarabande — B278

Minuetto — B279

Anglaise — B280

French Suite, No. 4, in E Flat, Pft. — Sarabande — B281

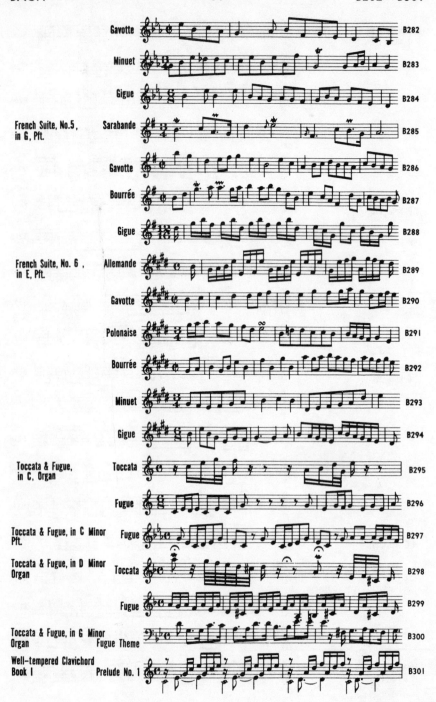

Fugue No. 1 — B302

Prelude No. 2 — B303

Fugue No. 2 — B304

Prelude No. 3 — B305

Fugue No. 3 — B306

Prelude No. 4 — B307

Fugue No. 4 — B308

Prelude No. 5 — B309

Fugue No. 5 — B310

Prelude No. 6 — B311

Fugue No. 6 — B312

Prelude No. 7 — B313

Fugue No. 7 — B314

Prelude No. 8 — B315

Fugue No. 8 — B316

Prelude No. 9 — B317

Fugue No. 9 — B318

Prelude No. 10 — B319

Fugue No. 10 — B320

Prelude No. 11 — B321

Fugue No. 11 — B322
Prelude No. 12 — B323
Fugue No. 12 — B324
Prelude No. 13 — B325
Fugue No. 13 — B326
Prelude No. 14 — B327
Fugue No. 14 — B328
Prelude No. 15 — B329
Fugue No. 15 — B330
Prelude No. 16 — B331
Fugue No. 16 — B332
Prelude No. 17 — B333
Fugue No. 17 — B334
Prelude No. 18 — B335
Fugue No. 18 — B336
Prelude No. 19 — B337
Fugue No. 19 — B338
Prelude No. 20 — B339
Fugue No. 20 — B340
Prelude No. 21 — B341

Fugue No. 21 — B342
Prelude No. 22 — B343
Fugue No. 22 — B344
Prelude No. 23 — B345
Fugue No. 23 — B346
Prelude No. 24 — B347
Fugue No. 24 — B348

Well Tempered Clavichord
Book II
Prelude No. 1 — B349
Fugue No. 1 — B350
Prelude No. 2 — B351
Fugue No. 2 — B352
Prelude No. 3 A — B353
B — B354
Fugue No. 3 — B355
Prelude No. 4 — B356
Fugue No. 4 — B357
Prelude No. 5 — B358
Fugue No. 5 — B359
Prelude No. 6 — B360
Fugue No. 6 — B361

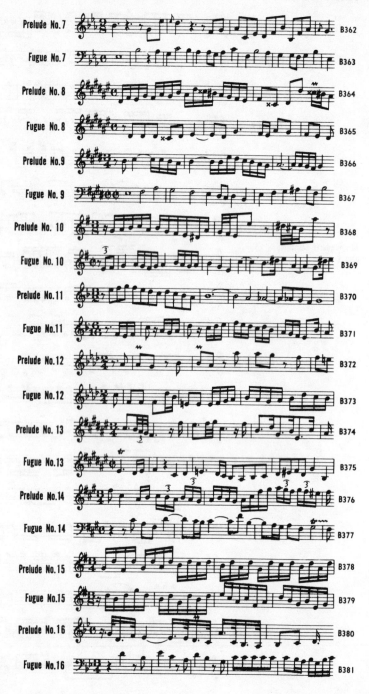

Prelude No. 7 — B362
Fugue No. 7 — B363
Prelude No. 8 — B364
Fugue No. 8 — B365
Prelude No. 9 — B366
Fugue No. 9 — B367
Prelude No. 10 — B368
Fugue No. 10 — B369
Prelude No. 11 — B370
Fugue No. 11 — B371
Prelude No. 12 — B372
Fugue No. 12 — B373
Prelude No. 13 — B374
Fugue No. 13 — B375
Prelude No. 14 — B376
Fugue No. 14 — B377
Prelude No. 15 — B378
Fugue No. 15 — B379
Prelude No. 16 — B380
Fugue No. 16 — B381

BACH   41   B382—B400

Prelude No.17 ... B382
Fugue No.17 ... B383
Prelude No.18 ... B384
Fugue No.18 ... B385
Prelude No. 19 ... B386
Fugue No. 19 ... B387
Prelude No. 20 ... B388
Fugue No. 20 ... B389
Prelude No. 21 ... B390
Fugue No. 21 ... B391
Prelude No. 22 ... B392
Fugue No. 22 ... B393
Prelude No. 23 ... B394
Fugue No. 23 ... B395
Prelude No. 24 ... B396
Fugue No. 24 ... B397

BACH, Karl Philipp Emanuel (1714-1788)

Abschied Von Meinem
Silbermannischen Klaviere , Pft. ... B398

Concerto No. 3 , in A
Cello & Str. Orch.   1st Movement ... B399

2nd Movement ... B400

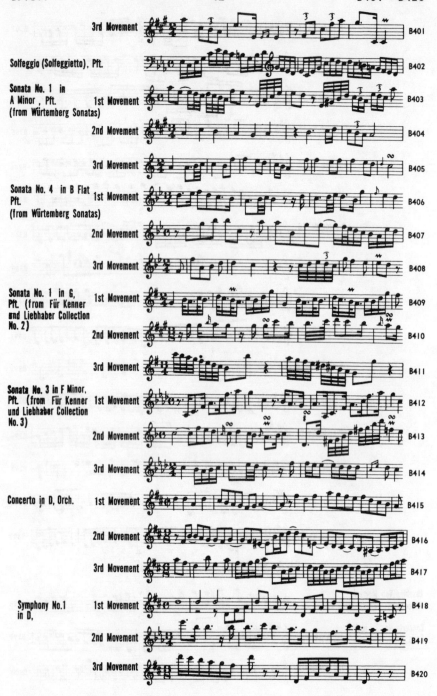

3rd Movement — B401

Solfeggio (Solfeggietto), Pft. — B402

Sonata No. 1 in
A Minor , Pft.   1st Movement — B403
(from Würtemberg Sonatas)

2nd Movement — B404

3rd Movement — B405

Sonata No. 4 in B Flat
Pft.   1st Movement — B406
(from Würtemberg Sonatas)

2nd Movement — B407

3rd Movement — B408

Sonata No. 1 in G,
Pft. (from Für Kenner   1st Movement — B409
und Liebhaber Collection
No. 2)   2nd Movement — B410

3rd Movement — B411

Sonata No. 3 in F Minor,
Pft. (from Für Kenner   1st Movement — B412
und Liebhaber Collection
No. 3)   2nd Movement — B413

3rd Movement — B414

Concerto in D, Orch.   1st Movement — B415

2nd Movement — B416

3rd Movement — B417

Symphony No.1
in D,   1st Movement — B418

2nd Movement — B419

3rd Movement — B420

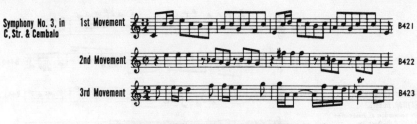

Symphony No. 3, in C, Str. & Cembalo — 1st Movement — B421

2nd Movement — B422

3rd Movement — B423

BACH, Wilhelm Friedemann (1710-1784)

Concerto in D Minor, (also attributed to Vivaldi), Pft. — 1st Movement Intro. — B424

1st Movement Fugue — B425

2nd Movement — B426

3rd Movement — B427

Sonata in C, Harpsi. — 1st Movement — B428

2nd Movement — B429

3rd Movement — B430

Sonata in F (Concerto) 2 Pfts. — 1st Movement — B431

2nd Movement — B432

3rd Movement — B433

BALAKIREFF, Mily (1837-1910)

Islamey (Oriental Fantasy) Pft.
By permission of Associated Music Publishers, Inc. — 1st Theme — B434

2nd Theme, A — B435

2nd Theme, B — B436

Russia (symph. poem) — 1st Theme — B437

2nd Theme — B438

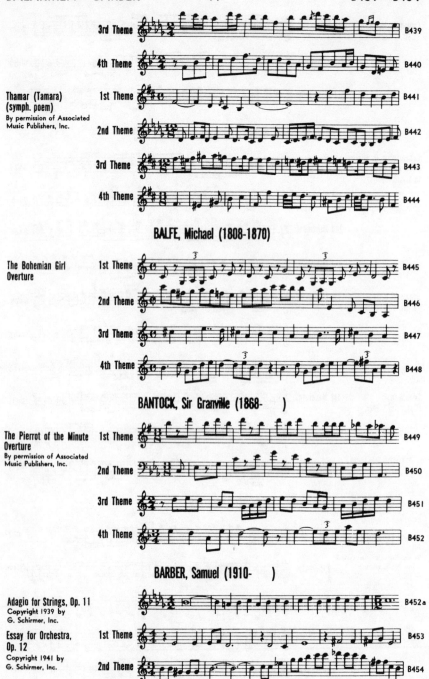

3rd Theme   B439

4th Theme   B440

Thamar (Tamara)
(symph. poem)
By permission of Associated
Music Publishers, Inc.

1st Theme   B441

2nd Theme   B442

3rd Theme   B443

4th Theme   B444

BALFE, Michael (1808-1870)

The Bohemian Girl
Overture

1st Theme   B445

2nd Theme   B446

3rd Theme   B447

4th Theme   B448

BANTOCK, Sir Granville (1868-   )

The Pierrot of the Minute
Overture
By permission of Associated
Music Publishers, Inc.

1st Theme   B449

2nd Theme   B450

3rd Theme   B451

4th Theme   B452

BARBER, Samuel (1910-   )

Adagio for Strings, Op. 11
Copyright 1939 by
G. Schirmer, Inc.   B452a

Essay for Orchestra,
Op. 12
Copyright 1941 by
G. Schirmer, Inc.

1st Theme   B453

2nd Theme   B454

First Symphony Op. 9
Copyright 1943 by G. Schirmer, Inc.
1st Theme — B454a
2nd Theme — B454b
3rd Theme — B454c
4th Theme — B454d
5th Theme — B454e
6th Theme — B454f
7th Theme — B454g

The School for Scandal Overture
Copyright 1941 by G. Schirmer, Inc.
1st Theme — B455
2nd Theme — B456

BARTÓK, Béla (1881-1945)

Allegro Barbaro, Pft.
1st Theme — B457
2nd Theme — B458
By permission of the copyright owner, Boosey and Hawkes, Inc.

Bagatelle, Op.2, Pft. — B459

Burlesque (A Bit Drunk) Op.8c, No.2 — B460

Concerto for Vn. & Orch.
1st Movement 1st Theme — B461
By permission of the copyright owner, Boosey and Hawkes, Inc.
1st Movement 2nd Theme — B462
2nd Movement — B463
3rd Movement 1st Theme — B464
3rd Movement 2nd Theme — B465

Contrasts, Vn., Cl. & Pft.
1st Movement 1st Theme Recruiting Dance — B466
By permission of the copyright owner, Boosey and Hawkes, Inc.

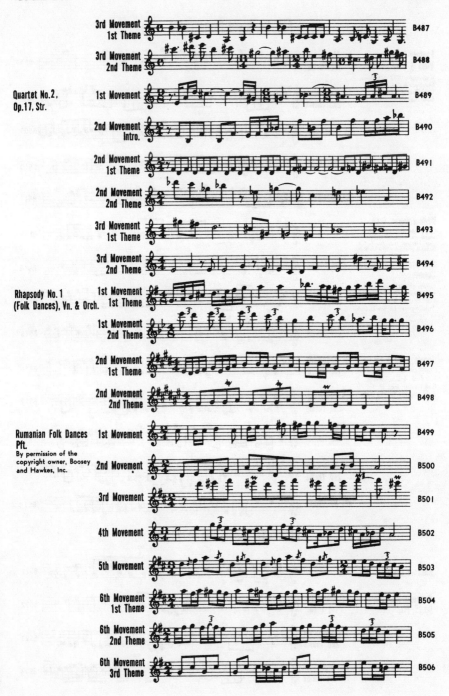

Quartet No.2,
Op.17, Str.

Rhapsody No.1
(Folk Dances), Vn. & Orch.

Rumanian Folk Dances
Pft.
By permission of the
copyright owner, Boosey
and Hawkes, Inc.

3rd Movement 1st Theme — B487
3rd Movement 2nd Theme — B488
1st Movement — B489
2nd Movement Intro. — B490
2nd Movement 1st Theme — B491
2nd Movement 2nd Theme — B492
3rd Movement 1st Theme — B493
3rd Movement 2nd Theme — B494
1st Movement 1st Theme — B495
1st Movement 2nd Theme — B496
2nd Movement 1st Theme — B497
2nd Movement 2nd Theme — B498
1st Movement — B499
2nd Movement — B500
3rd Movement — B501
4th Movement — B502
5th Movement — B503
6th Movement 1st Theme — B504
6th Movement 2nd Theme — B505
6th Movement 3rd Theme — B506

BAX, Sir Arnold Trevor (1883-   )

Fantasy-Sonata, Viola & Harp
Copyright 1922 Murdock, Murdock & Co., London. Carl Fischer, Inc., N. Y., Sole Agents for the U. S. A.

1st Movement 1st Theme — B507

1st Movement 2nd Theme — B508

2nd Movement — B509

3rd Movement — B510

4th Movement — B511

Mediterranean, Orch.
Copyright 1923 Murdock, Murdock & Co., London. Carl Fischer, Inc., N. Y., Sole Agents for the U. S. A. — B512

Overture to a Picaresque Comedy
Copyright 1934 Murdock, Murdock & Co., London. Carl Fischer, Inc., N. Y., Sole Agents for the U. S. A.

1st Theme — B513

2nd Theme — B514

3rd Theme — B515

Sonata, Viola & Pft.
Copyright 1923 Murdock, Murdock & Co., London. Carl Fischer, Inc., N. Y., Sole Agents for the U. S. A.

1st Movement 1st Theme — B516

1st Movement 2nd Theme — B517

2nd Movement 1st Theme — B518

2nd Movement 2nd Theme — B519

3rd Movement — B520

BEETHOVEN, Ludwig Van (1770-1827)

Andante Favori, F — B521

Concerto No. 1, in C Op.15, Pft.

1st Movement 1st Theme — B522

1st Movement 2nd Theme — B523

2nd Movement 1st Theme — B524

2nd Movement / 2nd Theme — B525

3rd Movement / 1st Theme — B526

3rd Movement / 2nd Theme — B527

3rd Movement / 3rd Theme — B528

Concerto No. 2, in B Flat Op. 19, Pft.

1st Movement / 1st Theme — B529

1st Movement / 2nd Theme — B530

2nd Movement — B531

3rd Movement — B532

Concerto No. 3, in C Minor, Op.37, Pft.

1st Movement / 1st Theme — B533

1st Movement / 2nd Theme — B534

2nd Movement — B535

3rd Movement — B536

Concerto No. 4, in G, Op.58, Pft.

1st Movement / 1st Theme — B537

1st Movement / 2nd Theme — B538

2nd Movement — B539

3rd Movement / 1st Theme, A — B540

3rd Movement / 1st Theme, B — B541

3rd Movement / 2nd Theme — B542

Concerto No. 5, in E Flat, Op.73,"Emperor"

1st Movement / 1st Theme — B543

1st Movement / 2nd Theme — B544

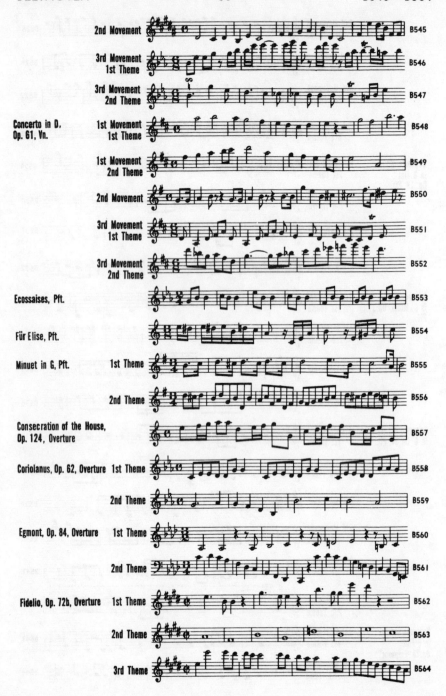

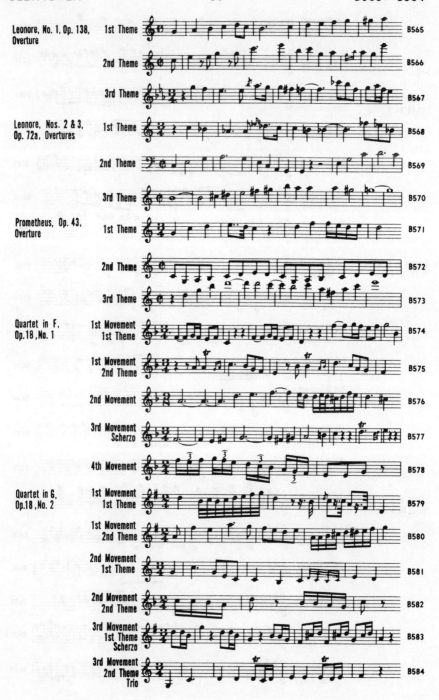

Leonore, No. 1, Op. 138, Overture	1st Theme	B565
	2nd Theme	B566
	3rd Theme	B567
Leonore, Nos. 2 & 3, Op. 72a, Overtures	1st Theme	B568
	2nd Theme	B569
	3rd Theme	B570
Prometheus, Op. 43, Overture	1st Theme	B571
	2nd Theme	B572
	3rd Theme	B573
Quartet in F, Op. 18, No. 1	1st Movement 1st Theme	B574
	1st Movement 2nd Theme	B575
	2nd Movement	B576
	3rd Movement Scherzo	B577
	4th Movement	B578
Quartet in G, Op. 18, No. 2	1st Movement 1st Theme	B579
	1st Movement 2nd Theme	B580
	2nd Movement 1st Theme	B581
	2nd Movement 2nd Theme	B582
	3rd Movement 1st Theme Scherzo	B583
	3rd Movement 2nd Theme Trio	B584

Quartet in B Flat, Op.18, No.6 — 1st Movement 1st Theme — B604
1st Movement 2nd Theme — B605
2nd Movement — B606
3rd Movement — B607
4th Movement La Malinconia Intro. — B608
4th Movement Theme — B609

Quartet in F Op.59, No.1 "Rasoumowsky" — 1st Movement — B610
2nd Movement — B611
3rd Movement — B612
4th Movement — B613

Quartet in E Minor, Op.59, No.2 "Rasoumowsky" — 1st Movement — B614
2nd Movement 1st Theme — B615
2nd Movement 2nd Theme — B616
3rd Movement 1st Theme — B617
3rd Movement 2nd Theme — B618
4th Movement — B619

Quartet in C, Op.59, No.3, "Rasoumowsky" — 1st Movement — B620
2nd Movement — B621
3rd Movement — B622
4th Movement — B623

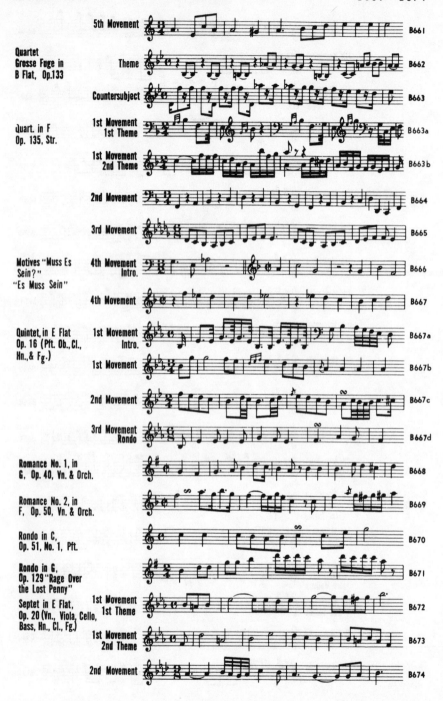

5th Movement — B661

Quartet
Grosse Fuge in
B Flat, Op.133 — Theme — B662

Countersubject — B663

Quart. in F
Op. 135, Str. — 1st Movement / 1st Theme — B663a

1st Movement / 2nd Theme — B663b

2nd Movement — B664

3rd Movement — B665

Motives "Muss Es
Sein?"
"Es Muss Sein" — 4th Movement Intro. — B666

4th Movement — B667

Quintet, in E Flat
Op. 16 (Pft. Ob., Cl.,
Hn., & Fg.) — 1st Movement Intro. — B667a

1st Movement — B667b

2nd Movement — B667c

3rd Movement Rondo — B667d

Romance No. 1, in
G, Op. 40, Vn. & Orch. — B668

Romance No. 2, in
F, Op. 50, Vn. & Orch. — B669

Rondo in C,
Op. 51, No. 1, Pft. — B670

Rondo in G,
Op. 129 "Rage Over
the Lost Penny" — B671

Septet in E Flat,
Op. 20 (Vn., Viola, Cello,
Bass, Hn., Cl., Fg.) — 1st Movement 1st Theme — B672

1st Movement 2nd Theme — B673

2nd Movement — B674

3rd Movement — B675
4th Movement — B676
5th Movement — B677
6th Movement — B678
7th Movement — B679

Serenade, Op. 8, Vn., Viola & Cello
1st Movement — B679a
2nd Movement — B679b
3rd Movement Minuet — B679c
4th Movement 1st Theme — B679d
4th Movement 2nd Theme — B679e
5th Movement Alla Polacca — B679f
6th Movement — B679g

Sonata No. 2, in G Minor, Op. 5, No. 2, Cello & Pft.
1st Movement Intro. — B679h
1st Movement — B680
2nd Movement — B680a

Sonata No. 3 in A, Op. 69, Cello & Pft.
1st Movement — B681
2nd Movement 1st Theme — B682
2nd Movement 2nd Theme — B683
3rd Movement — B684

Sonata No. 4, in C, Op. 102, No. 1, Cello & Pft.
1st Movement Intro. — B685

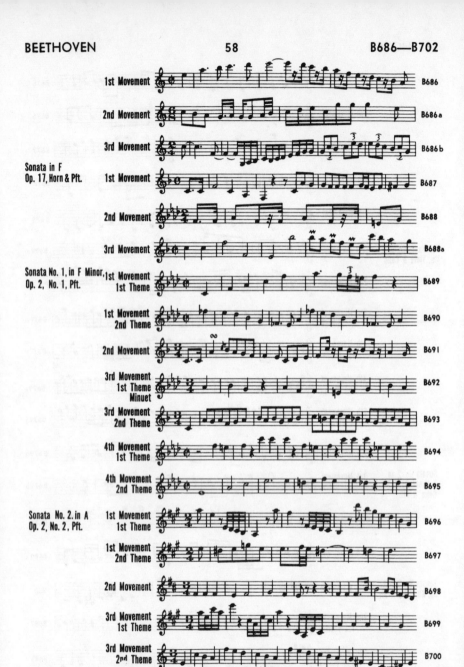

1st Movement B686

2nd Movement B686a

3rd Movement B686b

Sonata in F
Op. 17, Horn & Pft.   1st Movement B687

2nd Movement B688

3rd Movement B688a

Sonata No. 1, in F Minor, 1st Movement
Op. 2, No. 1, Pft.   1st Theme B689

1st Movement
2nd Theme B690

2nd Movement B691

3rd Movement
1st Theme
Minuet B692

3rd Movement
2nd Theme B693

4th Movement
1st Theme B694

4th Movement
2nd Theme B695

Sonata No. 2, in A   1st Movement
Op. 2, No. 2, Pft.   1st Theme B696

1st Movement
2nd Theme B697

2nd Movement B698

3rd Movement
1st Theme B699

3rd Movement
2nd Theme B700

4th Movement
1st Theme B701

4th Movement
2nd Theme B702

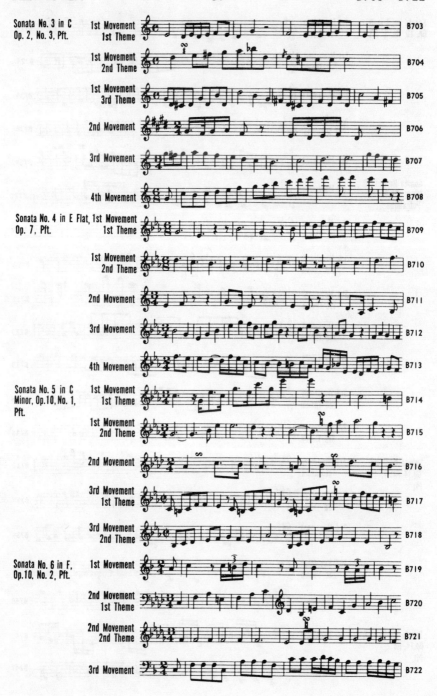

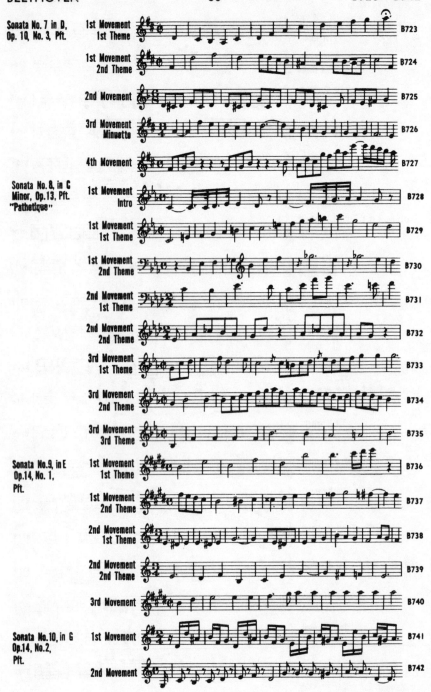

Sonata No. 7 in D, Op. 10, No. 3, Pft.	1st Movement 1st Theme	B723
	1st Movement 2nd Theme	B724
	2nd Movement	B725
	3rd Movement Minuetto	B726
	4th Movement	B727
Sonata No. 8, in C Minor, Op. 13, Pft. "Pathetique"	1st Movement Intro	B728
	1st Movement 1st Theme	B729
	1st Movement 2nd Theme	B730
	2nd Movement 1st Theme	B731
	2nd Movement 2nd Theme	B732
	3rd Movement 1st Theme	B733
	3rd Movement 2nd Theme	B734
	3rd Movement 3rd Theme	B735
Sonata No. 9, in E Op. 14, No. 1, Pft.	1st Movement 1st Theme	B736
	1st Movement 2nd Theme	B737
	2nd Movement 1st Theme	B738
	2nd Movement 2nd Theme	B739
	3rd Movement	B740
Sonata No. 10, in G Op. 14, No. 2, Pft.	1st Movement	B741
	2nd Movement	B742

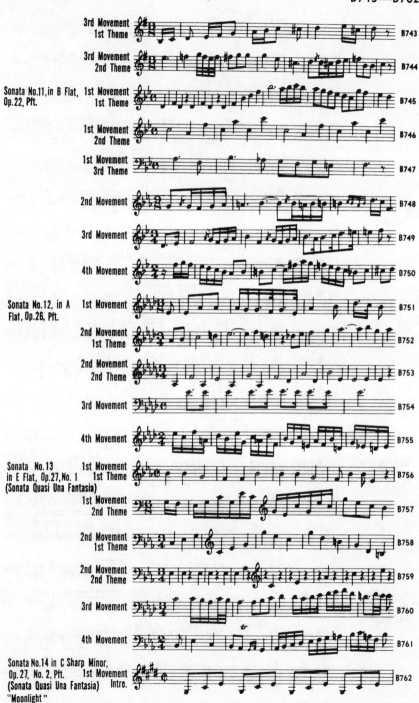

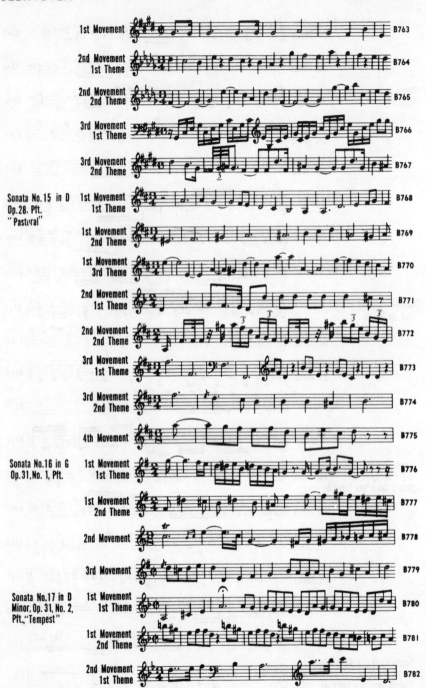

1st Movement — B763

2nd Movement 1st Theme — B764

2nd Movement 2nd Theme — B765

3rd Movement 1st Theme — B766

3rd Movement 2nd Theme — B767

Sonata No.15 in D Op.28. Pft. "Pastoral"

1st Movement 1st Theme — B768

1st Movement 2nd Theme — B769

1st Movement 3rd Theme — B770

2nd Movement 1st Theme — B771

2nd Movement 2nd Theme — B772

3rd Movement 1st Theme — B773

3rd Movement 2nd Theme — B774

4th Movement — B775

Sonata No.16 in G Op.31,No. 1, Pft.

1st Movement 1st Theme — B776

1st Movement 2nd Theme — B777

2nd Movement — B778

3rd Movement — B779

Sonata No.17 in D Minor, Op. 31, No. 2, Pft.,"Tempest"

1st Movement 1st Theme — B780

1st Movement 2nd Theme — B781

2nd Movement 1st Theme — B782

Sonata No. 18 in E Flat Op.31, No. 3, Pft.

Sonata No. 19 in G Minor Op.49, No.1, Pft.

Sonata No.20 in G Op.49, No.2, Pft.

Sonata No.21 in C Op.53, Pft. "Waldstein"

2nd Movement 2nd Theme — B783
3rd Movement 1st Theme — B784
3rd Movement 2nd Theme — B785
1st Movement 1st Theme — B786
1st Movement 2nd Theme — B787
2nd Movement — B788
3rd Movement 1st Theme Minuetto — B789
3rd Movement 2nd Theme — B790
4th Movement 1st Theme, A — B791
4th Movement 1st Theme, B — B792
1st Movement 1st Theme — B793
1st Movement 2nd Theme — B794
2nd Movement 1st Theme — B795
2nd Movement 2nd Theme — B796
1st Movement 1st Theme — B797
1st Movement 2nd Theme — B798
2nd Movement — B799
1st Movement 1st Theme — B800
1st Movement 2nd Theme — B801
2nd Movement Intro. — B802

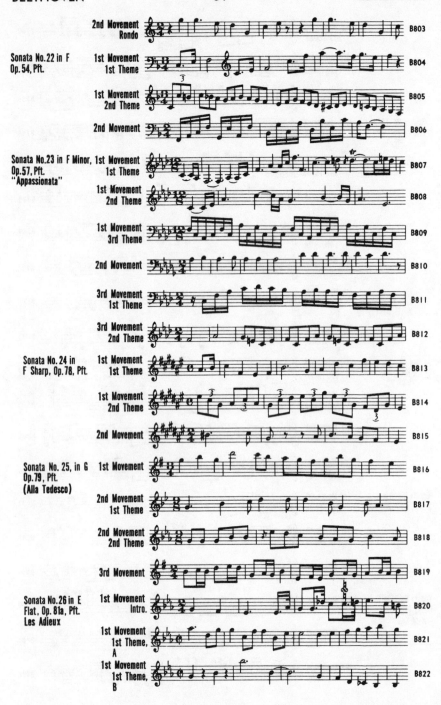

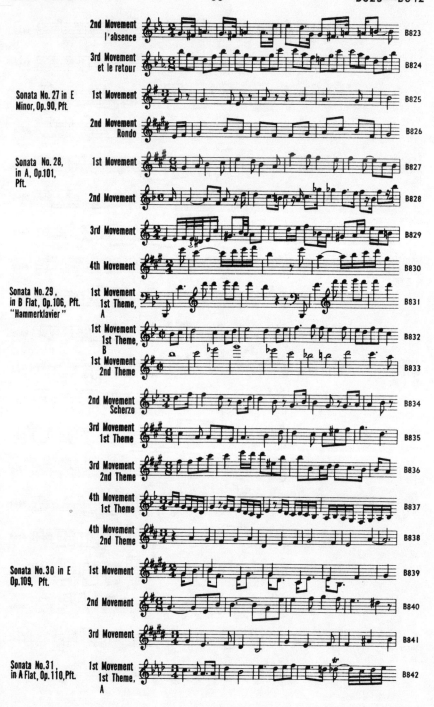

2nd Movement l'absence — B823

3rd Movement et le retour — B824

Sonata No. 27 in E Minor, Op. 90, Pft.
1st Movement — B825

2nd Movement Rondo — B826

Sonata No. 28, in A, Op. 101, Pft.
1st Movement — B827

2nd Movement — B828

3rd Movement — B829

4th Movement — B830

Sonata No. 29, in B Flat, Op. 106, Pft. "Hammerklavier"
1st Movement 1st Theme, A — B831

1st Movement 1st Theme, B — B832

1st Movement 2nd Theme — B833

2nd Movement Scherzo — B834

3rd Movement 1st Theme — B835

3rd Movement 2nd Theme — B836

4th Movement 1st Theme — B837

4th Movement 2nd Theme — B838

Sonata No. 30 in E Op. 109, Pft.
1st Movement — B839

2nd Movement — B840

3rd Movement — B841

Sonata No. 31, in A Flat, Op. 110, Pft.
1st Movement 1st Theme, A — B842

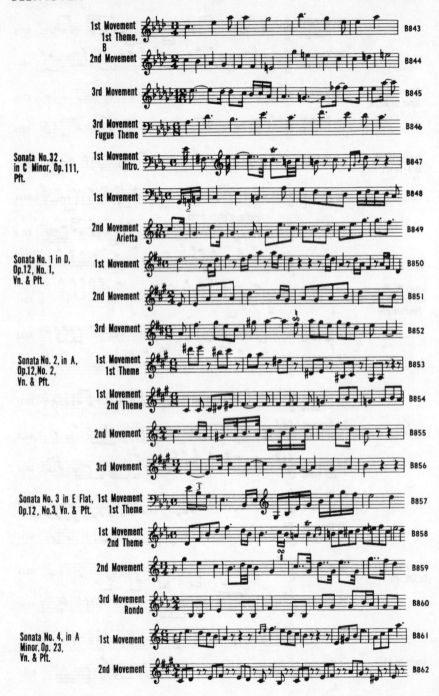

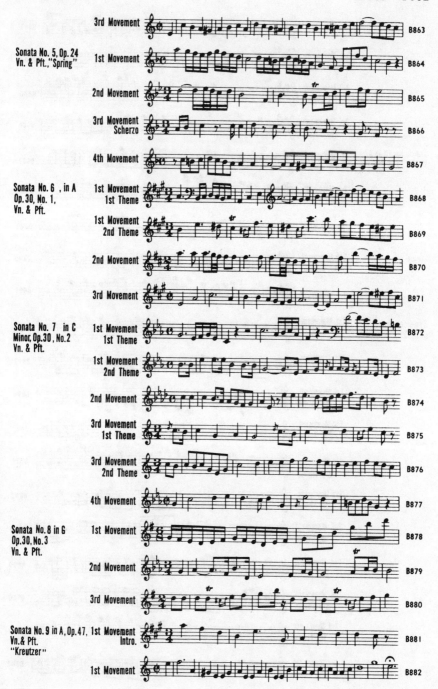

3rd Movement — B863

Sonata No. 5, Op. 24
Vn. & Pft., "Spring"   1st Movement — B864

2nd Movement — B865

3rd Movement
Scherzo — B866

4th Movement — B867

Sonata No. 6 , in A
Op. 30, No. 1,
Vn. & Pft.   1st Movement
1st Theme — B868

1st Movement
2nd Theme — B869

2nd Movement — B870

3rd Movement — B871

Sonata No. 7 in C
Minor, Op. 30 , No. 2
Vn. & Pft.   1st Movement
1st Theme — B872

1st Movement
2nd Theme — B873

2nd Movement — B874

3rd Movement
1st Theme — B875

3rd Movement
2nd Theme — B876

4th Movement — B877

Sonata No. 8 in G
Op. 30, No. 3
Vn. & Pft.   1st Movement — B878

2nd Movement — B879

3rd Movement — B880

Sonata No. 9 in A, Op. 47,
Vn. & Pft.
"Kreutzer"   1st Movement
Intro. — B881

1st Movement — B882

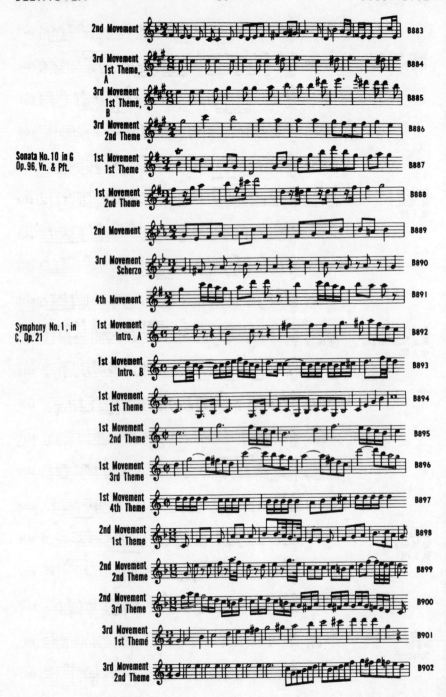

2nd Movement — B883

3rd Movement
1st Theme,
A — B884

3rd Movement
1st Theme,
B — B885

3rd Movement
2nd Theme — B886

Sonata No. 10 in G
Op. 96, Vn. & Pft.

1st Movement
1st Theme — B887

1st Movement
2nd Theme — B888

2nd Movement — B889

3rd Movement
Scherzo — B890

4th Movement — B891

Symphony No. 1, in
C, Op. 21

1st Movement
Intro. A — B892

1st Movement
Intro. B — B893

1st Movement
1st Theme — B894

1st Movement
2nd Theme — B895

1st Movement
3rd Theme — B896

1st Movement
4th Theme — B897

2nd Movement
1st Theme — B898

2nd Movement
2nd Theme — B899

2nd Movement
3rd Theme — B900

3rd Movement
1st Theme — B901

3rd Movement
2nd Theme — B902

4th Movement 1st Theme — B903
4th Movement 2nd Theme — B904

Symphony No.2, in D Op.36

1st Movement Intro. — B905
1st Movement 1st Theme — B906
1st Movement 2nd Theme — B907
2nd Movement 1st Theme, A — B908
2nd Movement 1st Theme, B — B909
2nd Movement 2nd Theme — B910
2nd Movement 3rd Theme — B911
2nd Movement 4th Theme — B912
3rd Movement 1st Theme — B913
3rd Movement 2nd Theme — B914
4th Movement 1st Theme — B915
4th Movement 2nd Theme — B916
4th Movement 3rd Theme — B917

Symphony No.3, in E Flat, Op.55 "Eroica"

1st Movement 1st Theme — B918
1st Movement 2nd Theme — B919
1st Movement 3rd Theme — B920
1st Movement 4th Theme — B921
1st Movement 5th Theme — B922

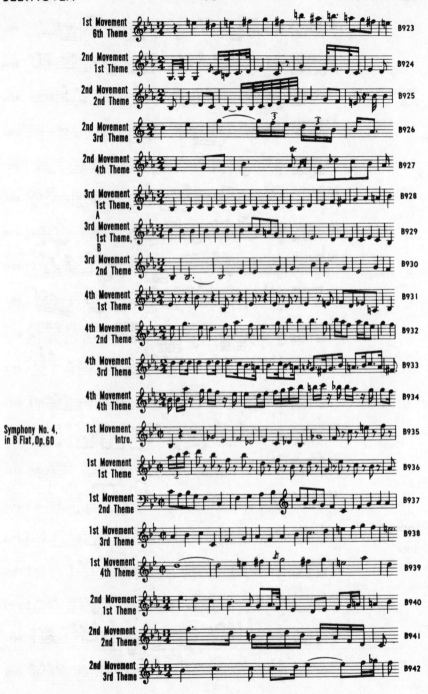

1st Movement 6th Theme — B923
2nd Movement 1st Theme — B924
2nd Movement 2nd Theme — B925
2nd Movement 3rd Theme — B926
2nd Movement 4th Theme — B927
3rd Movement 1st Theme, A — B928
3rd Movement 1st Theme, B — B929
3rd Movement 2nd Theme — B930
4th Movement 1st Theme — B931
4th Movement 2nd Theme — B932
4th Movement 3rd Theme — B933
4th Movement 4th Theme — B934

Symphony No. 4, in B Flat, Op. 60

1st Movement Intro. — B935
1st Movement 1st Theme — B936
1st Movement 2nd Theme — B937
1st Movement 3rd Theme — B938
1st Movement 4th Theme — B939
2nd Movement 1st Theme — B940
2nd Movement 2nd Theme — B941
2nd Movement 3rd Theme — B942

3rd Movement 1st Theme   B943

3rd Movement 2nd Theme   B944

4th Movement 1st Theme   B945

4th Movement 2nd Theme   B946

4th Movement 3rd Theme   B947

Symphony No. 5, in C Minor, Op. 67 "Fate"

1st Movement 1st Theme, A   B948

1st Movement 1st Theme, B   B949

1st Movement 1st Theme, C   B950

1st Movement 2nd Theme   B951

1st Movement 3rd Theme   B952

1st Movement 4th Theme   B953

2nd Movement 1st Theme   B954

2nd Movement 2nd Theme   B955

2nd Movement Coda   B956

3rd Movement 1st Theme   B957

3rd Movement 2nd Theme   B958

3rd Movement 3rd Theme   B959

4th Movement 1st Theme   B960

4th Movement 2nd Theme   B961

4th Movement 3rd Theme   B962

BEETHOVEN 72 B963—B982

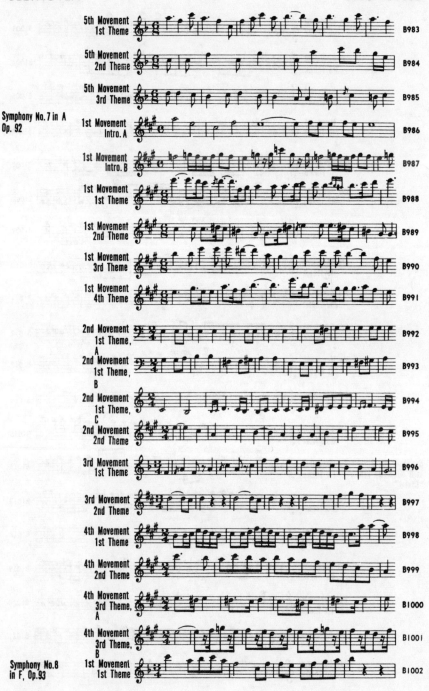

1st Movement
2nd Theme — B1003

1st Movement
3rd Theme — B1004

1st Movement
4th Theme,
A — B1005

1st Movement
4th Theme,
B — B1006

2nd Movement
1st Theme — B1007

2nd Movement
2nd Theme — B1008

2nd Movement
3rd Theme — B1009

3rd Movement
1st Theme — B1010

3rd Movement
2nd Theme — B1011

4th Movement
1st Theme,
A — B1012

4th Movement
1st Theme,
B — B1013

4th Movement
2nd Theme — B1014

4th Movement
3rd Theme — B1015

Symphony No. 9,
in D Minor, Op. 125,
"Choral"

1st Movement
1st Theme — B1016

1st Movement
2nd Theme — B1017

1st Movement
3rd Theme — B1018

1st Movement
4th Theme — B1019

2nd Movement
1st Theme — B1020

2nd Movement
2nd Theme — B1021

2nd Movement
3rd Theme
A — B1022

2nd Movement
3rd Theme,
B   B1023

3rd Movement
1st Theme   B1024

3rd Movement
2nd Theme   B1025

4th Movement
Intro.   B1026

4th Movement
1st Theme   B1027

4th Movement
2nd Theme   B1028

4th Movement
3rd Theme   B1029

4th Movement
4th Theme   B1030

Trio in B Flat,   1st Movement   B1031
Op.11, Cl., Cello & Pft.
Gassenhauer (Street Song)

2nd Movement   B1032

3rd Movement   B1033

Trio in C Minor,   1st Movement
Op.1, No.3, Str.   1st Theme,
                         A   B1034

1st Movement
1st Theme,
B   B1035

1st Movement
2nd Theme   B1036

2nd Movement   B1037

3rd Movement
1st Theme   B1038

3rd Movement
2nd Theme   B1039

4th Movement
1st Theme   B1040

4th Movement
2nd Theme   B1041

Trio in D,   1st Movement   B1042
Op.70, No. 1   1st Theme
"Geister"
Vn, Cello, Pft.

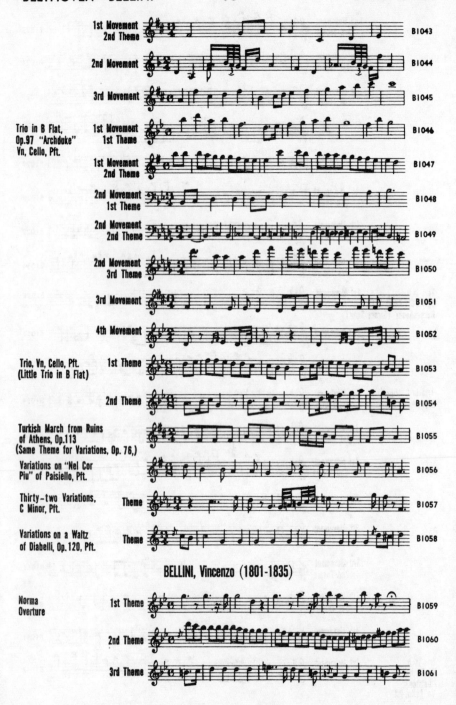

1st Movement 2nd Theme — B1043

2nd Movement — B1044

3rd Movement — B1045

Trio in B Flat, Op.97 "Archduke" Vn, Cello, Pft. — 1st Movement 1st Theme — B1046

1st Movement 2nd Theme — B1047

2nd Movement 1st Theme — B1048

2nd Movement 2nd Theme — B1049

2nd Movement 3rd Theme — B1050

3rd Movement — B1051

4th Movement — B1052

Trio, Vn, Cello, Pft. (Little Trio in B Flat) — 1st Theme — B1053

2nd Theme — B1054

Turkish March from Ruins of Athens, Op.113 (Same Theme for Variations, Op. 76,) — B1055

Variations on "Nel Cor Piu" of Paisiello, Pft. — B1056

Thirty-two Variations, C Minor, Pft. — Theme — B1057

Variations on a Waltz of Diabelli, Op.120, Pft. — Theme — B1058

BELLINI, Vincenzo (1801-1835)

Norma Overture — 1st Theme — B1059

2nd Theme — B1060

3rd Theme — B1061

BERLIOZ, Hector (1803-1869)

Beatrice and Benedict Overture — Intro. — B1062

1st Theme — B1063

2nd Theme Variant of Intro. — B1064

3rd Theme, A — B1065

3rd Theme, B — B1066

Benvenuto Cellini Overture, Op. 23 — 1st Theme — B1067

2nd Theme — B1068

3rd Theme — B1069

4th Theme — B1070

The Corsair Overture, Op. 21 — 1st Theme — B1071

2nd Theme — B1072

3rd Theme — B1073

Les Francs – Juges Overture, Op. 3 — Intro. A — B1074

Intro. B — B1075

1st Theme — B1076

2nd Theme — B1077

King Lear Overture, Op. 4 — 1st Theme — B1078

2nd Theme — B1079

3rd Theme — B1080

4th Movement
March to the Scaffold
1st Theme — B1101

4th Movement
2nd Theme — B1102

5th Movement
Witches' Sabbath
1st Theme — B1103

5th Movement
2nd Theme
Dies Irae — B1104

5th Movement
3rd Theme — B1105

Harold in Italy, Op.16   1st Movement
Orch.   Harold in the Mountains
Intro. A1 — B1106

1st Movement
Intro. A 2 — B1107

1st Movement
Intro. B — B1108

1st Movement
1st Theme — B1109

1st Movement
2nd Theme — B1110

1st Movement
3rd Theme — B1111

2nd Movement
March of the Pilgrims — B1112

3rd Movement
Serenade
1st Theme — B1113

3rd Movement
2nd Theme — B1114

4th Movement
Orgy of the Brigands
1st Theme — B1115

4th Movement
2nd Theme — B1116

4th Movement
3rd Theme — B1117

BERNSTEIN, Leonard (1918-)

Fancy Free
Ballet
Copyright 1946 by
Harms, Inc.
Reprinted by
special permission.

Opening Dance — B1117a

At the Bar
Intro. — B1117b

Theme — B1117c

Pas de Deux — B1117d

Variation 1
1st Theme — B1117e

2nd Theme — B1117f

Variation 2 — B1117g

Variation 3
1st Theme — B1117h

2nd Theme — B1117i

Finale — B1117j

Jeremiah, Symphony
Copyright 1943 by
Harms, Inc.
Reprinted by
special permission.

1st Movement
Prophecy
1st Theme — B1117k

1st Movement
2nd Theme — B1117l

1st Movement
3rd Theme — B1117m

2nd Movement
1st Theme — B1117n

2nd Movement
2nd Theme — B1117o

3rd Movement
1st Theme — B1117p

3rd Movement
2nd Theme — B1117q

3rd Movement
3rd Theme — B1117r

BIZET, Georges (1838-1875)

L'Arlesienne
Suite No.1, Orch.

Overture
1st Theme — B1118

2nd Theme — B1119

Minuetto
1st Theme — B1120

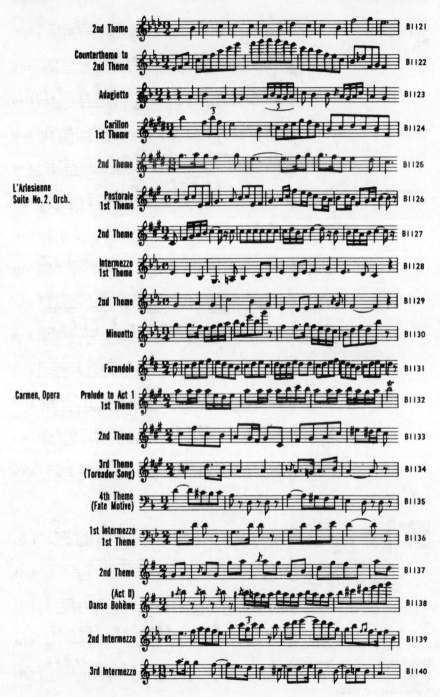

2nd Theme — B1121

Countertheme to 2nd Theme — B1122

Adagietto — B1123

Carillon 1st Theme — B1124

2nd Theme — B1125

L'Arlesienne Suite No. 2, Orch.

Pastorale 1st Theme — B1126

2nd Theme — B1127

Intermezzo 1st Theme — B1128

2nd Theme — B1129

Minuetto — B1130

Farandole — B1131

Carmen, Opera

Prelude to Act 1 1st Theme — B1132

2nd Theme — B1133

3rd Theme (Toreador Song) — B1134

4th Theme (Fate Motive) — B1135

1st Intermezzo 1st Theme — B1136

2nd Theme — B1137

(Act II) Danse Bohème — B1138

2nd Intermezzo — B1139

3rd Intermezzo — B1140

Petite Suite, Op. 22
"Jeux D'Enfants"
Orch.

Marche   B1141

Berceuse (Doll)   B1142

Impromptu   B1143

Duo (Petit Mari,
Petite Femme)   B1144

Galop (Le Bal)   B1145

Symphony No.1,
in C

1st Movement
1st Theme,
A   B1146

1st Movement
1st Theme,
B   B1147

1st Movement
2nd Theme   B1148

2nd Movement
1st Theme   B1149

2nd Movement
2nd Theme   B1150

3rd Movement   B1151

4th Movement
1st Theme   B1152

4th Movement
2nd Theme   B1153

4th Movement
3rd Theme   B1154

BLOCH, Ernest (1880-   )

Baal Shem, (Three
Pictures of Chassidic
Life) Vn. & Pft.

Vidui (Contrition)
Copyright 1924
by Carl Fischer,
Inc., N. Y.   B1155

Nigun (Improvisation)
1st Theme
Copyright 1924 by Carl Fischer,
Inc., N. Y.   B1156

2nd Theme   B1157

Simchas Torah
Copyright 1924 by Carl Fischer,
Inc., N. Y.   B1158

Concerto grosso
Str. Orch. & Pft.
Obbligato

1st Movement
(Prelude)   B1159

2nd Movement
(Dirge)
1st Theme A   B1160

1st Theme B   B1161

2nd Theme   B1162

3rd Theme   B1163

3rd Movement
Pastorale &
Rustic Dances
1st Theme   B1164

3rd Movement
2nd Theme   B1165

3rd Movement
3rd Theme   B1166

3rd Movement
4th Theme   B1167

3rd Movement
5th Theme   B1168

4th Movement
Fugue
1st Theme   B1169

4th Movement
2nd Theme   B1170

1st Movement
1st Theme   B1171

Quartet, Str.
Copyright renewal
assigned 1946 to
G. Schirmer, Inc.

1st Movement
2nd Theme   B1172

1st Movement
3rd Theme   B1173

2nd Movement
1st Theme   B1174

2nd Movement
2nd Theme   B1175

2nd Movement
3rd Theme   B1176

3rd Movement
1st Theme   B1177

3rd Movement
2nd Theme   B1178

4th Movement
1st Theme   B1179

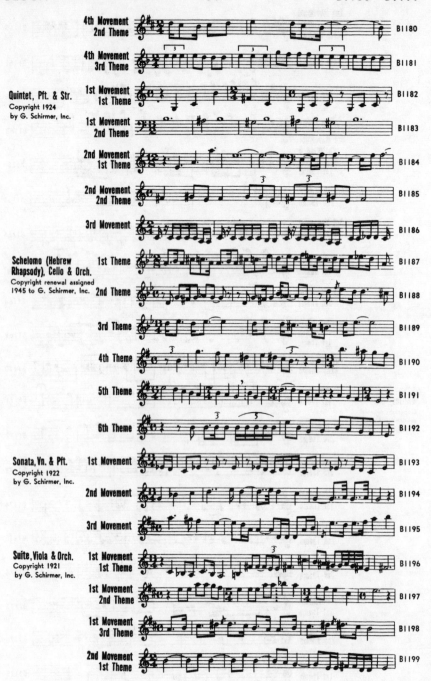

Quintet, Pft. & Str.
Copyright 1924
by G. Schirmer, Inc.

Schelomo (Hebrew
Rhapsody), Cello & Orch.
Copyright renewal assigned
1945 to G. Schirmer, Inc.

Sonata, Vn. & Pft.
Copyright 1922
by G. Schirmer, Inc.

Suite, Viola & Orch.
Copyright 1921
by G. Schirmer, Inc.

2nd Movement
2nd Theme — B1200

3rd Movement — B1201

4th Movement — B1202

Israel, Symphony
Copyright 1925
by G. Schirmer, Inc.

1st Theme — B1203

2nd Theme — B1204

3rd Theme — B1205

4th Theme — B1206

5th Theme — B1207

Three Nocturnes,
Vn., Cello, & Pft.
Copyright by Carl Fischer, Inc., N. Y.
Reprinted by permisssion.

I — B1208

II — B1209

III — B1210

BOCCHERINI, Luigi (1743-1805)

Concerto in B Flat
Cello & Orch.

1st Movement
1st Theme — B1211

1st Movement
2nd Theme — B1212

2nd Movement — B1213

3rd Movement — B1214

Concerto No. 2 in D
Cello & Orch..

1st Movement — B1215

2nd Movement
1st Theme — B1216

2nd Movement
2nd Theme — B1217

3rd Movement
1st Theme,
A — B1218

3rd Movement
1st Theme, B   B1219

Concerto No.3 in G
Cello & Str. Orch.   1st Movement   B1220

2nd Movement   B1221

3rd Movement   B1222

Quartet in D
Op.6, No.1, Str.   1st Movement
1st Theme   B1223

1st Movement
2nd Theme   B1224

2nd Movement   B1225

3rd Movement
1st Theme   B1226

3rd Movement
2nd Theme   B1227

3rd Movement
3rd Theme   B1228

Quartet in A
Op.33, No.6, Str.   1st Movement   B1229

2nd Movement   B1230

3rd Movement
1st Theme   B1231

3rd Movement
2nd Theme   B1232

4th Movement   B1233

Quintet in E,
Str.   1st Movement   B1234

2nd Movement   B1235

3rd Movement
1st Theme   B1236

3rd Movement
2nd Theme   B1237

4th Movement   B1238

Quintet in D, Op.37, Str.
1st Movement — B1239

2nd Movement — B1240

3rd Movement 1st Theme — B1241

3rd Movement 2nd Theme — B1242

Rondo, Cello & Pft.
1st Theme — B1243

2nd Theme — B1244

3rd Theme — B1245

Sonata No. 2 in C, Cello & Pft.
1st Movement — B1246

2nd Movement — B1247

3rd Movement — B1248

Sonata No. 6 in A, Cello & Pft.
1st Movement — B1249

2nd Movement 1st Theme — B1250

2nd Movement 2nd Theme — B1251

3rd Movement 1st Theme — B1252

3rd Movement 2nd Theme — B1253

Sonata in B Flat, Cello & Pft.
1st Movement — B1254

2nd Movement — B1255

3rd Movement 1st Theme — B1256

3rd Movement 2nd Theme — B1257

Sonata in C, Cello & Pft.
1st Movement — B1258

2nd Movement — B1259

3rd Movement — B1260

BOËLLMANN, Leon (1862-1897)

Suite Gothique,   1st Movement
Op. 25, Organ   Introduction-Choral — B1261
Permission for reprint
granted by Durand
& Cie, Paris.   2nd Movement
Elkan-Vogel Co., Inc.   Menuet Gothique — B1262
Philadelphia, Copyright
Owners

3rd Movement — B1263

4th Movement
Toccata — B1264

Variations Symphoniques,   Intro. — B1265
Op. 63, Cello & Orch.
Permission for reprint granted
by Durand & Cie, Paris.   Theme — B1266
Elkan-Vogel Co., Inc. Philadelphia,
Copyright Owners

BOÏELDIEU, Francois (1775-1834)

Le Calife De Bagdad   1st Theme — B1267
Overture

2nd Theme — B1268

3rd Theme — B1269

La Dame Blanche,   1st Theme — B1270
Overture,

2nd Theme — B1271

3rd Theme — B1272

BORODIN, Alexander (1833-1887)

On the Steppes of   1st Theme — B1273
Central Asia, Orch.

2nd Theme — B1274

Polovetsian Dances   1st Theme — B1275
from Prince Igor

2nd Theme — B1276
3rd Theme — B1277
3rd Theme — B1278
4th Theme — B1279

Quartet No.1, in A, Str.
1st Movement Intro. — B1280
1st Movement 1st Theme — B1281
1st Movement 2nd Theme — B1282
2nd Movement 1st Theme — B1283
2nd Movement 2nd Theme — B1284
2nd Movement 3rd Theme Fugato — B1285
3rd Movement 1st Theme — B1286
3rd Movement 2nd Theme — B1287
4th Movement 1st Theme — B1288
4th Movement 2nd Theme — B1289

Quartet No.2 in D, Str.
1st Movement 1st Theme — B1290
1st Movement 2nd Theme — B1291
1st Movement 3rd Theme — B1292
2nd Movement 1st Theme — B1293
2nd Movement 2nd Theme — B1294
3rd Movement 1st Theme Notturno — B1295

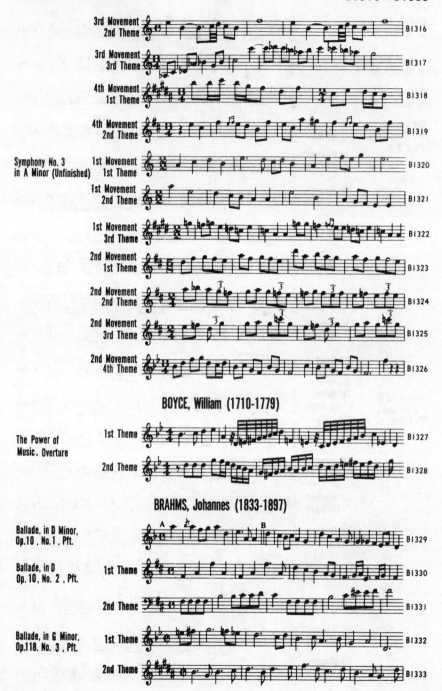

3rd Movement
2nd Theme   B1316

3rd Movement
3rd Theme   B1317

4th Movement
1st Theme   B1318

4th Movement
2nd Theme   B1319

Symphony No. 3   1st Movement
in A Minor (Unfinished) 1st Theme   B1320

1st Movement
2nd Theme   B1321

1st Movement
3rd Theme   B1322

2nd Movement
1st Theme   B1323

2nd Movement
2nd Theme   B1324

2nd Movement
3rd Theme   B1325

2nd Movement
4th Theme   B1326

BOYCE, William (1710-1779)

The Power of   1st Theme   B1327
Music, Overture

2nd Theme   B1328

BRAHMS, Johannes (1833-1897)

Ballade, in D Minor,   B1329
Op.10, No.1, Pft.

Ballade, in D   1st Theme   B1330
Op. 10, No. 2, Pft.

2nd Theme   B1331

Ballade, in G Minor, 1st Theme   B1332
Op.118. No. 3, Pft.

2nd Theme   B1333

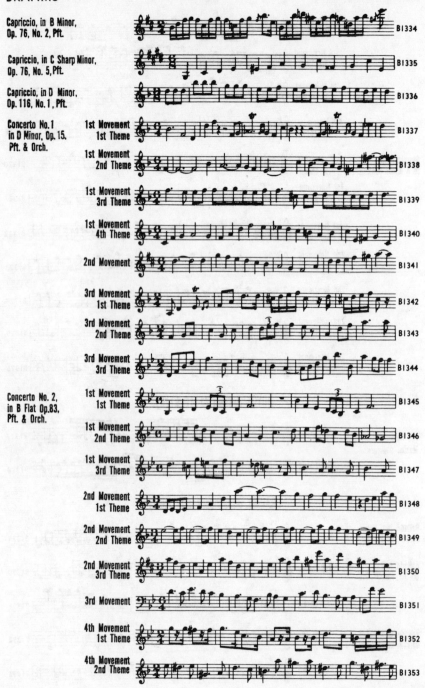

Capriccio, in B Minor, Op. 76, No. 2, Pft. — B1334

Capriccio, in C Sharp Minor, Op. 76, No. 5, Pft. — B1335

Capriccio, in D Minor, Op. 116, No. 1, Pft. — B1336

Concerto No. 1 in D Minor, Op. 15. Pft. & Orch.
1st Movement 1st Theme — B1337
1st Movement 2nd Theme — B1338
1st Movement 3rd Theme — B1339
1st Movement 4th Theme — B1340
2nd Movement — B1341
3rd Movement 1st Theme — B1342
3rd Movement 2nd Theme — B1343
3rd Movement 3rd Theme — B1344

Concerto No. 2, in B Flat Op. 83, Pft. & Orch.
1st Movement 1st Theme — B1345
1st Movement 2nd Theme — B1346
1st Movement 3rd Theme — B1347
2nd Movement 1st Theme — B1348
2nd Movement 2nd Theme — B1349
2nd Movement 3rd Theme — B1350
3rd Movement — B1351
4th Movement 1st Theme — B1352
4th Movement 2nd Theme — B1353

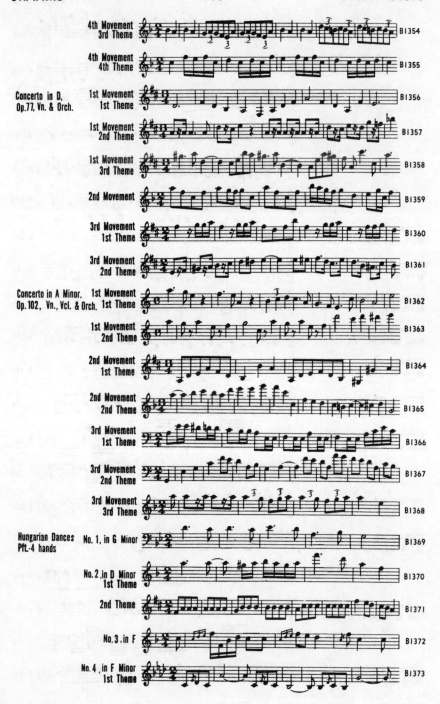

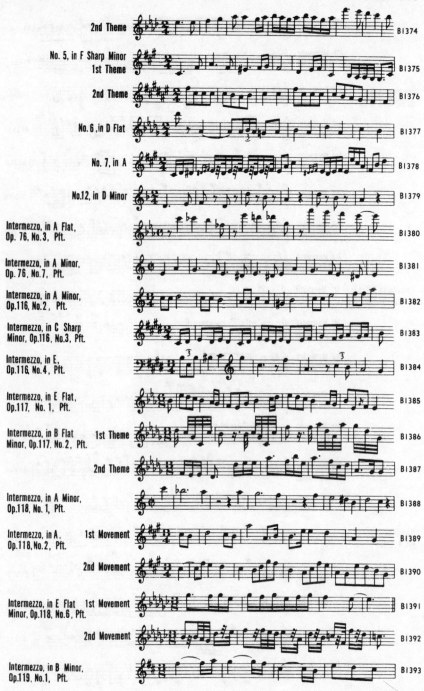

2nd Theme — B1374

No. 5, in F Sharp Minor
1st Theme — B1375

2nd Theme — B1376

No. 6, in D Flat — B1377

No. 7, in A — B1378

No.12, in D Minor — B1379

Intermezzo, in A Flat,
Op. 76, No.3, Pft. — B1380

Intermezzo, in A Minor,
Op. 76, No.7, Pft. — B1381

Intermezzo, in A Minor,
Op.116, No.2, Pft. — B1382

Intermezzo, in C Sharp
Minor, Op.116, No.3, Pft. — B1383

Intermezzo, in E,
Op.116, No.4, Pft. — B1384

Intermezzo, in E Flat,
Op.117, No.1, Pft. — B1385

Intermezzo, in B Flat
Minor, Op.117. No.2, Pft. 1st Theme — B1386

2nd Theme — B1387

Intermezzo, in A Minor,
Op.118, No.1, Pft. — B1388

Intermezzo, in A,
Op.118, No.2, Pft. 1st Movement — B1389

2nd Movement — B1390

Intermezzo, in E Flat 1st Movement
Minor, Op.118, No.6, Pft. — B1391

2nd Movement — B1392

Intermezzo, in B Minor,
Op.119, No.1, Pft. — B1393

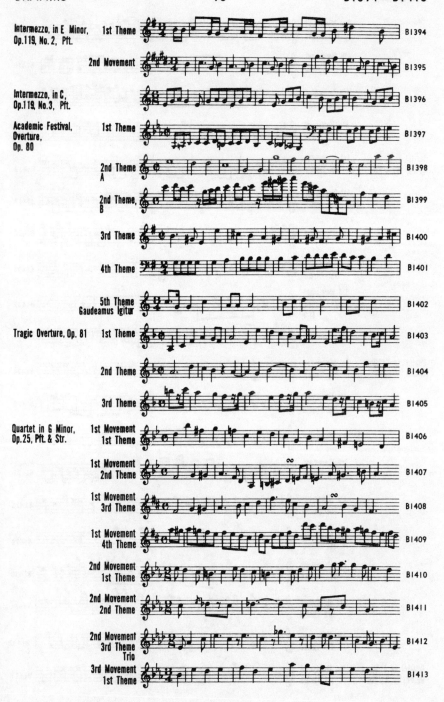

Intermezzo, in E Minor,   1st Theme   B1394
Op.119, No. 2, Pft.

                          2nd Movement   B1395

Intermezzo, in C,   B1396
Op.119, No.3, Pft.

Academic Festival,   1st Theme   B1397
Overture,
Op. 80

                          2nd Theme   B1398
                          A

                          2nd Theme,   B1399
                          B

                          3rd Theme   B1400

                          4th Theme   B1401

                          5th Theme   B1402
                          Gaudeamus Igitur

Tragic Overture, Op. 81   1st Theme   B1403

                          2nd Theme   B1404

                          3rd Theme   B1405

Quartet in G Minor,   1st Movement   B1406
Op.25, Pft. & Str.   1st Theme

                          1st Movement   B1407
                          2nd Theme

                          1st Movement   B1408
                          3rd Theme

                          1st Movement   B1409
                          4th Theme

                          2nd Movement   B1410
                          1st Theme

                          2nd Movement   B1411
                          2nd Theme

                          2nd Movement   B1412
                          3rd Theme
                          Trio

                          3rd Movement   B1413
                          1st Theme

Quartet in A,
Op. 26, Pft. & Str.

Quartet in C Minor
Op. 51, No. 1, Str.

Quartet in A Minor
Op. 51, No. 2, Str.

3rd Movement 2nd Theme — B1414
4th Movement 1st Theme — B1415
4th Movement 2nd Theme — B1416
4th Movement 3rd Theme — B1417
1st Movement 1st Theme — B1418
1st Movement 2nd Theme — B1419
2nd Movement — B1420
3rd Movement 1st Theme — B1421
3rd Movement 2nd Theme Trio — B1422
4th Movement — B1423
1st Movement 1st Theme — B1424
1st Movement 2nd Theme — B1425
2nd Movement — B1426
3rd Movement 1st Theme — B1427
3rd Movement 2nd Theme — B1428
4th Movement 1st Theme — B1429
4th Movement 2nd Theme — B1430
4th Movement 3rd Theme — B1431
4th Movement 4th Theme — B1432
1st Movement 1st Theme — B1433

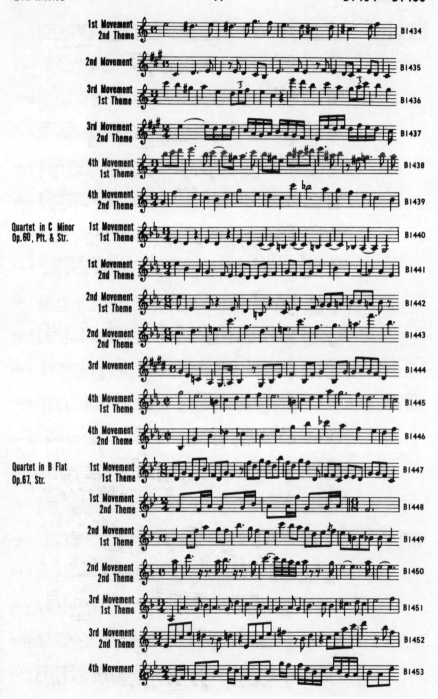

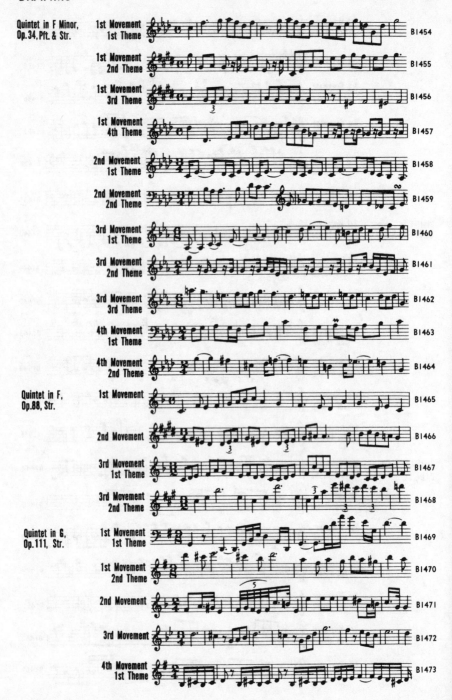

Quintet in F Minor, Op. 34, Pft. & Str.

1st Movement 1st Theme — B1454

1st Movement 2nd Theme — B1455

1st Movement 3rd Theme — B1456

1st Movement 4th Theme — B1457

2nd Movement 1st Theme — B1458

2nd Movement 2nd Theme — B1459

3rd Movement 1st Theme — B1460

3rd Movement 2nd Theme — B1461

3rd Movement 3rd Theme — B1462

4th Movement 1st Theme — B1463

4th Movement 2nd Theme — B1464

Quintet in F, Op. 88, Str.

1st Movement — B1465

2nd Movement — B1466

3rd Movement 1st Theme — B1467

3rd Movement 2nd Theme — B1468

Quintet in G, Op. 111, Str.

1st Movement 1st Theme — B1469

1st Movement 2nd Theme — B1470

2nd Movement — B1471

3rd Movement — B1472

4th Movement 1st Theme — B1473

3rd Movement / 3rd Theme   B1494

4th Movement / Minuet I   B1495

4th Movement / Minuet II   B1496

5th Movement / 1st Theme   B1497

5th Movement / 2nd Theme   B1498

6th Movement / 1st Theme   B1499

6th Movement / 2nd Theme   B1500

Serenade in A, Op. 16, Str.   1st Movement   B1501

2nd Movement / 1st Theme   B1502

2nd Movement / 2nd Theme   B1503

3rd Movement   B1504

4th Movement   B1505

5th Movement / 1st Theme   B1506

5th Movement / 2nd Theme   B1507

Sextet in B Flat, Op.18, Str.   1st Movement / 1st Theme   B1508

1st Movement / 2nd Theme   B1509

1st Movement / 3rd Theme   B1510

2nd Movement   B1511

3rd Movement / 1st Theme   B1512

3rd Movement / 2nd Theme   B1513

4th Movement   B1514

Sextet, in G, Op. 36, Str.

1st Movement 1st Theme   B1515

1st Movement 2nd Theme   B1516

2nd Movement 1st Theme   B1517

2nd Movement 2nd Theme   B1518

3rd Movement   B1519

4th Movement 1st Theme   B1520

4th Movement 2nd Theme   B1521

Sonata in E Minor, Op. 38, Cello & Pft.

1st Movement 1st Theme   B1522

1st Movement 2nd Theme   B1523

2nd Movement 1st Theme   B1524

2nd Movement 2nd Theme   B1525

3rd Movement 1st Theme   B1526

3rd Movement 2nd Theme   B1527

Sonata in F Op. 99, Cello & Pft.

1st Movement 1st Theme   B1528

1st Movement 2nd Theme   B1529

2nd Movement 1st Theme   B1530

2nd Movement 2nd Theme   B1531

3rd Movement 1st Theme   B1532

3rd Movement 2nd Theme   B1533

4th Movement — B1534

Sonata in F Minor, Op. 120, No. 1, Cl. or Viola & Pft.
By permission of Associated Music Publishers, Inc.

1st Movement — B1535

2nd Movement — B1536

3rd Movement — B1537

4th Movement — B1538

Sonata in E Flat Op. 120, No. 2, Cl. or Viola & Pft.
By permission of Associated Music Publishers, Inc.

1st Movement 1st Theme — B1539

1st Movement 2nd Theme — B1540

2nd Movement 1st Theme — B1541

2nd Movement 2nd Theme — B1542

3rd Movement — B1543

Sonata in F Minor, Op. 5, Pft.

1st Movement 1st Theme — B1544

1st Movement 2nd Theme — B1545

2nd Movement 1st Theme — B1546

2nd Movement 2nd Theme — B1547

2nd Movement 3rd Theme — B1548

3rd Movement 1st Theme — B1549

3rd Movement 2nd Theme — B1550

4th Movement 1st Theme — B1551

4th Movement 2nd Theme — B1552

Sonata in G Op. 78, Vn. & Pft.

1st Movement 1st Theme — B1553

1st Movement
2nd Theme — B1554

2nd Movement
1st Theme — B1555

2nd Movement
2nd Theme — B1556

3rd Movement
1st Theme — B1557

3rd Movement
2nd Theme — B1558

Sonata in A
Op. 100, Vn. & Pft.

1st Movement
1st Theme — B1559

1st Movement
2nd Theme — B1560

1st Movement
3rd Theme — B1561

1st Movement
4th Theme — B1562

2nd Movement
1st Theme — B1563

2nd Movement
2nd Theme — B1564

2nd Movement
3rd Theme — B1565

3rd Movement
1st Theme — B1566

3rd Movement
2nd Theme — B1567

Sonata in D Minor,
Op.108, Vn. & Pft.

1st Movement
1st Theme — B1568

1st Movement
2nd Theme — B1569

2nd Movement — B1570

3rd Movement — B1571

4th Movement
1st Theme — B1572

4th Movement
2nd Theme — B1573

4th Movement — B1574

Symphony No.1
in C Minor
Op.68

1st Movement
Intro. A 1 — B1575

Both Themes
Simultaneous
Intro. A 2 — B1576

1st Movement
Intro. B — B1577

1st Movement
1st Theme,
A — B1578

1st Movement
1st Theme,
B — B1579

1st Movement
1st Theme,
C — B1580

1st Movement
2nd Theme — B1581

1st Movement
3rd Theme — B1582

1st Movement
4th Theme — B1583

2nd Movement
1st Theme — B1584

2nd Movement
2nd Theme — B1585

2nd Movement
3rd Theme — B1586

2nd Movement
4th Theme — B1587

3rd Movement
1st Theme — B1588

3rd Movement
2nd Theme — B1589

3rd Movement
3rd Theme,
A — B1590

3rd Movement
3rd Theme,
B — B1591

3rd Movement
4th Theme — B1592

4th Movement
Intro. A — B1593

Symphony No. 2
in D, Op.73

3rd Movement 4th Theme — B1614

4th Movement 1st Theme, A — B1615

4th Movement 1st Theme, B — B1616

4th Movement 2nd Theme — B1617

4th Movement 3rd Theme — B1618

Symphony No. 3 in F Op. 90

1st Movement 1st Theme — B1619

1st Movement 2nd Theme — B1620

1st Movement 3rd Theme — B1621

1st Movement 4th Theme — B1622

2nd Movement 1st Theme — B1623

2nd Movement 2nd Theme — B1624

2nd Movement 3rd Theme — B1625

3rd Movement 1st Theme — B1626

3rd Movement 2nd Theme — B1627

3rd Movement 3rd Theme — B1628

4th Movement 1st Theme A — B1629

4th Movement 1st Theme B — B1630

4th Movement 2nd Theme — B1631

4th Movement 3rd Theme — B1632

4th Movement 4th Theme — B1633

Symphony No. 4 in E Minor, Op. 98

1st Movement 1st Theme A — B1634

1st Movement 1st Theme B — B1635

1st Movement 2nd Theme — B1636

1st Movement 3rd Theme — B1637

1st Movement 4th Theme — B1638

1st Movement 5th Theme — B1639

1st Movement 6th Theme — B1640

1st Movement 7th Theme — B1641

2nd Movement 1st Theme — B1642

2nd Movement 2nd Theme — B1643

2nd Movement 3rd Theme — B1644

3rd Movement 1st Theme A — B1645

3rd Movement 1st Theme B — B1646

3rd Movement 1st Theme C — B1647

3rd Movement 2nd Theme — B1648

4th Movement 1st Theme — B1649

4th Movement 2nd Theme — B1650

4th Movement 3rd Theme — B1651

4th Movement 4th Theme — B1652

4th Movement 5th Theme — B1653

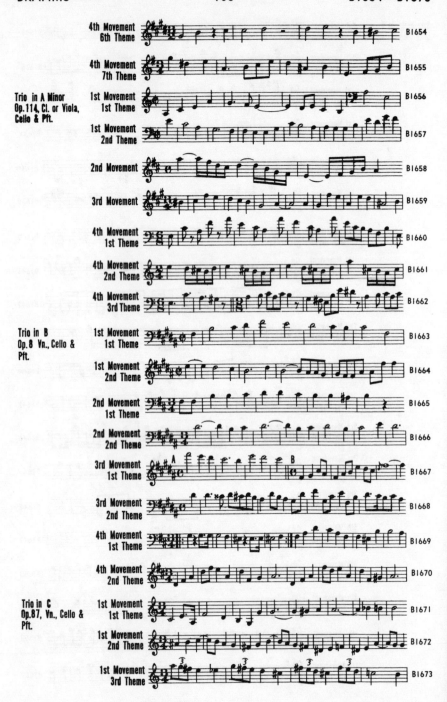

4th Movement 6th Theme — B1654

4th Movement 7th Theme — B1655

Trio in A Minor Op.114, Cl. or Viola, Cello & Pft.

1st Movement 1st Theme — B1656

1st Movement 2nd Theme — B1657

2nd Movement — B1658

3rd Movement — B1659

4th Movement 1st Theme — B1660

4th Movement 2nd Theme — B1661

4th Movement 3rd Theme — B1662

Trio in B Op.8 Vn., Cello & Pft.

1st Movement 1st Theme — B1663

1st Movement 2nd Theme — B1664

2nd Movement 1st Theme — B1665

2nd Movement 2nd Theme — B1666

3rd Movement 1st Theme — B1667

3rd Movement 2nd Theme — B1668

4th Movement 1st Theme — B1669

4th Movement 2nd Theme — B1670

Trio in C Op.87, Vn., Cello & Pft.

1st Movement 1st Theme — B1671

1st Movement 2nd Theme — B1672

1st Movement 3rd Theme — B1673

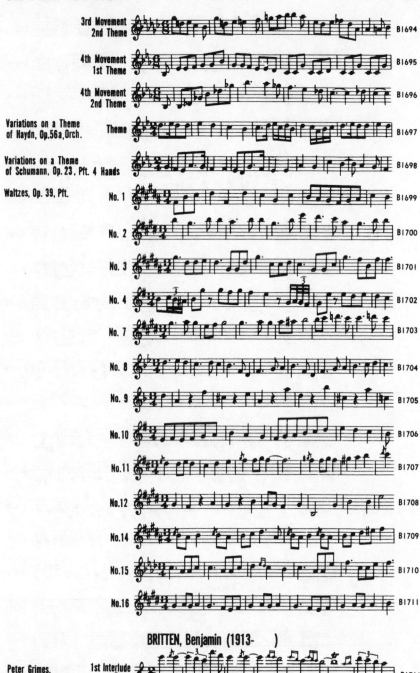

3rd Movement 2nd Theme — B1694

4th Movement 1st Theme — B1695

4th Movement 2nd Theme — B1696

Variations on a Theme of Haydn, Op.56a, Orch. — Theme — B1697

Variations on a Theme of Schumann, Op. 23, Pft. 4 Hands — B1698

Waltzes, Op. 39, Pft. — No. 1 — B1699

No. 2 — B1700

No. 3 — B1701

No. 4 — B1702

No. 7 — B1703

No. 8 — B1704

No. 9 — B1705

No. 10 — B1706

No. 11 — B1707

No. 12 — B1708

No. 14 — B1709

No. 15 — B1710

No. 16 — B1711

BRITTEN, Benjamin (1913-   )

Peter Grimes, Four Sea Interludes, Op. 33a, Orch. — 1st Interlude Dawn — B1711a

Variations on a Theme of
Frank Bridge, Op. 10, Orch.
By permission
of the copyright owner,
Boosey and Hawkes, Inc.

Theme — B1719a

BRUCH, Max (1838-1920)

Concerto No. 1
in G Minor, Vn. & Orch.

Permission for reprint
granted by Durand
& Cie, Paris.
Elkan-Vogel Co., Inc.
Philadelphia, Copyright
Owners.

1st Movement
Intro. — B1720

1st Movement
1st Theme — B1721

1st Movement
2nd Theme — B1722

1st Movement
2nd Theme — B1723

2nd Movement
1st Theme,
A — B1724

2nd Movement
1st Theme,
B — B1725

3rd Movement
1st Theme — B1726

3rd Movement
2nd Theme — B1727

Concerto No. 2
in D Minor, Vn. & Orch.
By permission of Associated
Music Publishers, Inc.

1st Movement
1st Theme — B1728

1st Movement
2nd Theme — B1729

2nd Movement
1st Theme — B1730

2nd Movement
2nd Theme — B1731

3rd Movement
1st Theme,
A — B1732

3rd Movement
1st Theme,
B — B1733

3rd Movement
2nd Theme — B1734

Kol Nidrei (Based on
Traditional Hebrew Themes)
Vn. & Pft.
By permission of Associated
Music Publishers, Inc.

1st Theme — B1735

2nd Theme — B1736

3rd Theme — B1737

BRUCKNER, Anton (1824-1896)

Overture in G Minor
By permission of Associated
Music Publishers, Inc.

1st Theme   B1738

2nd Theme   B1739

3rd Theme   B1740

Quintet in F, Str.
By permission of
International Music Co.

1st Movement
1st Theme   B1741

1st Movement
2nd Theme   B1742

2nd Movement
1st Theme   B1743

2nd Movement
2nd Theme   B1744

3rd Movement   B1745

4th Movement   B1746

**Symphony No. 3
in D Minor**
Copyright by Lienau,
Licensed by
SESAC, Inc., N. Y.

1st Movement
1st Theme   B1747

1st Movement
2nd Theme   B1748

1st Movement
3rd Theme   B1749

1st Movement
4th Theme   B1750

2nd Movement
1st Theme   B1751

2nd Movement
2nd Theme   B1752

2nd Movement
3rd Theme   B1753

3rd Movement
1st Theme   B1754

3rd Movement
2nd Theme,
A   B1755

3rd Movement
2nd Theme
B   B1756

4th Movement 1st Theme — B1757
4th Movement 2nd Theme — B1758
4th Movement 3rd Theme — B1759

Symphony No.4, in E Flat, "Romantic"
By permission of Associated Music Publishers, Inc.

1st Movement 1st Theme — B1760
1st Movement 2nd Theme — B1761
1st Movement 3rd Theme — B1762
2nd Movement 1st Theme — B1763
2nd Movement 2nd Theme — B1764
3rd Movement 1st Theme — B1765
3rd Movement 2nd Theme — B1766
3rd Movement 3rd Theme — B1767
4th Movement 1st Theme — B1768
4th Movement 2nd Theme — B1769
4th Movement 3rd Theme — B1770
4th Movement 4th Theme — B1771

Symphony No.5, in B Flat,
By permission of Associated Music Publishers, Inc.

1st Movement Intro. — B1772
1st Movement 1st Theme — B1773
1st Movement 2nd Theme — B1774
2nd Movement 1st Theme — B1775
2nd Movement 2nd Theme — B1776

Symphony No.7,
in E
By permission of Associated
Music Publishers, Inc.

Symphony No.9,
in D Minor
By permission of Associated
Music Publishers, Inc.

1st Movement
2nd Theme — B1797

1st Movement
3rd Theme — B1798

2nd Movement
1st Theme — B1799

2nd Movement
2nd Theme — B1800

3rd Movement
1st Theme — B1801

3rd Movement
2nd Theme — B1802

BULL, John (1563-1628)

A Gigge (Doctor Bull's My Selfe)
Pft.-Harpsi. — B1803

The King's Hunt, Pft.-Harpsi. — B1804

BUXTEHUDE, Dietrich (1637-1707)

Chaconne, in E Minor, Organ — B1805

Passacaglia, Organ — B1806

Prelude & Fugue, No.6
in E Minor, Organ   1st Theme
Prelude — B1807

2nd Theme
Fugue 1 — B1808

3rd Theme
Fugue 2 — B1809

4th Theme
Fugue 3 — B1810

Prelude & Fugue, No.8
in E, Organ   1st Theme
Prelude — B1811

2nd Theme
Fugue — B1812

Prelude & Fugue, No.14,
in G Minor, Organ   1st Theme
Prelude — B1813

2nd Theme
Fugue I — B1814

3rd Theme
Fugue II — B1815

Toccata No. 20 in F,
Organ — 1st Theme — B1816

2nd Theme — B1817

Toccata No. 21 in F,
Organ — 1st Theme — B1818

2nd Theme — B1819

Toccata No. 22 in G
Organ — B1820

BYRD, William (1543-1623)

The Bells
Fitzwilliam Virginal Book
No. 69, Harpsi. — 1st Theme — B1821

2nd Theme — B1822

3rd Theme — B1823

The Carman's Whistle
Fitzwilliam Virginal Book, No. 58
Variations for Harpsi. — B1824

Galliard
Fitzwilliam Virginal Book No. 92
Harpsi. — B1825

Galliard, The Earl of Salisbury
from The Parthenia, Harpsi. — B1826

Sir John Grayes' Galliard
Fitzwilliam Virginal Book No. 191,
Harpsi. — B1827

Miserere Fitzwilliam
Virginal Book No. 177
Organ or Harpsi. — 1st Theme — B1828

2nd Theme — B1829

O Mistris Myne Fitzwilliam Virginal
Book No. 66, Variations for Harpsi. — B1830

Pavan, The Earl of Salisbury
from The Parthenia
Harpsi. — Theme, A — B1831

Theme, B — B1832

Rowland, Harpsi.
Fitzwilliam Virginal Book No. 160 — B1833

Sellenger's Round, Harpsi.
Fitzwilliam Virginal Book No. 64   B1834

La Volta, Harpsi.
Fitzwilliam Virginal Book No. 155   B1835

Wolsey's Wilde, Harpsi.
Fitzwilliam Virginal Book No. 157   B1836

CABANILLAS, Juan (1644-1712)

Passacalles in D Minor, Organ   C1

Tiento De Falsas, Del 4° Tomo, Organ   C2

CABÉZON, Antonio de (1510-1566)

Tiento, Del 1° Tomo, Organ   C3

Tiento, Del 4° Tomo, Organ   C4

Variations on "El Canto Del Caballero"   C5

CADMAN, Charles Wakefield (1881-   )

Thunderbird Suite, Orch.   1st Movement
(Music for a Production   From the
of Norman Bel Geddes)   Village   C6
(Based on American   2nd Movement
Indian Tunes)   Before the Sunrise   C7

Copyright by
White-Smith
Music Publishers   3rd Movement
Co., Boston.   Nuwana's Love Song
                                  (Blackfeet Indian Tune)   C8
                                  4th Movement
Night Song (Blackfeet Indian Tune)   C9

                                  5th Movement
Wolf Song (War Dance)   C10

CAIX d'HERVELOIS, Louis de (1670-1760)

Suite No. 1, in A,   1st Movement
Cello & Pft.   La Milanese   C11

                                  2nd Movement
                                  Sarabande   C12

                                  3rd Movement
                                  Minuet   C13

3rd Movement
3rd Theme — C32

3rd Movement
4th Theme — C33

3rd Movement
5th Theme — C34

4th Movement
The Lake — C35

5th Movement
Dogs
1st Theme — C36

5th Movement
2nd Theme — C37

6th Movement
Dreams — C38

Quartet in A Minor,
Str.
Copyright 1928 by
G. Schirmer, Inc.

1st Movement
Intro. — C39

1st Movement
1st Theme — C40

1st Movement
2nd Theme — C41

2nd Movement — C42

3rd Movement
1st Theme — C43

3rd Movement
2nd Theme — C44

CASELLA, Alfredo (1883-   )

Il Convento
Veneziano, Ballet
Copyright 1919 by
G. Ricordi & Co., Inc.

Ronde D'Enfants
1st Theme — C45

2nd Theme — C46

Pas Des
Vieilles Dames — C47

La Giara, Ballet
By permission of Associated
Music Publishers, Inc.

Sicilian Dance
"Chiovu" — C48

General Dance — C49

Finale — C50

Pupazzetti, Orch.
By permission of the copyright holders,
J. & W. Chester, Ltd., 11
Great Marlborough
Street, London, W. 1.

1st Movement
1st Theme
Marcietta — C51

1st Movement
2nd Theme — C52

2nd Movement
Berceuse — C53

3rd Movement
Serenata — C54

4th Movement
Notturnino — C55

5th Movement
1st Theme
Polka — C56

5th Movement
2nd Theme — C57

Serenata
Cl., Fg., Tpt., Vn. & Cello
By permission of Associated
Music Publishers, Inc.

1st Movement
Marcia — C58

2nd Movement
Minuet — C59

3rd Movement
1st Theme
Notturno — C60

3rd Movement
2nd Theme — C61

4th Movement
1st Theme
Gavotte — C62

4th Movement
2nd Theme
Musette — C63

5th Movement
Cavatina — C64

6th Movement
Finale-Tarantella — C65

Siciliana E Burlesca,
Vn., Cello, Pft.
Copyright 1919 by
G. Ricordi & Co., Inc.

1st Movement
Siciliana — C66

2nd Movement
Burlesca — C67

CHABRÍER, Alexis Emmanuel (1841-1894)

Bourrée Fantasque,
Pft., Arr. for Orch., F. Mottl
By permission of
M M Enoch & Cie.,
Music Publishers,
27 Boulevard
des Italiens, Paris.

1st Theme — C68

2nd Theme,
A — C69

2nd Theme, B — C70

España, Rhapsody for Orch.
By permission of
M M Enoch & Cie.,
Music Publishers,
27 Boulevard
des Italiens, Paris.

1st Theme — C71

2nd Theme — C72

3rd Theme — C73

4th Theme — C74

5th Theme — C75

Habañera, Pft. or Orch.
By permission of M M Enoch & Cie.,
Music Publishers,
27 Boulevard des Italiens, Paris.
— C76

Joyeuse Marche, Orch.
By permission of
M M Enoch & Cie.,
Music Publishers,
27 Boulevard
des Italiens, Paris.

Intro. — C77

1st Theme — C78

2nd Theme — C79

3rd Theme — C80

Gwendoline, Overture
By permission of
M M Enoch & Cie.,
Music Publishers,
27 Boulevard
des Italiens, Paris.

1st Theme — C81

2nd Theme — C82

3rd Theme — C83

Pieces Pittoresques, Pft.
By permission of
M M Enoch & Cie.,
Music Publishers,
27 Boulevard
des Italiens, Paris.

No. 4 Sous Bois — C84

No. 6 Idylle — C85

No. 7 Danse Villageoise 1st Theme — C86

2nd Theme — C87

No. 8 , Improvisation — C88

No. 10 Scherzo-Valse 1st Theme — C89

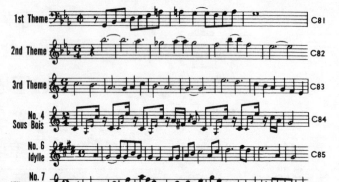
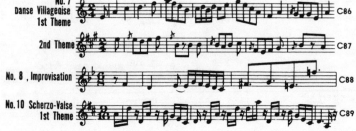

Le Roi Malgré Lui, Orch.
By permission of
M M Enoch & Cie.,
Music Publishers,
27 Boulevard
des Italiens, Paris

Symphonic Sketches
Copyright renewal assigned
1935 to G. Schirmer, Inc.

Air de Ballet, Pft.

Callirhoë, in G
Air de Ballet. Pft.

The Flatterer, Pft.

Scarf Dance, Pft.

CHADWICK, George W. (1854-1931)

CHAMINADE, Cécile (1857-1944)

3rd Theme (Orch. Version)   C108

Serenade, Pft.   C109

Spanish Serenade, Vn. & Pft. Arr. by Kreisler   C110

CHAUSSON, Ernest (1855-1899)

Concerto in D
Pft., Vn. &
Str. Quartet
Op. 21
Copyright by Editions
Salabert Editions Salabert,
22 Rue Chaucat, Paris
Salabert, Inc.,
I East 57 St., N. Y.

1st Movement 1st Theme   C111

1st Movement 2nd Theme   C112

2nd Movement Sicilienne   C113

3rd Movement 1st Theme   C114

3rd Movement 2nd Theme   C115

4th Movement 1st Theme   C116

4th Movement 2nd Theme   C117

Poème, Op. 25, Vn. & Orch.
By permission of Associated
Music Publishers, Inc.

Intro.   C118

1st Theme   C119

2nd Theme   C120

3rd Theme   C121

Quartet, Op. 30
Str. & Pft.
By permission of
International Music Co.

1st Movement 1st Theme   C122

1st Movement 2nd Theme   C123

1st Movement 3rd Theme   C124

2nd Movement 1st Theme   C125

2nd Movement 2nd Theme   C126

Symphony in B Flat, Op. 20

CHAVEZ, Carlos (1899-   )

Concerto
Pft. & Orch.
Copyright 1942
by G. Schirmer, Inc.

Sinfonia India
By permission of the
copyright owners,
G. Schirmer, Inc.

3rd Movement 1st Theme — C127
3rd Movement 2nd Theme — C128
4th Movement 1st Theme — C129
4th Movement 2nd Theme — C130
1st Movement 1st Theme — C131
1st Movement 2nd Theme — C132
1st Movement 3rd Theme — C133
1st Movement 4th Theme — C134
2nd Movement 1st Theme, A — C135
2nd Movement 1st Theme, B — C136
2nd Movement 2nd Theme — C137
3rd Movement 1st Theme — C138
3rd Movement 2nd Theme — C139
1st Movement 1st Theme — C140
1st Movement 2nd Theme — C141
2nd Movement — C142
3rd Movement 1st Theme — C143
3rd Movement 2nd Theme — C144
1st Theme A — C145

1st Theme, B — C146

2nd Theme — C147

3rd Theme — C148

4th Theme — C149

5th Theme — C150

CHERUBINI, Maria Luigi (1760-1842)

Les Abencerages Overture

Intro. — C151

1st Theme — C152

2nd Theme — C153

3rd Theme — C154

Anacreon Overture

Intro. — C155

1st Theme — C156

2nd Theme — C157

Medea Overture

1st Theme — C158

2nd Theme — C159

3rd Theme — C160

Der Wasserträger (Les Deux Journées) Overture

Intro. — C161

1st Theme — C162

2nd Theme — C163

CHOPIN, Frédéric (1810-1849)

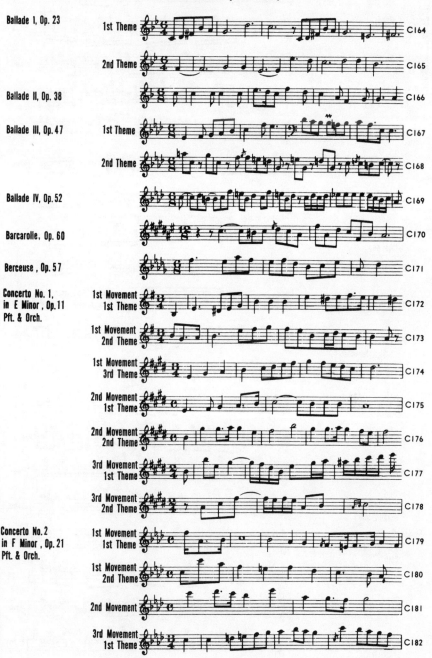

Ballade I, Op. 23 — 1st Theme — C164

2nd Theme — C165

Ballade II, Op. 38 — C166

Ballade III, Op. 47 — 1st Theme — C167

2nd Theme — C168

Ballade IV, Op. 52 — C169

Barcarolle, Op. 60 — C170

Berceuse, Op. 57 — C171

Concerto No. 1, in E Minor, Op. 11 Pft. & Orch. — 1st Movement 1st Theme — C172

1st Movement 2nd Theme — C173

1st Movement 3rd Theme — C174

2nd Movement 1st Theme — C175

2nd Movement 2nd Theme — C176

3rd Movement 1st Theme — C177

3rd Movement 2nd Theme — C178

Concerto No. 2 in F Minor, Op. 21 Pft. & Orch. — 1st Movement 1st Theme — C179

1st Movement 2nd Theme — C180

2nd Movement — C181

3rd Movement 1st Theme — C182

3rd Movement 2nd Theme — C183

Ecossaise, No. 1, Op. 72, No. 3 — C184

Ecossaise, No. 2, Op. 72, No. 4 — C185

Études, Op. 10 No. 1 in C — C186

No. 2 in A Minor — C187

No. 3 in E — C188

No. 4 in C Sharp Minor — C189

No. 5 in G Flat "Black Key" — C190

No. 6 in E Flat Minor — C191

No. 7 in C — C192

No. 8 in F {1st Theme — C193, Simultaneous 2nd Theme — C194}

No. 9 in F Minor — C195

No. 10 in A Flat — C196

No. 11 in E Flat — C197

No. 12 in C Minor "Revolutionary" — C198

Etudes, Op. 25 No. 1 in A Flat "Harp" — C198a

No. 2 in F Minor — C199

No. 3 in F — C200

No. 4 in A Minor — C201

No. 5 in E Minor   1st Theme   C202

2nd Theme   C203

No. 6 in G Sharp Minor   C204

No. 7 in C Sharp Minor   C205

No. 8 in D Flat   C206

No. 9 in G Flat "Butterfly"   C207

No. 10 in B Minor   Intro.   C208

1st Theme   C209

2nd Theme   C210

No. 11 in A Minor "Winter Wind"   C211

No. 12 in C Minor   C212

Posth. Etudes
No. 1 in F Minor   C213

No. 2 in D Flat   C214

No. 3 in A Flat   C215

Fantaisie in F Minor, Op. 49   1st Theme   C216

2nd Theme   C217

3rd Theme   C218

4th Theme   C219

Impromptu, Op. 29   1st Theme   2nd Theme   C220

3rd Theme   C221

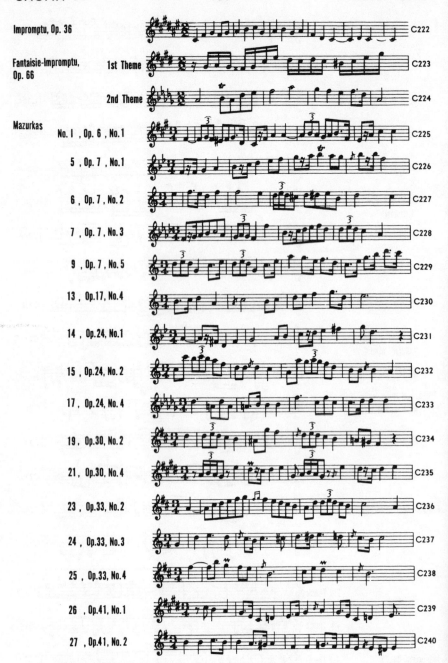

Impromptu, Op. 36   C222

Fantaisie-Impromptu, Op. 66   1st Theme   C223

2nd Theme   C224

Mazurkas

No. 1 , Op. 6 , No. 1   C225

5 , Op. 7 , No. 1   C226

6 , Op. 7 , No. 2   C227

7 , Op. 7 , No. 3   C228

9 , Op. 7 , No. 5   C229

13 , Op. 17, No. 4   C230

14 , Op. 24, No. 1   C231

15 , Op. 24, No. 2   C232

17 , Op. 24, No. 4   C233

19 , Op. 30, No. 2   C234

21 , Op. 30, No. 4   C235

23 , Op. 33, No. 2   C236

24 , Op. 33, No. 3   C237

25 , Op. 33, No. 4   C238

26 , Op. 41, No. 1   C239

27 , Op. 41, No. 2   C240

No. 30 , Op.50, No.1 — C241

31, Op.50, No.2 1st Theme — C242

2nd Theme — C243

32, Op.50, No.3 1st Theme — C244

2nd Theme — C245

36, Op.59, No.1 — C246

38, Op.59, No.3 — C247

39, Op.63, No.1 — C248

41, Op.63, No.3 — C249

42, Op.67, No.1 — C250

43, Op. 67 No.2 — C251

44, Op.67, No.3 — C252

45, Op.67, No.4 — C253

47, Op.68, No.2 1st Theme — C254

2nd Theme — C255

Nocturnes
Op. 9, No.1
in B Flat Minor, 1st Theme — C256

2nd Theme — C257

Op. 9 , No.2
in E Flat — C258

Op. 9, No.3 in B — C259

Op.15 , No.1 in F — C260
Op.15 , No. 2 in F Sharp — C261
Op.15 , No. 3 in G Minor — C262
Op. 27, No.1 in C Sharp Minor — C263
Op. 27, No. 2 in D Flat — C264
Op. 32, No. 1 in B — C265
Op. 32, No. 2 in A Flat — C266
Op. 37, No. 1 in G Minor — C267
Op. 37, No. 2 in G — C268
Op.48 , No.1 in C Minor   1st Theme — C269
2nd Theme — C270
Op.48, No. 2 in F Sharp Minor — C271
Op. 55, No. 1 in F Minor — C272
Op. 55, No. 2 in E Flat — C273
Op.62, No.1 in B — C274
Op.62 , No. 2 in E — C275
Op.72, No. 1 in E Minor — C276
Andante Spianato & Polonaise, Op. 22   1st Theme Andante — C277
2nd Theme Polonaise — C278

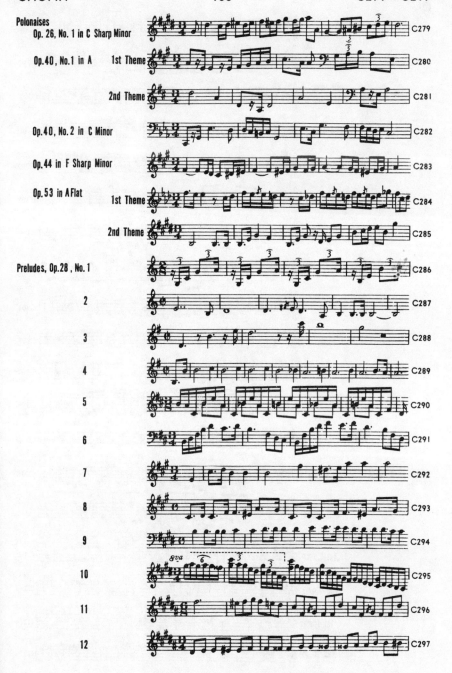

Polonaises
Op. 26, No. 1 in C Sharp Minor — C279

Op. 40, No. 1 in A   1st Theme — C280

2nd Theme — C281

Op. 40, No. 2 in C Minor — C282

Op. 44 in F Sharp Minor — C283

Op. 53 in A Flat   1st Theme — C284

2nd Theme — C285

Preludes, Op. 28, No. 1 — C286

2 — C287

3 — C288

4 — C289

5 — C290

6 — C291

7 — C292

8 — C293

9 — C294

10 — C295

11 — C296

12 — C297

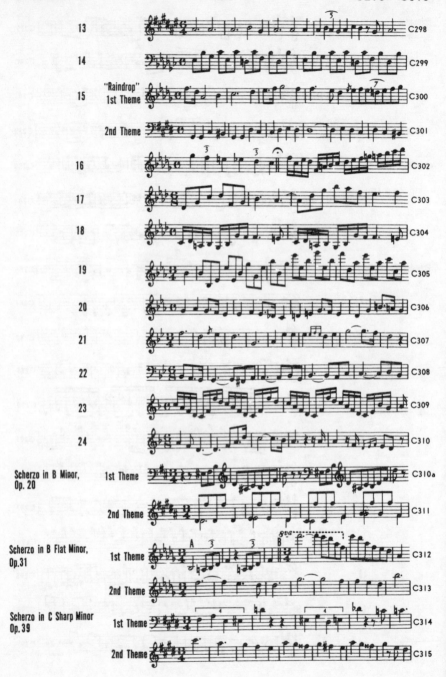

13 — C298

14 — C299

15 "Raindrop" 1st Theme — C300

2nd Theme — C301

16 — C302

17 — C303

18 — C304

19 — C305

20 — C306

21 — C307

22 — C308

23 — C309

24 — C310

Scherzo in B Minor, Op. 20 — 1st Theme — C310a

2nd Theme — C311

Scherzo in B Flat Minor, Op.31 — 1st Theme — C312

2nd Theme — C313

Scherzo in C Sharp Minor Op. 39 — 1st Theme — C314

2nd Theme — C315

3rd Theme — C316

Scherzo in E,
Op. 54 — 1st Theme — C317

2nd Theme — C318

3rd Theme — C319

Sonata in G Minor, Op. 65
Cello & Pft. — 1st Movement — C320

2nd Movement
1st Theme — C321

2nd Movement
2nd Theme — C322

3rd Movement — C323

Sonata in C Minor,
Op. 4 — 1st Movement — C324

2nd Movement
Minuet — C325

3rd Movement — C326

Sonata in B Flat Minor,
Op. 35 — 1st Movement
1st Theme — C327

1st Movement
2nd Theme — C328

2nd Movement
Scherzo
1st Theme — C329

2nd Movement
2nd Theme — C330

3rd Movement
Funeral March
1st Theme — C331

3rd Movement
2nd Theme — C332

Sonata in B Minor,
Op. 58 — 1st Movement
1st Theme — C333

1st Movement
2nd Theme — C334

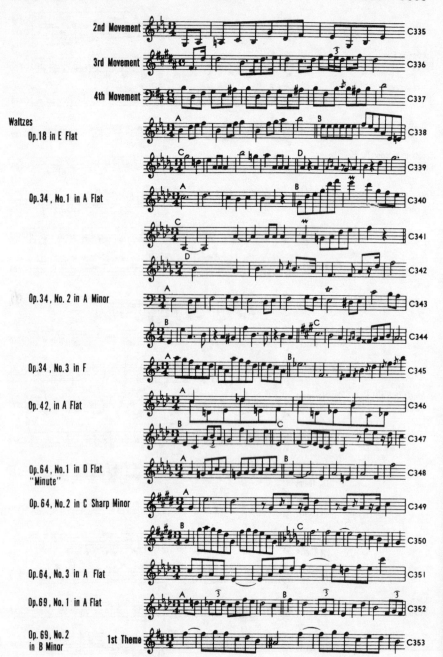

2nd Movement — C335

3rd Movement — C336

4th Movement — C337

Waltzes
Op.18 in E Flat — C338

— C339

Op.34, No.1 in A Flat — C340

— C341

— C342

Op.34, No.2 in A Minor — C343

— C344

Op.34, No.3 in F — C345

Op.42, in A Flat — C346

— C347

Op.64, No.1 in D Flat "Minute" — C348

Op.64, No.2 in C Sharp Minor — C349

— C350

Op.64, No.3 in A Flat — C351

Op.69, No.1 in A Flat — C352

Op.69, No.2 in B Minor — 1st Theme — C353

2nd Theme — C354

Op.70, No.1 in G Flat　1st Theme — C355

2nd Theme — C356

Op.70, No.2 in F Minor — C357

Op.70, No.3 in D Flat — C358

Waltz in E Minor, Posth.　1st Theme — C359

2nd Theme — C360

Waltz in E, Posth. — C361

CIMAROSA, Domenico (1749-1801)

Il Matrimonio Segreto Overture　1st Theme — C362

2nd Theme — C363

CLEMENTI, Muzio (1752-1832)

Sonata in B Flat, Pft. Op.47, No.2　1st Movement — C364

2nd Movement — C365

3rd Movement 1st Theme — C366

3rd Movement 2nd Theme — C367

Sonata in G Minor, Pft. Didone Abbandonata Op.50, No.3　1st Movement Intro. — C368

1st Movement — C369

2nd Movement — C370

3rd Movement — C371

Sonata No. 1 in B Flat
2 Pianos, 4 Hands
1st Movement
1st Theme — C372

1st Movement
2nd Theme — C373

2nd Movement — C374

3rd Movement — C375

Sonata No. 2 in B Flat
2 Pianos, 4 Hands
1st Movement
1st Theme — C376

1st Movement
2nd Theme — C377

2nd Movement
Tempo Di Minuetto — C378

COLERIDGE-TAYLOR, Samuel (1875-1912)

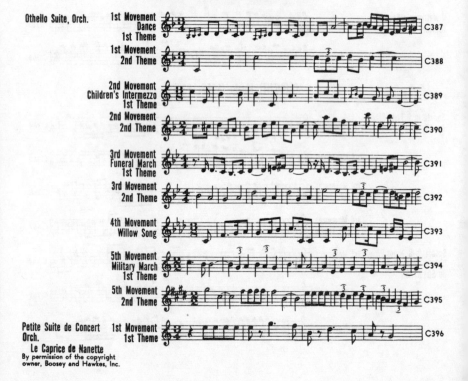

Othello Suite, Orch.
1st Movement
Dance
1st Theme — C387

1st Movement
2nd Theme — C388

2nd Movement
Children's Intermezzo
1st Theme — C389

2nd Movement
2nd Theme — C390

3rd Movement
Funeral March
1st Theme — C391

3rd Movement
2nd Theme — C392

4th Movement
Willow Song — C393

5th Movement
Military March
1st Theme — C394

5th Movement
2nd Theme — C395

Petite Suite de Concert
Orch.
1st Movement
1st Theme — C396

Le Caprice de Nanette

1st Movement / 2nd Theme — C397

Demande et Réponse — 2nd Movement / 1st Theme — C398

2nd Movement / 2nd Theme — C399

Un Sonnet D'Amour — 3rd Movement / 1st Theme — C400

La Tarantelle Frétillante — 3rd Movement / 2nd Theme — C401

4th Movement — C402

COPLAND, Aaron (1900-   )

Appalachian Spring Ballet
By permission of the copyright owner, Boosey and Hawkes, Inc. — 1st Theme — C403

2nd Theme — C404

3rd Theme — C405

4th Theme, A — C406

4th Theme, B — C407

Shaker Melody "The Gift To Be Simple" — 5th Theme — C408

6th Theme — C409

Billy the Kid, Ballet
The Open Prairie
By permission of the copyright owner, Boosey and Hawkes, Inc. — Intro. / 1st Theme — C410

Intro. / 2nd Theme — C411

Street in a Frontier Town (Cowboy Tune) — Scene I / 1st Theme — C412

The Streets of Laredo — 2nd Theme — C413

(Cowboy Tune) — 3rd Theme — C414

(Cowboy Tune) — 4th Theme — C415

COPLAND

The Card Game — Scene II, 1st Theme — C416

Macabre Dance — 3rd Theme — C417

Billy in Prison — 4th Theme — C418

Scene III — C419

Concerto for Orch. & Pft.
Copyright 1929,
Cos Cob Press, Inc.

1st Movement 1st Theme, A — C420

1st Movement 1st Theme, B — C421

1st Movement 2nd Theme — C422

2nd Movement 1st Theme — C423

2nd Movement 2nd Theme — C424

2nd Movement 3rd Theme — C425

2nd Movement 4th Theme — C426

Dance Symphony
Copyright 1931,
Cos Cob Press, Inc.

Intro. — C427

1st Movement 1st Theme — C428

1st Movement 2nd Theme — C429

1st Movement 3rd Theme — C430

2nd Movement 1st Theme — C431

2nd Movement 2nd Theme — C432

3rd Movement 1st Theme — C433

3rd Movement 2nd Theme — C434

3rd Movement 3rd Theme — C435

Music for the Theatre, Small Orch.
Copyright 1932, Cos Cob Press, Inc.

1st Movement Prologue 1st Theme — C436

1st Movement 2nd Theme — C437

2nd Movement Dance 1st Theme — C438

2nd Movement 2nd Theme — C439

3rd Movement Interlude 1st Theme — C440

3rd Movement 2nd Theme — C441

4th Movement Burlesque 1st Theme — C442

4th Movement 2nd Theme — C443

Nocturne, Vn. & Pft.
By permission of the copyright owner, Boosey and Hawkes, Inc.

1st Theme — C444

2nd Theme — C445

Passacaglia, Pft.
By permission of the copyright owner, Boosey and Hawkes, Inc.

— C446

Piano Variations
Copyright 1932, Cos Cob Press, Inc.

Theme — C447

El Salon Mexico, Orch.
By permission of the copyright owner, Boosey and Hawkes, Inc.

Intro. — C448

1st Theme — C449

2nd Theme Trumpet Solo — C450

3rd Theme — C451

4th Theme — C452

5th Theme — C453

6th Theme — C454

7th Theme Clarinet Solo — C455

Two Pieces, Str. Orch.
Copyright by Arrow
Music Press, Inc., N. Y.

1st Movement
Lento Molto
1st Theme
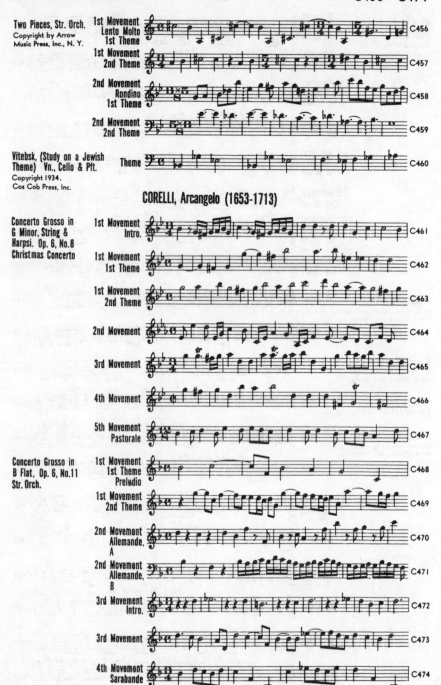 C456

1st Movement
2nd Theme
C457

2nd Movement
Rondino
1st Theme
C458

2nd Movement
2nd Theme
C459

Vitebsk, (Study on a Jewish
Theme) Vn., Cello & Pft.
Copyright 1934,
Cos Cob Press, Inc.

Theme
C460

CORELLI, Arcangelo (1653-1713)

Concerto Grosso in
G Minor, String &
Harpsi. Op. 6, No. 8
Christmas Concerto

1st Movement
Intro.
C461

1st Movement
1st Theme
C462

1st Movement
2nd Theme
C463

2nd Movement
C464

3rd Movement
C465

4th Movement
C466

5th Movement
Pastorale
C467

Concerto Grosso in
B Flat, Op. 6, No. 11
Str. Orch.

1st Movement
1st Theme
Preludio
C468

1st Movement
2nd Theme
C469

2nd Movement
Allemande,
A
C470

2nd Movement
Allemande,
B
C471

3rd Movement
Intro.
C472

3rd Movement
C473

4th Movement
Sarabande
C474

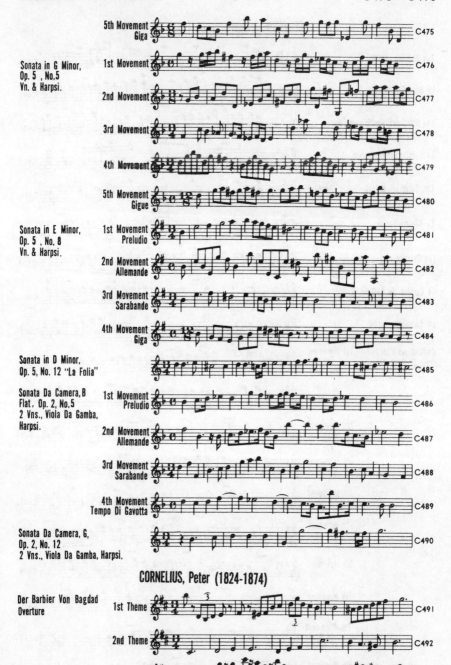

5th Movement
Giga — C475

Sonata in G Minor,
Op. 5 , No.5
Vn. & Harpsi.

1st Movement — C476

2nd Movement — C477

3rd Movement — C478

4th Movement — C479

5th Movement
Gigue — C480

Sonata in E Minor,
Op. 5 , No. 8
Vn. & Harpsi.

1st Movement
Preludio — C481

2nd Movement
Allemande — C482

3rd Movement
Sarabande — C483

4th Movement
Giga — C484

Sonata in D Minor,
Op. 5, No. 12 "La Folia" — C485

Sonata Da Camera, B
Flat , Op. 2, No,5
2 Vns., Viola Da Gamba,
Harpsi.

1st Movement
Preludio — C486

2nd Movement
Allemande — C487

3rd Movement
Sarabande — C488

4th Movement
Tempo Di Gavotta — C489

Sonata Da Camera, G,
Op. 2, No. 12
2 Vns., Viola Da Gamba, Harpsi. — C490

CORNELIUS, Peter (1824-1874)

Der Barbier Von Bagdad
Overture

1st Theme — C491

2nd Theme — C492

3rd Theme — C493

COUPERIN, François (1668-1733)

Les Abeilles, Harpsi.

La Bandoline, Harpsi.

Les Baricades Misterieuses, Harpsi.

Le Bavolet-Flotant, Harpsi.

Les Bergeries, Harpsi.   Rondeau

La Bersan, Harpsi.

Les Calotins et Les Calotines, Harpsi.

Le Carillon de Cythere, Harpsi.

La Commére, Harpsi.

Concert No. 8 in G,   1st Movement
Dans Le Goût Théatral   Overture
                               1st Theme

                               2nd Theme

                        2nd Movement
                        Grande Retournele

                        3rd Movement
                        Air No. 1

                        4th Movement
                        Air Tendre No. 1

                        5th Movement
                        Air Léger No. 1

                        6th Movement
                        Loure

                        7th Movement
                        Air No. 2

                        8th Movement
                        Sarabande Brave
                        Et Tendre

                        9th Movement
                        Air Leger No. 2

C494
C495
C496
C497
C498
C499
C500
C501
C502
C503
C504
C505
C506
C507
C508
C509
C510
C511
C512

Concert Royal, No. 4
in E Minor, Chamber Orch. 1st Movement Prelude C533

2nd Movement Allemande C534

3rd Movement Courante Françoise C535

4th Movement Courante a L'Italiéne C536

5th Movement Sarabande C537

6th Movement Rigaudon C538

7th Movement Forlane C539

La Croûilli ou La Couperinéte, Harpsi. C540

Le Dodo, Harpsi. C541

Les Fastes de La Grande Et Ancienne Ménestrandises, Harpsi.
Act I (Les Notables et Jurés-Ménestrandises) C542

Act II (Les Viéleux et Les Gueux) 1st Theme C543

2nd Theme C544

Act III (Les Jongleurs, Sauteurs, et Saltimbiques) C545

Act IV (Les Invalides) C546

Act V (Desordre et Deroute de Toute La Troupe) C547

La Fleurie ou La Tendre Nanètte Harpsi. C548

Les Folies Françaises Harpsi. 1st Movement La Virginité C549

2nd Movement La Pudeur C550

3rd Movement L'Ardeur C551

4th Movement L'Esperance C552

5th Movement
La Fidelité — C553

6th Movement
Le Perseverance — C554

7th Movement
La Langueur — C555

8th Movement
Le Coqueterie — C556

9th Movement
Les Vieux Galans — C557

10th Movement
Les Coucous Bénévoles — C558

11th Movement
La Jalousie Taciturne — C559

12th Movement
La Frénésie — C560

Le Gazouillement, Harpsi. — C561

L'Himen-Amour, Harpsi. — C562

La Julliet,
Harpsi. or Fl., Cello & Harpsi. — C563

Les Langueurs-Tendres, Harpsi. — C564

Les Moissonneurs, Harpsi. — C565

Le Moucheron, Harpsi. — C566

Musétte de Choisi, Harpsi. — C567

Musétte de Taverni, Harpsi. — C568

La Nanète, Harpsi. — C569

Passacaille, Harpsi.   1st Theme, A — C570

1st Theme, B — C571

Les Petits Moulins à Vent
Harpsi. — C572

Le Rossignol en Amour, Harpsi   C573

Soeur Monique, Harpsi.   C574

Les Tambourins, Harpsi.   C575

Le Tic-Toc-Chic ou Les Maillotins, Harpsi.   C576

Les Vergers Fleuris, Harpsi.   C577

Messe Pour Les Convents, Organ   Offertoire Sur Les Grands Jeux   C578

Recit de Chromhorne   C579

Messe Pour Les Paroisses, Organ   Fugue on the Kyrie   C580

Recit de Chromhorne   C581

Offertoire Sur Les Grands Jeux   1st Theme   C582

2nd Theme   C583

CUI César (1835-1918)

Orientale, Op. 50, No.9, Vn. & Pft.
Copyright renewal assigned 1945
to G. Schirmer, Inc.   C584

Tarantella, Op. 12, Orch.
By permission of Associated
Music Publishers, Inc.   1st Theme   C585

2nd Theme   C586

3rd Theme   C587

4th Theme   C588

DAQUIN, Louis Claude (1694-1772)

Le Coucou, Harpsi.   1st Theme   D1

2nd Theme   D2

La Guitarre, Harpsi.   D3

L'Hirondelle, Harpsi.   D4

Musette Et Tambourin   1st Theme Musette   D5
Harpsi.

   2nd Theme Tambourin   D6

Noël No. 9, (Sur Les Flutes), Organ   D7

Noël No. 10, Organ   D8

DARGOMIJSKY, Alexander Sergeivich (1813-1869)

Roussalka, Opera   Danse Slave   D9

   Gypsy Dance   D10

   Dance of the Nymphs 1st Theme   D11

   2nd Theme   D12

DEBUSSY, Claude (1862-1918)

Prélude A L'Après-Midi
D'Un Faune
(Afternoon of A Faun)   1st Theme   D13
Orch.
Permission for reprint granted   2nd Theme   D14
by Jean Jobert, Paris. Elkan-Vogel Co.
Inc., Philadelphia, Copyright Owners

Arabesque No. 1,
in E, Pft.   1st Theme A   D15
Permission for reprint granted
by Durand & Cie, Paris.
Elkan-Vogel Co., Inc.,   1st Theme B   D16
Philadelphia, Copyright Owners

   2nd Theme   D17

Arabesque No. 2,
in G, Pft.   1st Theme   D18
Permission for reprint granted
by Durand & Cie, Paris.
Elkan-Vogel Co., Inc.,   2nd Theme   D19
Philadelphia, Copyright Owners.

Ballade, Pft.   1st Theme   D20
Permission for reprint granted
by Jean Jobert, Paris.
Elkan-Vogel Co., Philadelphia, Inc.
Copyright Owners.

2nd Theme — D21

Children's Corner Suite, Pft.
Permission for reprint granted by Durand & Cie, Paris. Elkan-Vogel Co., Inc., Philadelphia, Copyright Owners.

Doctor Gradus Ad Parnassum — D22

Jimbo's Lullaby — D23

Serenade of the Doll — D24

The Little Shepherd 1st Theme — D25

2nd Theme — D26

Golliwogg's Cake Walk 1st Theme — D27

2nd Theme — D28

3rd Theme (Parody on Tristan) — D29

Danses, Harp
Permission for reprint granted by Durand & Cie, Paris. Elkan-Vogel Co., Inc., Philadelphia, Copyright Owners.

I Danse Sacrée — D30

II Danse Profane — D31

Danse (Tarantelle Styrienne), Pft.
Permission for reprint granted by Jean Jobert, Paris. Elkan-Vogel Co., Inc. Philadelphia, Copyright Owners.

1st Theme — D32

2nd Theme — D33

Estampes, Pft.
Permission for reprint granted by Durand & Cie, Paris. Elkan-Vogel Co. Inc. Philadelphia, Copyright Owners.

Pagodes — D34

La Soirée dans Grenade 1st Theme — D35

2nd Theme — D36

3rd Theme — D37

Jardins Sous La Pluie (Gardens in the Rain) 1st Theme — D38

2nd Theme — D39

L'Isle Joyeuse, Pft.
Permission for reprint granted by Durand & Cie, Inc., Philadelphia, Copyright Owners.

Intro. — D40

1st Theme — D41
2nd Theme — D42
3rd Theme — D43

Gigues, from Images,
Orch., No. 1
Permission for reprint granted
by Durand & Cie, Paris.
Elkan-Vogel Co., Inc.
Philadelphia, Copyright Owners.

1st Theme — D44
2nd Theme — D45
3rd Theme — D46

Iberia, from Images,
Orch., No. 2
   Par Les Rues et
   Par Les Chemins
   (Along the
   Streets and Roads)

Permission for reprint
granted by Durand
& Cie, Paris. Elkan-Vogel
Co., Inc. Philadelphia,
Copyright Owners.

1st Movement
1st Theme — D47

1st Movement
2nd Theme — D48

1st Movement
3rd Theme — D49

1st Movement
4th Theme — D50

1st Movement
5th Theme — D51

1st Movement
6th Theme — D52

Les Parfums
de La Nuit
(Perfumes of the Night)

2nd Movement
Intro. — D53

2nd Movement
1st Theme — D54

2nd Movement
2nd Theme — D55

2nd Movement
3rd Theme — D56

2nd Movement
4th Theme — D57

2nd Movement
5th Theme — D58

2nd Movement
6th Theme — D59

Le Matin D'Un Jour
De Fête (The
Morning of a Holiday)

3rd Movement
1st Theme — D60

3rd Movement 2nd Theme — D61
3rd Movement 3rd Theme — D62

I Reflets Dans L'Eau from Images—1st Series, Pft. Permission for reprint granted by Durand & Cie, Paris. Elkan-Vogel Co., Inc. Philadelphia, Copyright Owners. — 1st Theme — D63, 2nd Theme — D64

II Hommage à Rameau from Images—1st Series, Pft. Permission for reprint granted by Durand & Cie, Paris. Elkan-Vogel Co., Inc. Philadelphia, Copyright Owners. — 1st Theme — D65, 2nd Theme — D66

Poissons D'Or (Goldfish) from Images—2nd Series, Pft. Permission for reprint granted by Durand & Cie, Paris. Elkan-Vogel Co., Inc. Philadelphia, Copyright Owners. — D67

Mazurka, Pft. Permission for reprint granted by Jean Jobert, Paris. Elkan-Vogel Co., Inc. Philadelphia, Copyright Owners. — D68

La Mer, Orch. De L'Aube A Midi Sur La Mer (From Dawn to Noon on the Sea) Permission for reprint granted by Durand & Cie, Paris. Elkan-Vogel Co., Inc. Philadelphia, Copyright Owners, — 1st Movement 1st Theme — D69, 1st Movement 2nd Theme — D70, 1st Movement 3rd Theme — D71, 1st Movement 4th Theme — D72, 1st Movement 5th Theme — D73, 1st Movement 6th Theme — D74

Jeux De Vagues (Play of the Waves) — 2nd Movement 1st Theme — D75, 2nd Movement 2nd Theme — D76, 2nd Movement 3rd Theme — D77

Dialogue du Vent et de la Mer (Dialogue of the Wind and the Sea) — 3rd Movement 1st Theme — D78, 3rd Movement 2nd Theme — D79

Nocturnes, Orch. Permission for reprint granted by Jean Jobert, Paris. Elkan-Vogel Co., Inc. Philadelphia, Copyright Owners. — Nuages (Clouds) 1st Theme — D80

DEBUSSY

2nd Theme — D81
3rd Theme — D82
Fêtes 1st Theme — D83
2nd Theme — D84
3rd Theme — D85
4th Theme — D86
Sirènes 1st Theme — D87
2nd Theme — D88
En Bateau 1st Theme — D89
2nd Theme — D90
Cortège 1st Theme — D91
2nd Theme — D92
Menuet 1st Theme — D93
2nd Theme — D94
Ballet 1st Theme — D95
2nd Theme — D96
Prelude 1st Theme — D97
2nd Theme — D98
Sarabande — D99
Toccata — D100

Petite Suite, 2 Pianos
Permission for reprint granted
by Durand & Cie, Paris.
Elkan-Vogel Co., Inc.
Philadelphia, Copyright
Owners,

Pour le Piano, Suite
Permission for reprint
granted by Durand & Cie, Paris.
Elkan-Vogel Co., Inc.
Philadelphia, Copyright
Owners,

La Plus Que Lente, Waltz, Pft. — 1st Theme — D101
Permission for reprint granted by Durand & Cie, Paris. Elkan-Vogel Co., Inc. Philadelphia, Copyright Owners.

2nd Theme — D102

Préludes, Book 1, Pft. Permission for reprint granted by Durand & Cie, Paris. Elkan-Vogel Co., Inc. Philadelphia, Copyright Owners,
No. 1 — D103
Danseuses De Delphes

No. 2
Voiles (Veils) — 1st Theme — D104

2nd Theme — D105

No. 5
Les Collines D'Anacapri
(The Hills of Anacapri) — D106

No. 8
La Fille Aux Cheveux De Lin
(The Girl With the Flaxen Hair) — D107

No. 10
La Cathedrale Engloutie
(The Sunken Cathedral) — 1st Theme — D108

2nd Theme — D109

No. 11
La Danse De Puck — D110

No. 12
Minstrels — D111

Préludes, Book ii, Pft. Permission for reprint granted by Durand & Cie, Paris. Elkan-Vogel Co., Inc. Philadelphia, Copyright Owners,
No. 3
La Puerta Del Vino — D112

No. 5
Bruyères (Heather) — D113

No. 6
General Lavine-Eccentric — D114

No. 9, Hommage à
S. Pickwick, Esq., P.P.M.P.C.
(Parody on God Save the King) — D115

Printemps Symphonic Suite, Orch. — 1st Movement 1st Theme — D116
Permission for reprint granted by Durand & Cie, Paris. Elkan-Vogel Co., Inc. Philadelphia, Copyright Owners.

1st Movement 2nd Theme — D117

2nd Movement 1st Theme — D118

2nd Movement 2nd Theme — D119

Quartet in G Minor, Str. — 1st Movement 1st Theme — D120
Permission for reprint granted by Durand & Cie, Paris. Elkan-Vogel Co., Inc. Philadelphia, Copyright Owners.

Suite Bergamasque, Pft.
Permission for reprint granted
by Jean Jobert, Paris.
Elkan-Vogel Co., Inc.
Philadelphia, Copyright Owners.

Prelude — D141

Menuet
1st Theme — D142

2nd Theme — D143

Clair de Lune
1st Theme — D144

2nd Theme — D145

Passepied
1st Theme — D146

2nd Theme — D147

Valse Romantique, Pft.
Permission for reprint granted
by Jean Jobert, Paris.
Elkan-Vogel Co., Inc.
Philadelphia, Copyright Owners, — D148

DELIBES, Clement Philibert Leo (1836-1891)

Coppelia, Ballet
Act I

Prelude
1st Theme — D149

2nd Theme — D150

3rd Theme
(Also Mazurka Theme) — D151

Waltz — D152

Scene — D153

Thème Slave — D154

Czardas
1st Theme — D155

2nd Theme — D156

Act II   Musique des Automates — D157

Valse de la Poupée — D158

Act III   Marche de la Cloche
1st Theme — D159

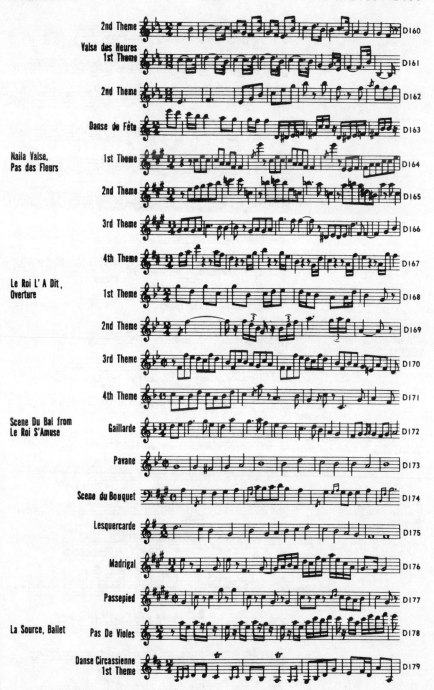

2nd Theme	D160
Valse des Heures 1st Theme	D161
2nd Theme	D162
Danse de Fête	D163
Naila Valse, Pas des Fleurs — 1st Theme	D164
2nd Theme	D165
3rd Theme	D166
4th Theme	D167
Le Roi L' A Dit, Overture — 1st Theme	D168
2nd Theme	D169
3rd Theme	D170
4th Theme	D171
Scene Du Bal from Le Roi S'Amuse — Gaillarde	D172
Pavane	D173
Scene du Bouquet	D174
Lesquercarde	D175
Madrigal	D176
Passepied	D177
La Source, Ballet — Pas De Violes	D178
Danse Circassienne 1st Theme	D179

2nd Theme — D180

Scherzo — Polka — D181

Sylvia, Ballet   Prelude — D182

Les Chasseresses — D183

Valse Lente — D184

Marche de Bacchus
1st Theme — D185

2nd Theme — D186

Pizzicato — D187

DELIUS, Frederick (1862-1934)

Appalachia, Orch.
By permission of the
copyright owner,
Boosey and Hawkes, Inc.   Intro. — D188

1st Theme — D189

2nd Theme
(March Variant of
1st Theme) — D190

Brigg Fair, Orch.
By permission of the
copyright owner,
Boosey and Hawkes, Inc.   1st Theme — D191

2nd Theme — D192

Concerto, Vn. & Orch.
By permission of Augener,
Ltd., London   1st Theme — D193

2nd Theme — D194

3rd Theme — D195

4th Theme — D196

5th Theme — D197

6th Theme — D198

Eventyr
"Once Upon a Time", Orch.
By permission of Augener,
Ltd., London — 1st Theme — D199

2nd Theme — D200

3rd Theme — D201

Hassan,
Suite for Orch.
By permission of the
copyright owner,
Boosey and Hawkes, Inc. — Intermezzo — D202

Serenade — D203

In a Summer Garden, Orch.
By permission of Associated
Music Publishers, Inc. — 1st Theme, A — D204

1st Theme, B — D205

2nd Theme — D206

3rd Theme — D207

4th Theme — D208

Irmelin–Prelude, Orch.
By permission of the copyright
owner, Boosey and Hawkes, Inc. — D209

Paris, Nocturne, Orch.
By permission of Associated
Music Publishers, Inc. — 1st Theme — D210

2nd Theme — D211

3rd Theme — D212

4th Theme — D213

Sonata No. 2, Vn. & Pft.
By permission of the
copyright owner,
Boosey and Hawkes, Inc. — 1st Theme — D214

2nd Theme — D215

3rd Theme — D216

4th Theme — D217

Two Pieces
for Small
Orchestra — No. 1, On Hearing the First Cuckoo in Spring — D218
Copyright by the
Oxford University Press
Reproduced by permission.

No.II Summer Night on the River — D219

The Walk to the Paradise Garden, from A Village Romeo & Juliet, Orch.
By permission of the copyright owner, Boosey and Hawkes, Inc.

1st Theme — D220

2nd Theme — D221

DETT, Robert Nathaniel (1882-1943)

Juba Dance, Pft. from In the Bottoms
By permission of Clayton F. Summy Co., owners of the copyright.

1st Theme — D222

2nd Theme — D223

DIAMOND, David (1915-   )

Rounds, Str. Orch.
Permission granted by Elkan-Vogel Co., Inc. Philadelphia, Pa. Copyright 1946

1st Movement 1st Theme — D223a

1st Movement 2nd Theme — D223b

1st Movement 3rd Theme — D223c

2nd Movement — D223d

3rd Movement 1st Theme — D223e

3rd Movement 2nd Theme — D223f

DINICU, ARR. BY HEIFETZ

Hora Staccato, Vn. & Pft.
Copyright 1930 by Carl Fischer, Inc., N. Y.

1st Theme — D224

2nd Theme — D225

DITTERSDORF, Carl Ditters von (1739-1799)

Quartet, No. 5, in E Flat, Str.

1st Movement — D226

2nd Movement 1st Theme — D227

2nd Movement 2nd Theme — D228

3rd Movement — D229

Quartet, No. 6, in A, Str. — 1st Movement — D230

2nd Movement — D231

3rd Movement — D232

DOHNÁNYI, Ernest von (1877-   )

Capriccio, Op. 28, Pft. — D233

Rhapsody, Op. 11, No. 3, Pft.
By permission of Associated Music Publishers, Inc. — 1st Theme — D234

2nd Theme — D235

Ruralia Hungarica, Op. 32a, No. 1 — D236

Ruralia Hungarica, Op. 32a, No. 2 — 1st Theme — D237

2nd Theme — D238

Ruralia Hungarica, Op. 32a, No. 7 — D239

Suite, Op. 19, Orch.
By permission of Associated Music Publishers, Inc. — Andante con Variazioni — D240

Scherzo 1st Theme — D241

2nd Theme — D242

Romance 1st Theme — D243

2nd Theme — D244

Rondo 1st Theme — D245

2nd Theme — D246

DONIZETTI, Alfredo (1867-1921)

Daughter of the Regiment
Overture   1st Theme  D247

2nd Theme · D248

3rd Theme · D249

4th Theme · D250

La Favorita
Overture   1st Theme · D251

2nd Theme · D252

Don Pasquale
Overture   1st Theme · D253

2nd Theme · D254

DOWLAND, John (1563-1626)

M. George Whitehead, His Almand
Lute & Strings · D255

Mrs. Nichols' Almand
Lute & Strings · D256

M. Henry Nöel, His Galliard
Lute & Strings · D257

M. Thomas Collier, His Galliard
Lute & Strings · D258

M. John Langton's Pavan
Lute & Strings · D259

The King of Denmark's Galliard
Lute & Strings · D260

The Earl of Essex Galliard
Lute & Strings · D261

DRDLA, Franz (1868-   )

Souvenir, Vn. & Pft.   1st Theme  D261a

2nd Theme · D261b

DRIGO, Riccardo (1846-1930)

Les Millions
d'Arlequin, Serenade
Vn. & Pft.
1st Theme — D261c

2nd Theme — D261d

Valse Bluette, Vn. & Pft. — D261e

DUKAS, Paul (1865-1935)

L'Apprenti Sorcier
(The Sorcerer's Apprentice)
Scherzo for Orch.
Permission for reprint granted
by Durand & Cie, Paris.
Elkan-Vogel Co., Inc.
Philadelphia, Copyright Owners.
Intro. — D262
1st Theme — D263
2nd Theme — D264

La Péri
Dance Poem for Orch.
Permission for reprint granted
by Durand & Cie, Paris.
Elkan-Vogel Co., Inc.
Philadelphia, Copyright Owners.
1st Theme — D265
2nd Theme — D266
3rd Theme — D267
4th Theme — D268

DVOŘÁK, Antonin (1841-1904)

Bagatelles, Op. 47,
Pft. & Str.
By permission of Associated
Music Publishers, Inc.
1st Movement — D269
2nd Movement — D270
4th Movement — D271
5th Movement
1st Theme — D272
5th Movement
2nd Theme — D273

Carnaval Overture, Op. 92
By permission of Associated
Music Publishers, Inc.
1st Theme — D274
2nd Theme — D275

3rd Theme — D276

4th Theme — D277

Concerto in B Minor,
Op.104, Cello & Orch.
Copyright 1930
by G. Schirmer, Inc.

1st Movement
1st Theme — D278

1st Movement
2nd Theme — D279

2nd Movement
1st Theme — D280

2nd Movement
2nd Theme — D281

3rd Movement
1st Theme — D282

3rd Movement
2nd Theme — D283

Concerto in A Minor,
Op. 53, Vn. & Orch.
By permission of Associated
Music Publishers, Inc.

1st Movement
1st Theme,
A — D284

1st Movement
1st Theme,
B — D285

1st Movement
2nd Theme — D286

2nd Movement
1st Theme — D287

2nd Movement
2nd Theme — D288

3rd Movement
1st Theme — D289

3rd Movement
2nd Theme — D290

3rd Movement
3rd Theme — D291

Humoresque, Op. 101,
No. 7, Pft.
By permission of Associated
Music Publishers, Inc.

1st Theme — D292

2nd Theme — D293

3rd Theme — D294

Quartet in D,
Op. 23, Pft. & Str.
By permission of Associated
Music Publishers, Inc.

1st Movement
1st Theme — D295

Quartet in E Flat,
Op. 87, Pft. & Str.
By permission of
Associated Music
Publishers, Inc.

Quart., in F, Op. 96
Str.,"American"
By permission of
Associated Music
Publishers, Inc.

1st Movement 2nd Theme — D296
2nd Movement — D297
3rd Movement 1st Theme — D298
3rd Movement 2nd Theme — D299
1st Movement 1st Theme — D300
1st Movement 2nd Theme — D301
2nd Movement — D302
3rd Movement 1st Theme — D303
3rd Movement 2nd Theme — D304
4th Movement 1st Theme — D305
4th Movement 2nd Theme — D306
1st Movement 1st Theme — D307
1st Movement 2nd Theme — D308
2nd Movement — D309
3rd Movement 1st Theme — D310
3rd Movement 2nd Theme A — D311
3rd Movement 2nd Theme B — D312
4th Movement Intro. — D313
4th Movement 1st Theme — D314
4th Movement 2nd Theme — D315

DVORAK

DVORAK — 166 — D316—D332c

Quartet in A Flat, Op. 105, Str.
By permission of Associated Music Publishers, Inc.

- 1st Movement 1st Theme — D316
- 1st Movement 2nd Theme — D317
- 2nd Movement 1st Theme — D318
- 2nd Movement 2nd Theme — D319
- 3rd Movement — D320
- 4th Movement 1st Theme — D321
- 4th Movement 2nd Theme — D322
- 4th Movement 3rd Theme — D323

Quartet in G, Op. 106, Str.
By permission of Associated Music Publishers, Inc.

- 1st Movement 1st Theme — D324
- 1st Movement 2nd Theme — D325
- 2nd Movement — D326
- 3rd Movement 1st Theme — D327
- 3rd Movement 2nd Theme — D328
- 3rd Movement 3rd Theme — D329
- 4th Movement 1st Theme — D330
- 4th Movement 2nd Theme — D331
- 4th Movement 3rd Theme — D332

Quintet, Op. 81 Pft. & Str.

- 1st Movement 1st Theme — D332a
- 1st Movement 2nd Theme — D332b
- 2nd Movement Dumka 1st Theme, A — D332c

2nd Movement 1st Theme, B — D332d

2nd Movement 1st Theme, C — D332e

2nd Movement 2nd Theme — D332f

3rd Movement — D332g

4th Movement 1st Theme — D332h

4th Movement 2nd Theme — D332i

Quintet in E Flat, Op. 97, Str.
By permission of Associated Music Publishers, Inc.

1st Movement 1st Theme — D333

1st Movement 2nd Theme — D334

2nd Movement 1st Theme — D335

2nd Movement 2nd Theme — D336

3rd Movement — D337

4th Movement — D338

Scherzo Capriccioso, Op. 66, Orch.
By permission of Associated Music Publishers, Inc.

1st Theme — D339

2nd Theme — D340

3rd Theme — D341

4th Theme — D342

Serenade for Strings, in E, Op. 22
By permission of Associated Music Publishers, Inc.

1st Movement 1st Theme — D343

1st Movement 2nd Theme — D344

2nd Movement 1st Theme — D345

2nd Movement 2nd Theme — D346

2nd Theme D387
No. 6 **1st Theme** D388
2nd Theme D389
No. 7 **1st Theme** D390
2nd Theme D391
3rd Theme D392
4th Theme D393
No. 8 **1st Theme** D394
2nd Theme D395
3rd Theme D396
4th Theme D397
5th Theme D398
Slavonic Rhapsody, Op. 45, No. 3, Orch.
By permission of Associated Music Publishers, Inc.
1st Theme D399
2nd Theme D400
3rd Theme D401
Sonatina in G, Op. 100, Vn. & Pft.
By permission of Associated Music Publishers, Inc.
1st Movement 1st Theme D402
1st Movement 2nd Theme D403
(Arr. by Kreisler as "Indian Lament")
2nd Movement 1st Theme D404
2nd Movement 2nd Theme D405
3rd Movement D406

Symphony No. 1, in D.
Op. 60
By permission of
Associated Music
Publishers, Inc.

Symphony No. 2
in D Minor, Op. 70
By permission of
Associated Music
Publishers, Inc.

Symphony No. 4
in G, Op. 88
By permission of
Novello & Co., Ltd.,
London

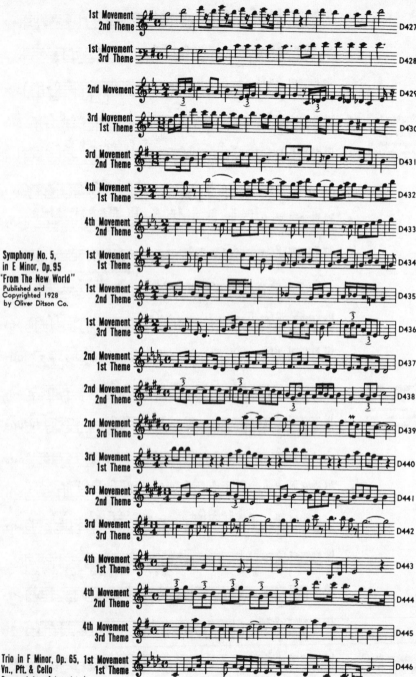

1st Movement 2nd Theme — D427

1st Movement 3rd Theme — D428

2nd Movement — D429

3rd Movement 1st Theme — D430

3rd Movement 2nd Theme — D431

4th Movement 1st Theme — D432

4th Movement 2nd Theme — D433

Symphony No. 5, in E Minor, Op. 95 "From The New World" Published and Copyrighted 1928 by Oliver Ditson Co.

1st Movement 1st Theme — D434

1st Movement 2nd Theme — D435

1st Movement 3rd Theme — D436

2nd Movement 1st Theme — D437

2nd Movement 2nd Theme — D438

2nd Movement 3rd Theme — D439

3rd Movement 1st Theme — D440

3rd Movement 2nd Theme — D441

3rd Movement 3rd Theme — D442

4th Movement 1st Theme — D443

4th Movement 2nd Theme — D444

4th Movement 3rd Theme — D445

Trio in F Minor, Op. 65, Vn., Pft. & Cello By permission of Associated Music Publishers, Inc.

1st Movement 1st Theme — D446

1st Movement
2nd Theme   D447

2nd Movement   D448

3rd Movement   D449

4th Movement
1st Theme   D450

4th Movement
2nd Theme   D451

Trio, Op. 90 Vn.
Pft. & Cello,"Dumky"
By permission of
Associated Music
Publishers, Inc.

1st Movement
Intro.   D452

1st Movement
1st Theme,
A   D453

1st Movement
1st Theme,
B   D454

1st Movement
2nd Theme   D455

1st Movement
3rd Theme   D456

2nd Movement   D457

3rd Movement
1st Theme   D458

3rd Movement
2nd Theme   D459

4th Movement
1st Theme   D460

4th Movement
2nd Theme   D461

5th Movement
Intro.   D462

5th Movement   D463

Wedding Dance From
Die Waldtaube, Op. 110,
Orch.
By permission of Associated
Music Publishers, Inc.

1st Theme   D464

2nd Theme   D465

Waltzes, Op. 54, Pft.
No. 1
By permission of Associated
Music Publishers, Inc.   D466

No. 3   1st Theme   D467

2nd Theme   D468

No. 6   D469

ELGAR, Sir Edward (1857-1934)

Chanson de Nuit, Op. 15, No. 1, Orch.
By permission of Novello & Co., Ltd., London.   E1

Cockaigne, In London Town Op. 40, Concert Overture, Orch.   1st Theme   E2
By permission of the copyright owner, Boosey and Hawkes, Inc.

2nd Theme   E3

3rd Theme   E4

4th Theme   E5

Concerto in E Minor, Op. 85, Cello & Orch.   1st Movement Intro.   E6
By permission of Novello & Co., Ltd., London.

1st Movement 1st Theme   E7

1st Movement 2nd Theme   E8

2nd Movement 1st Theme   E9

2nd Movement 2nd Theme   E10

3rd Movement   E11

4th Movement   E12

Concerto in B Minor, Op. 61, Vn. & Orch.   1st Movement 1st Theme, A   E13
By permission of Novello & Co., Ltd., London.

1st Movement 1st Theme, B   E14

1st Movement 2nd Theme   E15

2nd Movement 1st Theme   E16

2nd Movement 2nd Theme — E17
3rd Movement 1st Theme — E18
3rd Movement 2nd Theme — E19

Contrasts, Op. 10, No. 3, Orch.
By permission of Novello & Co., Ltd., London.

1st Theme — E20
2nd Theme — E21

"Enigma" Variations, Op. 36, Orch.
By permission of Novello & Co., Ltd., London.

Theme — E22

Falstaff, Op. 68, Symphonic Study
By Permission of Novello & Co., Ltd., London

1st Theme — E23
2nd Theme — E24
3rd Theme — E25
4th Theme — E26
5th Theme — E27
6th Theme — E28
7th Theme — E29
8th Theme — E30
9th Theme — E31

Introduction and Allegro, Op. 47, Str. Quart. & Str. Orch.
By permission of Novello & Co., Ltd., London.

Intro. — E32
1st Theme — E33
2nd Theme — E34
3rd Theme — E35

May Song, Orch.

1st Theme — E36

Pomp and Circumstance,
Military Marches, Op. 39
No. 1
By permission of the
copyright owner,
Boosey and Hawkes, Inc.

No. 2

No. 3

No. 4

Salut D'Amour, Op. 12, Orch.
By permission of Associated
Music Publishers, Inc.

Serenade, Op. 20.
Str. Orch.
By permission of Associated
Music Publishers, Inc.

Sonata in E Minor,
Op. 82, Vn. & Pft.
By permission of
Novello & Co., Ltd.,
London.

2nd Movement 2nd Theme — E57

3rd Movement 1st Theme — E58

3rd Movement 2nd Theme — E59

Symphony No. 1, in A Flat, Op. 55
By permission of Novello & Co., Ltd., London.

1st Movement Intro. — E60

1st Movement 1st Theme — E61

1st Movement 2nd Theme — E62

2nd Movement 1st Theme — E63

2nd Movement 2nd Theme — E64

2nd Movement 3rd Theme — E65

2nd Movement 4th Theme — E66

3rd Movement 1st Theme — E67

3rd Movement 2nd Theme, A — E68

3rd Movement 2nd Theme, B — E69

3rd Movement 3rd Theme — E70

4th Movement 1st Theme — E71

4th Movement 2nd Theme — E72

4th Movement 3rd Theme — E73

The Wand of Youth Suite No. 1, Op. 1a, Orch.
By permission of Novello & Co., Ltd., London.

Overture — E74

Serenade — E75

Minuet (Old Style) — E76

Sun Dance — E77

Fairy Pipers — E78

Slumber Scene — E79

ENESCO, Georges (1881-   )

Poème Roumain, Op. 1
Symphonic Suite
By permission of
M M Enoch & Cie.,
Music Publishers,
27 Boulevard
des Italiens, Paris.

1st Movement
1st Theme — E80

1st Movement
2nd Theme — E81

1st Movement
3rd Theme — E82

2nd Movement
1st Theme — E83

2nd Movement
2nd Theme — E84

2nd Movement
Roumanian Folk Song
3rd Theme — E85

2nd Movement
4th Theme — E86

2nd Movement
5th Theme — E87

2nd Movement
Roumanian National Anthem — E88

Roumanian Rhapsody No. 1,
Op. 11, Orch.
By permission of
M M Enoch & Cie.,
Music Publishers,
27 Boulevard
des Italiens, Paris.

1st Theme,
A — E89

1st Theme,
B — E90

2nd Theme — E91

3rd Theme,
A — E92

3rd Theme,
B — E93

4th Theme — E94

5th Theme — E95

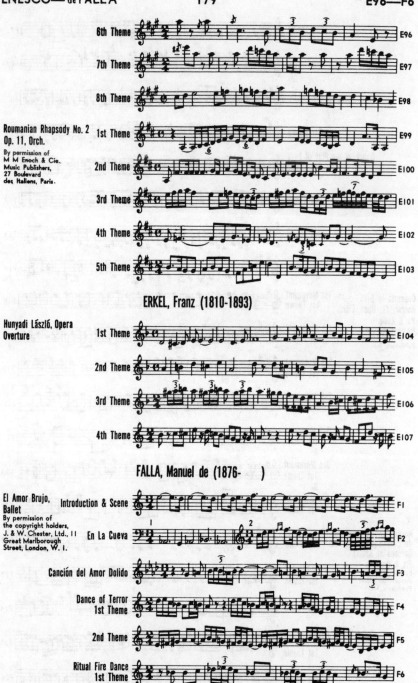

6th Theme — E96
7th Theme — E97
8th Theme — E98

Roumanian Rhapsody No. 2 Op. 11, Orch.

By permission of M M Enoch & Cie. Music Publishers, 27 Boulevard des Italiens, Paris.

1st Theme — E99
2nd Theme — E100
3rd Theme — E101
4th Theme — E102
5th Theme — E103

ERKEL, Franz (1810-1893)

Hunyadi László, Opera Overture

1st Theme — E104
2nd Theme — E105
3rd Theme — E106
4th Theme — E107

FALLA, Manuel de (1876-)

El Amor Brujo, Ballet

By permission of the copyright holders, J. & W. Chester, Ltd., 11 Great Marlborough Street, London, W. 1.

Introduction & Scene — F1
En La Cueva — F2
Canción del Amor Dolido — F3
Dance of Terror 1st Theme — F4
2nd Theme — F5
Ritual Fire Dance 1st Theme — F6

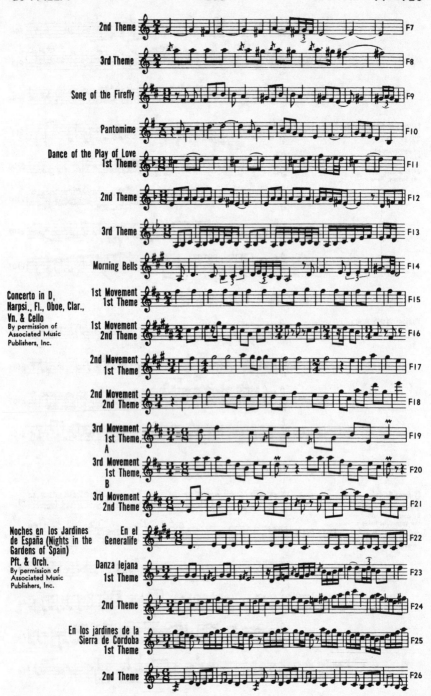

4 Pieces Espagñoles, Pft.
Permission for reprint
granted by Durand & Cie, Paris.
Elkan-Vogel Co., Inc.
Philadelphia, Copyright Owners.

3 Dances from El Sombrero de Tres Picos (The Three Cornered Hat), Orch.
By permission of the copyright holders, J. & W. Chester, Ltd., 11 Great Marlborough Street, London, W. 1.

Suite Populaire Espagñole, Vn. & Pft.
By permission of the copyright holders, J. & W. Chester, Ltd., 11 Great Marlborough Street, London, W. 1.

Aragonesa F27
Cubana F28
Montañesa 1st Theme F29
2nd Theme F30
Andaluza 1st Theme F31
2nd Theme F32
Dance of the Neighbors 1st Theme F33
2nd Theme F34
Danse du Corregidor (Mayor's Dance) 1st Theme F35
2nd Theme F36
Jota 1st Theme F37
2nd Theme F38
3rd Theme F39
4th Theme F40
Miller's Dance F41
El Pano Moruno F42
Nana F43
Canción F44
Polo F45
Asturiana F46

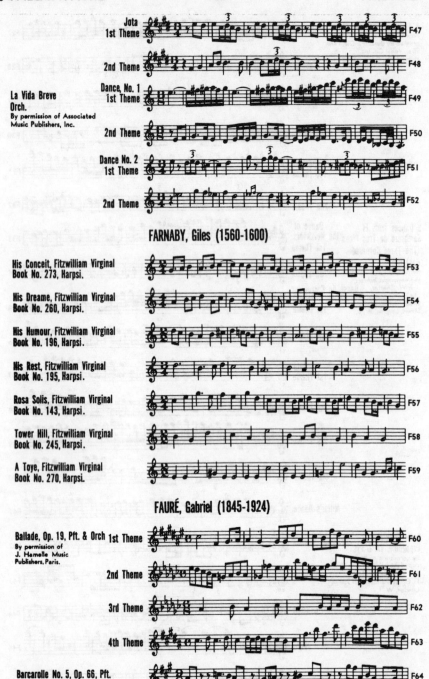

Jota 1st Theme   F47

2nd Theme   F48

La Vida Breve
Orch.
By permission of Associated
Music Publishers, Inc.

Dance, No. 1 1st Theme   F49

2nd Theme   F50

Dance No. 2 1st Theme   F51

2nd Theme   F52

FARNABY, Giles (1560-1600)

His Conceit, Fitzwilliam Virginal
Book No. 273, Harpsi.   F53

His Dreame, Fitzwilliam Virginal
Book No. 260, Harpsi.   F54

His Humour, Fitzwilliam Virginal
Book No. 196, Harpsi.   F55

His Rest, Fitzwilliam Virginal
Book No. 195, Harpsi.   F56

Rosa Solis, Fitzwilliam Virginal
Book No. 143, Harpsi.   F57

Tower Hill, Fitzwilliam Virginal
Book No. 245, Harpsi.   F58

A Toye, Fitzwilliam Virginal
Book No. 270, Harpsi.   F59

FAURÉ, Gabriel (1845-1924)

Ballade, Op. 19, Pft. & Orch 1st Theme
By permission of
J. Hamelle Music
Publishers, Paris.   F60

2nd Theme   F61

3rd Theme   F62

4th Theme   F63

Barcarolle No. 5, Op. 66, Pft.
By permission of J. Hamelle
Music Publishers, Paris.   F64

FAURE   183   F65—F80

Barcarolle No. 6, Op. 70, Pft.   F65
By permission of
J. Hamelle Music
Publishers, Paris.

Dolly, Op. 56, Pft.,   Berceuse   F66
4 Hands
By permission of
J. Hamelle Music
Publishers, Paris.

                            Mi-a-ou   F67
                            1st Theme

                            2nd Theme   F68

                     Le Jardin de Dolly   F69

                            Kitty-Valse   F70
                            1st Theme

                            2nd Theme   F71

                            Tendresse   F72

                     Le Pas Espagnol   F73
                            1st Theme

                            2nd Theme   F74

Elégie, Op. 24,   1st Theme   F75
Cello & Orch.
By permission of
J. Hamelle Music
Publishers, Paris.

                            2nd Theme   F76

Impromptu, No. 2,   1st Theme   F76a
Op. 34, Pft.
By permission of
International Music Co.

                            2nd Theme   F76b

Impromptu, No.3,   1st Theme   F76c
Op. 34, Pft.
By permission of
International Music Co.

                            2nd Theme   F76d

3rd Nocturne, Op. 33, No. 3, Pft.   F77
By permission of
J. Hamelle Music
Publishers, Paris.

4th Nocturne, Op. 36, Pft.   F78
By permission of
J. Hamelle Music
Publishers, Paris.

6th Nocturne, Op. 63, Pft. 1st Theme   F79
By permission of
J. Hamelle Music
Publishers, Paris.

                            2nd Theme   F80

Pelléas and Mélisande,
Op. 80, Orch.
By permission of
J. Hamelle Music
Publishers, Paris.

Prélude / 1st Theme — F81

2nd Theme — F82

Fileuse — F83

Quartet in C Minor,
Op. 15, Pft. & Str.
By permission of
J. Hamelle Music
Publishers, Paris.

1st Movement / 1st Theme — F84

1st Movement / 2nd Theme — F85

2nd Movement / 1st Theme — F86

2nd Movement / 2nd Theme — F87

3rd Movement — F88

4th Movement / 1st Theme — F89

4th Movement / 2nd Theme — F90

4th Movement / 3rd Theme — F91

Quartet in E Minor,
Op. 121, Str.
Permission for reprint
granted by Durand & Cie,
Paris. Elkan-Vogel Co., Inc.
Philadelphia, Copyright
Owners,

1st Movement / 1st Theme — F92

1st Movement / 2nd Theme — F93

2nd Movement — F94

3rd Movement — F95

Sicilienne, Op. 78, Cello & Pft.
By permission of
J. Hamelle Music
Publishers, Paris.

Sicilienne — F96

Sonata in A,
Op. 13, Vn. & Pft.
By permission of The
Boston Music Co.,
copyright owner.

1st Movement / 1st Theme — F97

1st Movement / 2nd Theme — F98

2nd Movement / 1st Theme, A — F99

2nd Movement / 1st Theme, B — F100

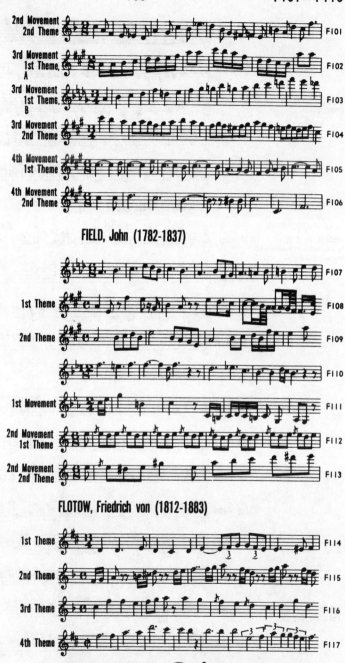

2nd Movement 2nd Theme   F101

3rd Movement 1st Theme, A   F102

3rd Movement 1st Theme, B   F103

3rd Movement 2nd Theme   F104

4th Movement 1st Theme   F105

4th Movement 2nd Theme   F106

FIELD, John (1782-1837)

Nocturne No. 3, Pft.   F107

Nocturne No. 4, Pft.   1st Theme   F108

2nd Theme   F109

Nocturne No. 5, Pft.   F110

Sonata in C Minor, Op. 1, No. 3, Pft.   1st Movement   F111

2nd Movement 1st Theme   F112

2nd Movement 2nd Theme   F113

FLOTOW, Friedrich von (1812-1883)

Alessandro Stradella Overture   1st Theme   F114

2nd Theme   F115

3rd Theme   F116

4th Theme   F117

Fatme (Zilda) Overture   1st Theme   F118

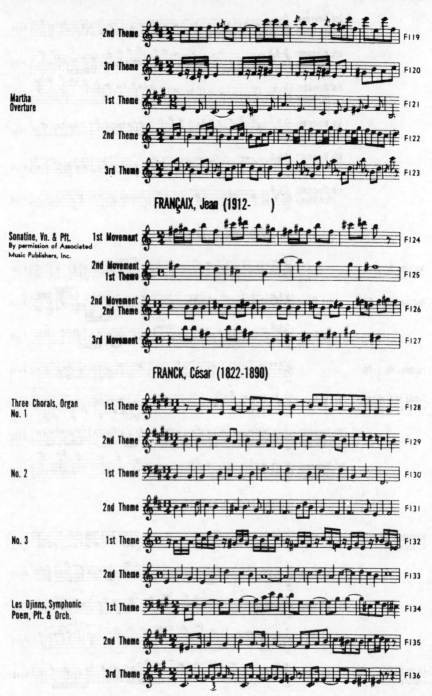

2nd Theme — F119

3rd Theme — F120

Martha
Overture — 1st Theme — F121

2nd Theme — F122

3rd Theme — F123

FRANÇAIX, Jean (1912-   )

Sonatine, Vn. & Pft. — 1st Movement — F124
By permission of Associated
Music Publishers, Inc.

2nd Movement
1st Theme — F125

2nd Movement
2nd Theme — F126

3rd Movement — F127

FRANCK, César (1822-1890)

Three Chorals, Organ — 1st Theme — F128
No. 1

2nd Theme — F129

No. 2 — 1st Theme — F130

2nd Theme — F131

No. 3 — 1st Theme — F132

2nd Theme — F133

Les Djinns, Symphonic — 1st Theme — F134
Poem, Pft. & Orch.

2nd Theme — F135

3rd Theme — F136

4th Theme   F137

Les Éolides, Symphonic Poem   1st Theme   F138

2nd Theme   F139

3rd Theme   F140

Grande Pièce Symphonique, Op. 17, Organ   1st Theme   F141

2nd Theme   F142

3rd Theme   F143

4th Theme   F144

5th Theme   F145

6th Theme   F146

Pastorale, Op. 19, Organ   1st Theme   F147

1st Theme   F148

2nd Theme   F149

Piece Héroïque, Organ   1st Theme   F150

2nd Theme   F151

Prélude, Aria, & Finale, Pft.   Prélude 1st Theme   F152

2nd Theme   F153

Aria   F154

Finale 1st Theme   F155

2nd Theme   F156

Prélude, Chorale & Fugue, Pft.

Prélude 1st Theme   F157

2nd Theme   F158

Chorale 1st Theme   F159

2nd Theme   F160

Fugue   F161

Prélude, Fugue & Variations, Op. 18 Organ or Pft.

Prélude & Variations   F162

Fugue   F163

Quartet in D, Str.

1st Movement 1st Theme   F164

1st Movement 2nd Theme   F165

1st Movement 3rd Theme   F166

2nd Movement 1st Theme   F167

2nd Movement 2nd Theme   F168

3rd Movement 1st Theme   F169

3rd Movement 2nd Theme   F170

4th Movement 1st Theme   F171

4th Movement 2nd Theme   F172

4th Movement 3rd Theme   F173

Quintet in F Minor, Pft. & Str.

1st Movement Intro. A   F174

1st Movement Intro. B   F175

1st Movement 1st Theme   F176

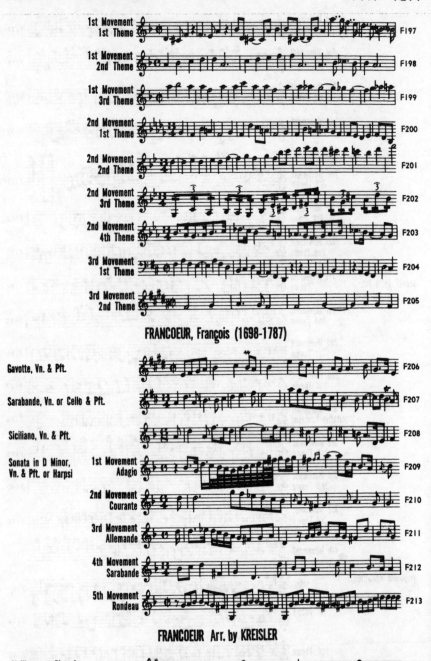

1st Movement 1st Theme — F197
1st Movement 2nd Theme — F198
1st Movement 3rd Theme — F199
2nd Movement 1st Theme — F200
2nd Movement 2nd Theme — F201
2nd Movement 3rd Theme — F202
2nd Movement 4th Theme — F203
3rd Movement 1st Theme — F204
3rd Movement 2nd Theme — F205

FRANCOEUR, François (1698-1787)

Gavotte, Vn. & Pft. — F206
Sarabande, Vn. or Cello & Pft. — F207
Siciliano, Vn. & Pft. — F208
Sonata in D Minor, Vn. & Pft. or Harpsi — 1st Movement Adagio — F209
2nd Movement Courante — F210
3rd Movement Allemande — F211
4th Movement Sarabande — F212
5th Movement Rondeau — F213

FRANCOEUR Arr. by KREISLER

Sicilienne et Rigaudon, Vn. & Pft. — Sicilienne — F214

Rigaudon 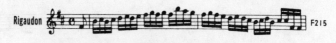 F215

FREDERICK II, King of Prussia (1712-1786)

Concerto No. 2, in
G, Flute & Str.

1st Movement
1st Theme

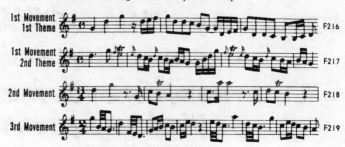

F216

1st Movement
2nd Theme

F217

2nd Movement

F218

3rd Movement

F219

FRESCOBALDI, Girolamo (1583-1643)

Capriccio on the Cuckoe,
Harpsi.

F220

Capriccio on La Girolometa
Harpsi.

F221

Capriccio on L'Aria di Ruggiero
Harpsi.

F222

Capriccio: La Spagnoletta
Harpsi.

F223

Fugue in G Minor, Organ & Str.

F224

Ricercar Cromatico Post II Credo
Organ

F225

Toccata, Spinet or Lute

F226

FUCÎK, Julius (1872-1916)

Entry of the Gladiators,
March

1st Theme

F227

2nd Theme

F228

3rd Theme

F229

GABRIEL-MARIE (1852-   )

La Cinquantaine, Air Dans
Le Style Ancien, Pft.

1st Theme

GI

2nd Theme — G2

GADE, Niels (1817-1890)

Bridal Waltz from "Et Folkesagn," Ballet   1st Theme — G3

2nd Theme — G4

Trio, Op. 42, Vn., Cello & Pft.   1st Movement — G5

2nd Movement — G6

3rd Movement — G7

4th Movement Theme, A — G8

4th Movement Theme, B — G9

GALLOT, Jacques de (17th Cent.)

La Colombe (The Dove) Harpsi. — G10

GALUPPI, Baldassare (1706-1785)

Sonata in A, Pft. or Harpsi.   1st Movement — G11

2nd Movement — G12

3rd Movement — G13

Sonata in C Minor, Pft. or Harpsi.   1st Movement — G14

2nd Movement — G15

3rd Movement — G16

Sonata in D Harpsi.   1st Movement — G17

2nd Movement — G18

3rd Movement 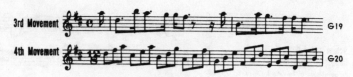 G19

4th Movement G20

GANNÉ, Louis (1862-1923)

La Czarina, Mazurka   1st Theme 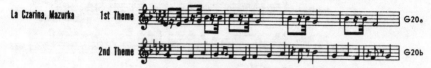 G20a

2nd Theme G20b

GAUTIER, Jean (1822-1878)

The Secret, Vn. & Pft.   1st Theme 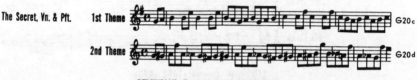 G20c

2nd Theme G20d

GEMINIANI, Francesco (1687-1762)

Sonata in C Minor,
Vn. & Pft.   1st Movement  G21

2nd Movement

3rd Movement
Siciliano G23

4th Movement G24

GERMAN, Sir Edward (1862-1936)

As You Like It
Incidental Music
By permission of
Novello & Co., Ltd.,
London.   1st Movement
Woodland Dance  G25

2nd Movement
Children's Dance G26

3rd Movement
Rustic Dance G27

Henry VIII
Incidental Music
By permission of
Novello & Co., Ltd., London   Morris Dance
1st Theme G28

2nd Theme G29

Shepherd's Dance G30

Torch Dance — G31

Romeo and Juliet
Incidental Music, Orch.
By permission of Novello & Co., Ltd., London.
Pavane — G32

Welsh Rhapsody, Orch.
By permission of
Novello & Co., Ltd., London.
1st Theme
Loudly Proclaim — G33

2nd Theme — G34

3rd Theme
Hunting the Hare — G35

4th Theme
Bells of Aberdovy — G36

5th Theme
David of the White Rock — G37

6th Theme
Men of Harlech — G38

GERSHWIN, George (1898-1937)

An American in Paris,
Orch.
Copyright 1930 by
New World Music Corp.
Reprinted by
special permission.
1st Theme — G39

2nd Theme — G40

3rd Theme
Blues Theme — G41

4th Theme — G42

Concerto in F,
Pft. & Orch.
Copyright 1927
by Harms, Inc.
Reprinted by
special permission.
1st Movement
1st Theme — G43

1st Movement
2nd Theme — G44

1st Movement
3rd Theme — G45

2nd Movement
1st Theme,
A — G46

2nd Movement
1st Theme,
B — G47

2nd Movement
2nd Theme — G48

2nd Movement
3rd Theme — G49

3rd Movement 1st Theme — G50

3rd Movement 2nd Theme — G51

Prelude No. 1, Pft.
Copyright 1927 by New
World Music Corp.
Reprinted by special permission. — G52

Prelude No. 2, Pft.
Copyright 1927 by New
World Music Corp.
Reprinted by special permission.
1st Theme — G53

2nd Theme — G54

Prelude No. 3, Pft.
Copyright 1927 by New
World Music Corp.
Reprinted by special permission. — G55

Rhapsody in Blue,
Pft. & Orch.
Copyright 1924 by
Harms, Inc.
Reprinted by special permission
1st Theme — G56

2nd Theme — G57

3rd Theme — G58

4th Theme — G59

5th Theme — G60

GIBBONS, Orlando (1583-1625)

The Lord of Salisbury, His Pavane,
Harpsi. — G61

The Queen's Command, Harpsi. — G62

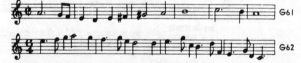

GLAZUNOFF, Alexander (1865-1936)

Carnaval, Overture,
Op. 45, Orch.
By permission of Associated
Music Publishers, Inc.
1st Theme — G63

2nd Theme — G64

3rd Theme — G65

4th Theme — G66

5th Theme — G67

Concerto in A Minor, Op. 82, Vn. & Orch. By permission of Associated Music Publishers, Inc. — 1st Theme G68 / 2nd Theme G69 / 3rd Theme G70 / 4th Theme G71 / 5th Theme G72

Une Fête Slave, from Slav Str. Quartet Op. 26, No. 4, Orch. By permission of Associated Music Publishers, Inc. — 1st Theme G73 / 2nd Theme G74 / 3rd Theme G75

Méditation, Op. 32, Vn. & Pft. By permission of Associated Music Publishers, Inc. G76

Mélodie Arabe, Op. 20, No. 1, Cello & Pft. By permission of Associated Music Publishers, Inc. — 1st Theme G77 / 2nd Theme G78

Novelettes, Op. 15, Str. Quart. By permission of Associated Music Publishers, Inc. — 1st Movement Alla Spagnuola 1st Theme G78a / 1st Movement 2nd Theme G78b / 2nd Movement Orientale 1st Theme G78c / 2nd Movement 2nd Theme G78d / 3rd Movement Interludium in Modo Antico G78e / 4th Movement Waltz 1st Theme G78f / 4th Movement 2nd Theme G78g / 5th Movement All 'Ungherese G78h

Ouverture Solennelle 1st Theme By permission of Associated Music Publishers, Inc. G79

2nd Theme — G80

3rd Theme — G81

4th Theme — G82

Rêverie, Op. 24
Fr. Horn & Pft.
By permission of Associated
Music Publishers, Inc. — G83

The Seasons (Ballet), Bacchanal
Op. 67
By permission of Associated
Music Publishers, Inc. — G84

Stenka Razin, Op. 13,   1st Theme
Symphonic Poem,   Volga Boat Song — G85
Orch.
By permission of Associated
Music Publishers, Inc.   2nd Theme — G86

Valsa de Concert,
Op. 47, Orch.   1st Theme — G87
By permission of Associated
Music Publishers, Inc.
                        2nd Theme — G88

                        3rd Theme — G89

GLIÈRE, Reinhold (1875-   )

Russian Sailors' Dance
from the Red Poppy, Ballet — G90

Symphony No. 3, Op. 42   Scherzo
"Ilia Mourometz"   1st Theme — G91

                        2nd Theme — G92

GLINKA, Michael (1804-1857)

Capriccio Brilliant on the   1st Theme — G92a
Jota Aragonesa, Orch.

                        2nd Theme — G93

Kamarinskaya, Orch.   1st Theme — G94

                        2nd Theme,
                        A — G95

                        2nd Theme,
                        B — G96

The Lark, (Arr. by Balakirev), Pft.

A Life for the Czar or
Ivan Soussanine, Overture   Intro.

                                 1st Theme

                                 2nd Theme

                                 3rd Theme

                                 4th Theme

Quartet in F, Str.   1st Movement
                      1st Theme

                      1st Movement
                      2nd Theme

                      2nd Movement

                      3rd Movement
                      1st Theme

                      3rd Movement
                      2nd Theme

                      4th Movement

Romance, Pft., Vn. & Cello
(Also as Song)

Russian and Ludmilla,
Overture   1st Theme

                      2nd Theme

Souvenir of a Night in   1st Theme
Madrid, Orch.   Jota

                          2nd Theme
                          Punto Muruno

                          3rd Theme
                  Seguidillas Manchegas

                          4th Theme
                  Seguidillas Manchegas

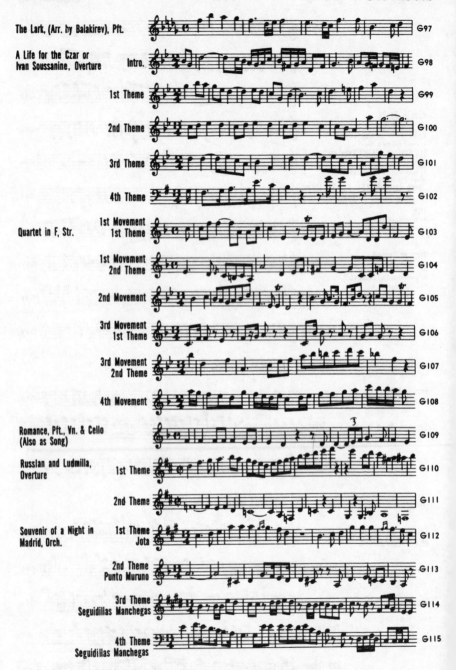

G97
G98
G99
G100
G101
G102
G103
G104
G105
G106
G107
G108
G109
G110
G111
G112
G113
G114
G115

GLUCK, Christoph (1714-1787)

Alceste, Overture — 1st Theme G116
2nd Theme G117
3rd Theme G118
Air de Ballet (also theme for Saint-Saëns Caprice for Pft.) G119
Ballet, Act II — 1st Movement G120
2nd Movement G121
3rd Movement G122
Ballet, Act IV — 1st Movement G123
2nd Movement March G124
3rd Movement G125
4th Movement Minuet G126
5th Movement Gavotte G127
6th Movement Chaconne G128
Armide, Musette from Ballet, Act IV G129
Iphigenia in Aulis, Overture 1st Theme G130
2nd Theme G131
3rd Theme G132
3rd Theme G133
4th Theme G134

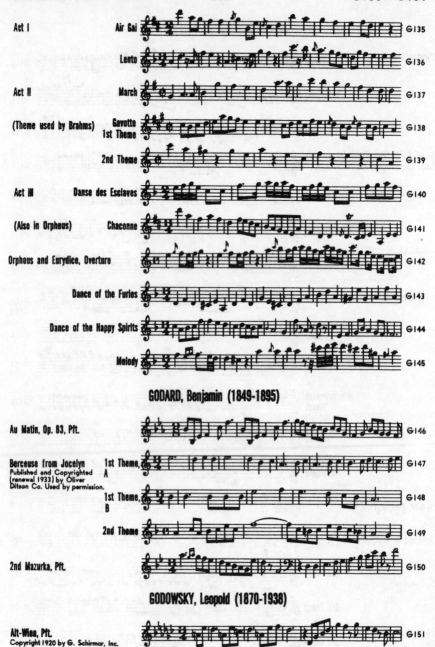

Act I   Air Gai   G135

Lento   G136

Act II   March   G137

(Theme used by Brahms)   Gavotte 1st Theme   G138

2nd Theme   G139

Act III   Danse des Esclaves   G140

(Also in Orpheus)   Chaconne   G141

Orpheus and Eurydice, Overture   G142

Dance of the Furies   G143

Dance of the Happy Spirits   G144

Melody   G145

GODARD, Benjamin (1849-1895)

Au Matin, Op. 83, Pft.   G146

Berceuse from Jocelyn
Published and Copyrighted
(renewal 1933) by Oliver
Ditson Co. Used by permission.   1st Theme, A   G147

1st Theme, B   G148

2nd Theme   G149

2nd Mazurka, Pft.   G150

GODOWSKY, Leopold (1870-1938)

Alt-Wien, Pft.
Copyright 1920 by G. Schirmer, Inc.   G151

GOLDMARK, Karl (1830-1915)

Im Frühling, Op. 36, Overture
By permission of Associated Music Publishers, Inc.
- 1st Theme — G152
- 2nd Theme — G153

Sakuntala, Op. 13, Overture
By permission of Associated Music Publishers, Inc.
- 1st Theme — G154
- 2nd Theme — G155
- 3rd Theme — G156
- 4th Theme — G157

Symphony, Op. 26, "Rustic Wedding"
By permission of Associated Music Publishers, Inc.
- 1st Movement Wedding March — G158
- 2nd Movement Bridal Song — G159
- 3rd Movement Serenade 1st Theme — G160
- 3rd Movement 2nd Theme — G161
- 4th Movement In the Garden 1st Theme — G162
- 4th Movement 2nd Theme — G163
- 5th Movement Dance 1st Theme — G164
- 5th Movement 2nd Theme — G165

GOOSSENS, Eugene (1845-1906)

The Hurdy-Gurdy Man, Op. 18, No. 3, Pft.
By permission of the copyright holders, J. & W. Chester, Ltd., 11 Great Marlborough Street, London, W. 1.
- G166

GOSSEC, François Joseph (1734-1829)

Gavotte in D, Vn. & Pft.
- 1st Theme — G167
- 2nd Theme — G168

Tambourin, Vn. & Pft. — G169

GOTTSCHALK, Louis (1829-1869)

The Dying Poet, Pft. — G169a

GOUNOD, Charles Francois (1818-1893)

Faust, Ballet Music, Act V   1st Theme — G170

2nd Theme — G171

3rd Theme — G172

4th Theme — G173

5th Theme — G174

6th Theme — G175

Funeral March of a Marionette, Orch.   1st Theme — G176

2nd Theme — G177

The Queen of Sheba   Cortège — G178

GRAENER, Paul (1872-1944)

Die Flöte von Sans-Souci, Op. 88, Orch.
Copyright by Eulenburg, Licensed by SESAC, Inc., N. Y.   Intro. 1st Theme — G179

Intro. 2nd Theme — G180

1st Movement Sarabande — G181

2nd Movement Gavotte — G182

3rd Movement Air — G183

4th Movement Rigaudon — G184

GRAINGER, Percy (1882-   )

Colonial Song, Orch. or Pft. 1st Theme — G185

2nd Theme — G186

Country Gardens, Eng. Morris Dance
Pft. Copyright renewed 1946
by Percy Grainger — G187

Handel in the Strand,
Clog Dance, Pft. or Orch. — G188

In A Nutshell, Suite Platform Humlet
Pft. & Orch.   1st Theme
Copyright renewal assigned
1944 to G. Schirmer, Inc.

Arrival — G189

2nd Theme — G190

3rd Theme — G191

Gay But Wistful
1st Theme — G192

2nd Theme — G193

Pastoral — G194

"Gum Suckers" March
1st Theme — G195

2nd Theme — G196

Londonderry Air,
Irish Folk Song Setting
Pft. or Orch. — G197

Mock Morris, Pft. or Orch. — G198

Molly on the Shore
Irish Reel, Orch. or Pft. 1st Theme — G199

2nd Theme — G200

Shepherd's Hey, Eng. Morris Dance , Pft. — G201
Copyright 1922
by G. Schirmer, Inc.

GRANADOS, Enrique (1867-1916)

Goyescas, Opera   Intermezzo
Copyright renewal assigned 1st Theme — G202
1944 to G. Schirmer, Inc.

2nd Theme — G203

3rd Theme — G204

The Maiden and the Nightingale,
Goyescas No. 4, Pft.
Copyright renewal assigned
1944 to G. Schirmer, Inc. — G205

Spanish Dance, No. 2, Pft.
Copyright renewal assigned
1943 to G. Schirmer, Inc.   1st Theme — G206

2nd Theme — G207

Spanish Dance, No. 4,
Villanesca, Pft.
Copyright renewal assigned
1943 to G. Schirmer, Inc.   1st Theme — G208

2nd Theme — G209

Spanish Dance, No. 5,
Playera-Andaluza, Pft.
Copyright renewal assigned
1943 to G. Schirmer, Inc.   1st Theme — G210

2nd Theme — G211

Spanish Dance, No. 6,
Rondalla Aragonesa
Copyright renewal assigned
1943 to G. Schirmer, Inc.   1st Theme — G212

2nd Theme — G213

GRETRY, André (1741-1813)

Ballet Suite from
Cephale et Procris   Gavotte — G214

Tambourin
1st Theme,
A — G215

1st Theme,
B — G216

2nd Theme — G217

Minuet
Nymphes de Diane — G218

Gigue — G219

Colinette à la Cour
Opera   Tambourin — G220

Gavotte — G221

Richard Coeur-de-Lion Opera — Rustic Dance — G222

La Rosière de Salency Opera — 1st Entr'acte 1st Theme — G223

2nd Theme — G224

2nd Entr'acte — G225

Ballet Suite from La Rosière Républicaine — Danse Legere — G226

Gavotte Gracieuse — G227

Contre Danse — G228

Romance — G229

Danse Generale — G230

Carmagnole — G231

Ballet Suite From Zémire et Azor — 1st Movement Air — G232

2nd Movement Pantomime — G233

3rd Movement Passepied — G234

GRIEG, Edvard (1843-1907)

Album Leaf, Op. 12, No. 7, Pft. — G235

Ballade, Op. 24, Pft.
By Permission of C. F. Peters,
Clayton F. Summy Co., Chicago, Agents in the U. S. — G236

Concerto, Op. 16, Pft. & Orch. — 1st Movement Intro. — G237

1st Movement 1st Theme, A — G238

1st Movement 1st Theme, B — G239

1st Movement 2nd Theme — G240

1st Movement 3rd Theme, A   G241

1st Movement 3rd Theme B   G242

2nd Movement 1st Theme   G243

2nd Movement 2nd Theme   G244

3rd Movement 1st Theme   G245

3rd Movement 2nd Theme   G246

Cradle Song, Op. 68, No. 5, Pft.
By Permission of C. F. Peters,
Clayton F. Summy Co., Chicago,
Agents in the U. S.   G247

Dance Caprice, Op. 28, No. 3, Pft.   1st Theme   G248

2nd Theme   G249

Elfin Dance, Op. 12, No. 4, Pft.   G250

Erotic, Op. 43, No. 5, Pft.
By Permission of C. F. Peters,
Clayton F. Summy Co., Chicago,
Agents in the U. S.   G251

French Serenade, Op. 62, No. 3, Pft.
By Permission of C. F. Peters, Clayton F.
Summy Co., Chicago, Agents in the U. S.   G252

Holberg Suite, Op. 40, Str. Orch.   1st Movement Prelude   G253

2nd Movement Sarabande   G254

3rd Movement 1st Theme Gavotte   G255

3rd Movement 2nd Theme Musette   G256

4th Movement Air   G257

5th Movement Rigaudon   G258

In Der Heimat, Op. 43, No. 3, Pft.   G259

Little Bird, Op. 43, No. 4, Pft.   G260

The Lonely Wanderer, Op. 43, No. 2, Pft.   G261

Lyric Suite, Op. 54, Pft.   Shepherd Boy   G262
By Permission of C. F. Peters,
Clayton F. Summy Co., Chicago,
Agents in the U. S.
  Norwegian Rustic March   G263

March of the Dwarfs
1st Theme   G264

2nd Theme   G265

Nocturne   G266

Melancholy, Op. 65, No. 3, Pft.   G267
By Permission of C. F. Peters,
Clayton F. Summy Co., Chicago,
Agents in the U. S.
Mélodie, Op. 47, No. 3, Pft.   G268
By Permission of C. F. Peters, Clayton F.
Summy Co., Chicago, Agents in the U. S.
Norwegian Bridal Procession,
Op. 19, No. 2, Pft.   G269
By Permission of C. F. Peters, Clayton F.
Summy Co., Chicago, Agents in the U. S.
Norwegian Dances,   No. 1
Op. 35, Pft. or Str. Orch.   1st Theme   G270
By Permission of C. F. Peters,
Clayton F. Summy Co., Chicago,
Agents in the U. S.
2nd Theme   G271

No. 2
1st Theme   G272

2nd Theme   G273

No. 3   G274

No. 4
1st Theme   G275

2nd Theme   G276

Norwegian Melody, Op. 12,
No. 7, Pft.   1st Theme   G277
Copyright 1899
by G. Schirmer, Inc.
2nd Theme   G278

Norwegian Melodies,   1st Movement
Op. 63, Str. Orch.   Popular Song   G279
By Permission of C. F.
Peters, Clayton F. Summy   2nd Movement
Co., Chicago,   1st Theme   G280
Agents in the U. S.   Cow Keeper's Tune

2nd Movement
2nd Theme
Peasant Dance — G281

Papilion (Butterfly), Op. 43, No. 1, Pft. — G282

Peer Gynt, Suite No. 1,
Op. 46, Orch.
1st Movement
Morning Mood — G283

2nd Movement
Ase's Death — G284

3rd Movement
Anitra's Dance
1st Theme — G285

3rd Movement
2nd Theme — G286

4th Movement
In the Hall of the Mountain King — G287

Peer Gynt,
Suite No. 2, Op. 55
Orch.
Copyright 1899
by G. Schirmer, Inc.
1st Movement
Ingrid's Complaint
1st Theme — G288

1st Movement
2nd Theme — G289

2nd Movement
Arabian Dance
1st Theme — G290

2nd Movement
2nd Theme — G291

3rd Movement
Peer Gynt's Return Home — G292

4th Movement
Solvejg's Song
Intro. — G293

4th Movement
1st Theme — G294

4th Movement
2nd Theme — G295

Puck, Op. 71, No. 3, Pft.
By Permission of C. F. Peters, Clayton F.
Summy Co., Chicago, Agents in the U. S. — G296

Quartet in G Minor,
Op. 27, Str.
By permission of
International Music Co.
1st Movement
1st Theme — G297

1st Movement
2nd Theme — G298

2nd Movement
Romanze
1st Theme — G298a

2nd Movement
2nd Theme — G299

3rd Movement Intermezzo 1st Theme — G300

3rd Movement 2nd Theme — G301

4th Movement 1st Theme — G302

4th Movement 2nd Theme — G303

Scherzo-Impromptu, Op. 73, No. 2, Pft.
By Permission of C. F. Peters, Clayton
F. Summy Co., Chicago, Agents in the U. S. — G304

Sigurd Jorsalfar, Orch. 1st Movement
Op. 56, In the King's Hall (Prelude)
(Incidental Music), — G305

By Permission of C. F.
Peters, Clayton F. Summy 1st Movement
Co., Chicago, 2nd Theme — G306
Agents in the U. S.

2nd Movement
Borghild's Dream (Intermezzo) — G307

3rd Movement
Triumphal March 1st Theme — G308

3rd Movement 2nd Theme — G309

Sonata in A Minor, 1st Movement
Op. 36, Cello & Pft. 1st Theme — G310
By Permission of
C. F. Peters, Clayton 1st Movement
F. Summy Co., Chicago, 2nd Theme — G311
Agents in the U. S.

2nd Movement — G312

3rd Movement 1st Theme — G313

3rd Movement 2nd Theme — G314

3rd Movement 3rd Theme — G315

Sonata in E Minor, 1st Movement
Op. 7, Pft. 1st Theme — G316
Published and Copyrighted
(renewal 1936) 1st Movement
by Oliver Ditson Co. 2nd Theme — G317
Used by permission.

1st Movement 3rd Theme — G318

2nd Movement — G319

3rd Movement — G320

4th Movement — G321

Sonata in G, Op. 13, No. 2, Vn. & Pft.
1st Movement Intro. — G322

1st Movement 1st Theme — G323

1st Movement 2nd Theme — G324

1st Movement 3rd Theme — G325

2nd Movement — G326

3rd Movement 1st Theme — G327

3rd Movement 2nd Theme — G328

Sonata in C Minor, Op. 45, No. 3, Vn. & Pft.
Copyright 1917 by
Carl Fischer, Inc., N. Y.
1st Movement Intro. — G329

1st Movement 1st Theme — G330

1st Movement 2nd Theme — G331

2nd Movement 1st Theme — G332

2nd Movement 2nd Theme — G333

3rd Movement 1st Theme — G334

3rd Movement 2nd Theme — G335

Summer's Eve, Op. 71, No. 2, Pft.
By Permission of C. F. Peters, Clayton F.
Summy Co., Chicago, Agents in the U. S.
— G336

Symphonic Dances, Op. 64, Orch.
By Permission of C. F. Peters,
Clayton F. Summy Co., Chicago,
Agents in the U. S.
No. 1 — G337

No. 2 1st Theme A — G338

1st Theme B — G339

2nd Theme — G340

No. 3 — G341

No. 4
1st Theme — G342

2nd Theme — G343

To Spring, Op. 43, No. 6, Pft. — G344

Two Elegaic Melodies,
Op. 34, Str. Orch.   No. 1
By Permission of C. F.   Heart Wounds — G345
Peters, Clayton F. Summy Co.,
Chicago, Agents in the U. S.   No. 2
                                Springtime — G346

Two Melodies, Op. 53,   No. 1
Str. Orch.   Norwegian — G347
By Permission of C. F.
Peters, Clayton F. Summy Co.,
Chicago, Agents   No. 2
in the U. S.   The First Meeting — G348

Waltz, Op. 12, No. 2, Pft. 1st Theme — G349
By Permission of C. F.
Peters, Clayton F. Summy Co.,
Chicago, Agents in the U. S. 2nd Theme — G350

Wedding Day at Troldhaugen,
Op. 65, No. 6, Pft. — G351
By Permission of C. F.
Peters, Clayton F. Summy Co.,
Chicago, Agents in the U. S.

GRIFFES, Charles Tomlinson (1884-1920)

The Pleasure Dome of
Kubla Khan, Orch.   1st Theme — G352
Copyright 1920
by G. Schirmer, Inc.

                           2nd Theme — G353

                           3rd Theme — G354

                           4th Theme — G355

Two Sketches (Based on   1st Movement
Indian Themes),   Farewell Song of — G356
Str. Quart.   Chippewa Indians
Copyright 1922   2nd Movement
by G. Schirmer, Inc.   1st Theme — G357

                           2nd Movement
                           2nd Theme — G358

2nd Movement 3rd Theme — G359

The White Peacock, Op. 7, No. 1, Pft.
Copyright renewal assigned
1945 to G. Schirmer, Inc. — G362

GROFÉ, Ferde (1892-   )

Grand Canyon Suite, Orch.
Copyright 1932 Robbins
Music Corp.
Used by special
permission Copyright
Proprietor.

1st Movement Sunrise — G361

2nd Movement Painted Desert — G362

3rd Movement On the Trail 1st Theme — G363

3rd Movement 2nd Theme — G364

Mississippi Suite, Orch.
Copyright 1926
Leo Feist, Inc.
Used by Special
Permission Copyright
Proprietor.

1st Movement Father of Waters — G365

2nd Movement Huckleberry Finn — G366

3rd Movement Old Creole Days — G367

4th Movement Mardi Gras 1st Theme — G368

4th Movement 2nd Theme — G369

HALVORSEN, Johan (1864-1935)

Andante Religioso Vn. & Orch.
By permission of Associated
Music Publishers, Inc.

1st Theme — H1

2nd Theme — H2

Triumphal Entry of the Boyars Orch.
By permission of Associated
Music Publishers, Inc.

1st Theme — H3

2nd Theme — H4

HANDEL, George Frederick (1685-1759)

Concerto No. 1 in B Flat, Oboe & Orch.

1st Movement — H5

2nd Movement Fugue — H6

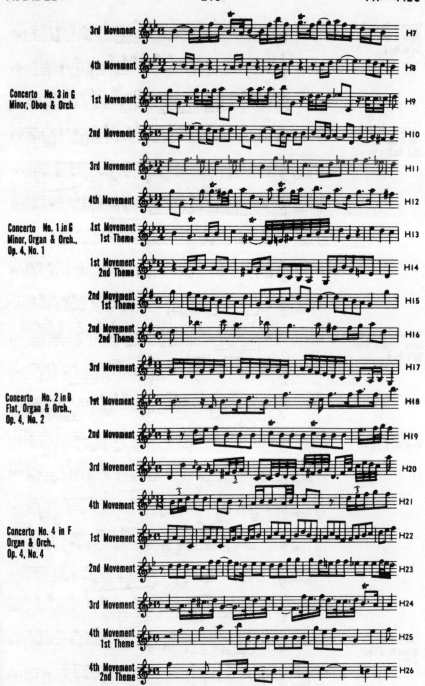

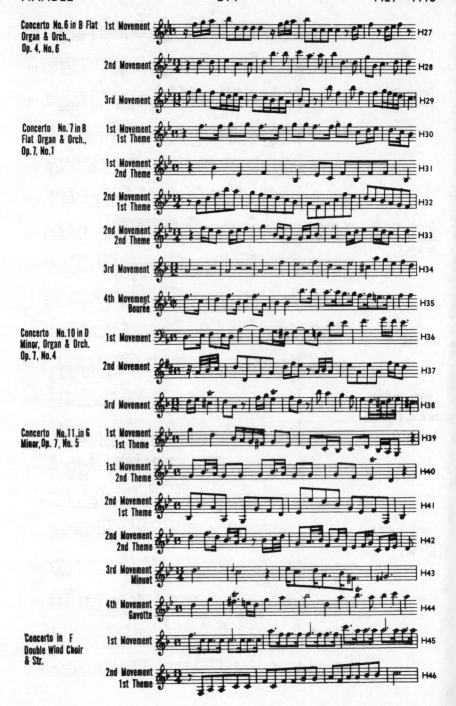

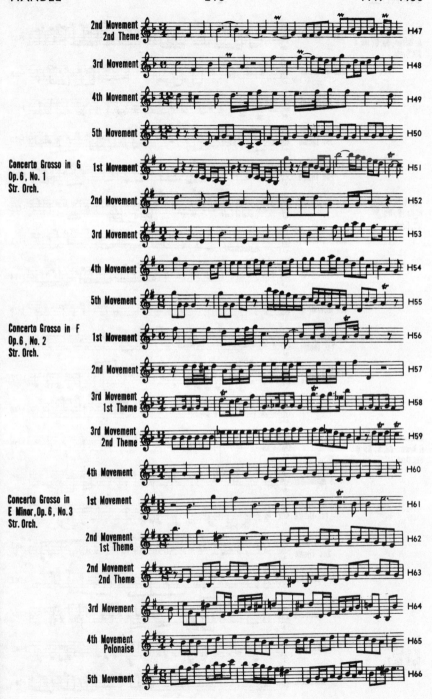

Concerto Grosso in A Minor, Op. 6, No. 4 Str. Orch.

1st Movement   H67

2nd Movement   H68

3rd Movement   H69

4th Movement 1st Theme   H70

4th Movement 2nd Theme   H71

Concerto Grosso in D, Op. 6, No. 5 Str. Orch.

1st Movement   H72

2nd Movement   H73

3rd Movement   H74

4th Movement   H75

5th Movement 1st Theme   H76

5th Movement 2nd Theme   H77

6th Movement   H78

Concerto Grosso in G Minor Op. 6, No. 6 Str. Orch.

1st Movement   H79

2nd Movement   H80

3rd Movement 1st Theme   H81

3rd Movement 2nd Theme   H82

4th Movement   H83

5th Movement   H84

Concerto Grosso in B flat Op. 6, No. 7 Str. Orch.

1st Movement   H85

2nd Movement   H86

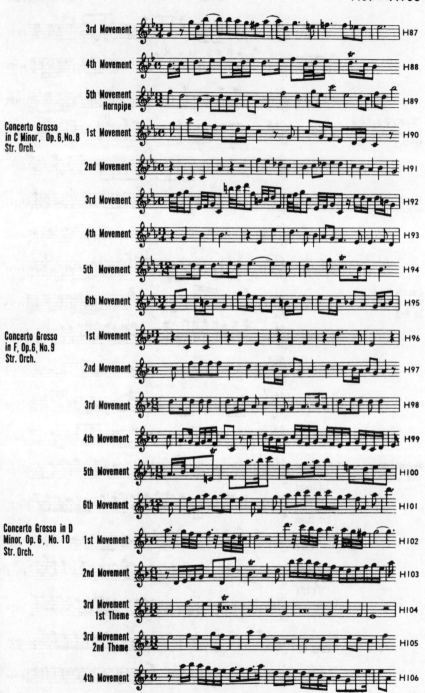

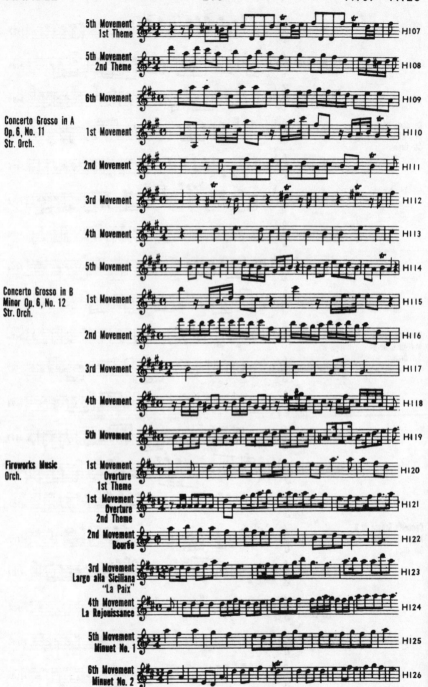

Concerto Grosso in A
Op. 6, No. 11
Str. Orch.

Concerto Grosso in B
Minor Op. 6, No. 12
Str. Orch.

Fireworks Music
Orch.

HANDEL

Alcina, Opera — Overture 1st Theme — H127

Overture 2nd Theme — H128

Musette — H129

Minuet — H130

Gavotte From Ballet — H131

Sarabande From Ballet — H132

Minuet From Ballet — H133

Gavotte No. 2 From Ballet — H134

Tamburino — H135

Oratorios — March from Joseph — H136

March from Judas Maccabeus — H137

Dead March from Saul — H138

Messiah — Overture 1st Theme — H139

2nd Theme — H140

Pt. 1 (Pastoral Symphony) — H141

Sonata in G, Flute & Fig. Bass Op. 1, No. 5 — 1st Movement — H142

2nd Movement — H143

3rd Movement — H144

4th Movement — H145

5th Movement — H146

Sonata in C,
Flute & Fig. Bass
Op. 1, No. 7

1st Movement   H147

2nd Movement   H148

3rd Movement   H149

4th Movement   H150

5th Movement   H151

Sonata in B Minor,
Flute & Fig. Bass
Op. 1, No. 9

1st Movement   H152

2nd Movement   H153

3rd Movement   H154

4th Movement   H155

5th Movement   H156

6th Movement   H157

7th Movement   H158

Sonata in F,
Flute & Fig. Bass
Op. 1, No. 11

1st Movement   H159

2nd Movement   H160

3rd Movement   H161

4th Movement   H162

Sonata in C Minor,
Fl., Vn., & Fig. Bass
Op. 2, No. 1

1st Movement   H163

2nd Movement   H164

3rd Movement   H165

4th Movement   H166

Sonata, G Minor,
2 Fls. or 2 Vns.
& Fig. Bass, Op. 2, No. 2

1st Movement — H167

2nd Movement — H168

3rd Movement — H169

4th Movement — H170

Sonata in G Minor,
Oboe & Fig. Bass
Op. 1, No. 6

1st Movement — H171

2nd Movement — H172

3rd Movement — H173

4th Movement — H174

Sonata in E,
Oboe or Vn. & Fig. Bass
Op. 1, No. 15

1st Movement — H175

2nd Movement — H176

3rd Movement — H177

4th Movement — H178

Sonata in E Flat
2 Vns. or 2 Oboes
& Fig. Bass

1st Movement — H179

2nd Movement — H180

3rd Movement — H181

4th Movement — H182

Sonata in A
Op. 1, No. 3
Vn. & Fig. Bass

1st Movement — H183

2nd Movement — H184

3rd Movement — H185

4th Movement — H186

Sonata in F
Op. 1, No. 12
Vn. & Fig. Bass

Sonata in D
Op. 1, No. 13
Vn. & Fig. Bass

Sonata in A
Op. 1, No. 14
Vn. & Fig. Bass

Suite No. 1 in B Flat
Pft., 2nd Set.

Suite No. 2 in F
Pft.

Suite No. 3 in D Minor
Pft.

1st Movement H187
2nd Movement H188
3rd Movement H189
4th Movement H190
1st Movement H191
2nd Movement H192
3rd Movement H193
4th Movement H194
1st Movement H195
2nd Movement H196
3rd Movement H197
4th Movement H198
Air and Variations H199
1st Movement H200
2nd Movement H201
3rd Movement H202
4th Movement H203
1st Movement Allemande H204
2nd Movement H205
3rd Movement Air H206

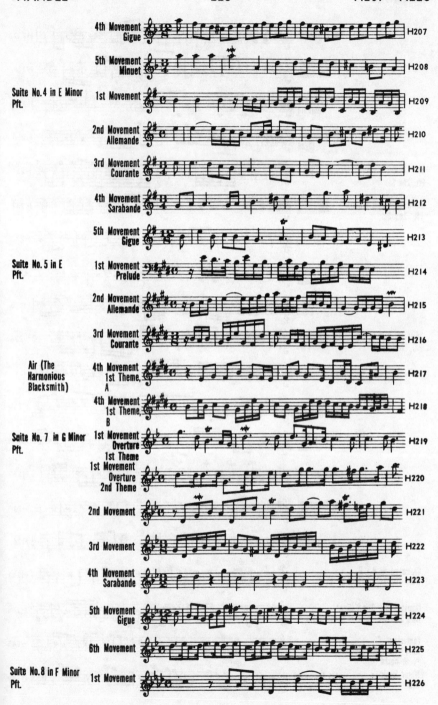

4th Movement Gigue — H207

5th Movement Minuet — H208

Suite No. 4 in E Minor Pft.
1st Movement — H209

2nd Movement Allemande — H210

3rd Movement Courante — H211

4th Movement Sarabande — H212

5th Movement Gigue — H213

Suite No. 5 in E Pft.
1st Movement Prelude — H214

2nd Movement Allemande — H215

3rd Movement Courante — H216

Air (The Harmonious Blacksmith)
4th Movement 1st Theme, A — H217

4th Movement 1st Theme, B — H218

Suite No. 7 in G Minor Pft.
1st Movement Overture 1st Theme — H219

1st Movement Overture 2nd Theme — H220

2nd Movement — H221

3rd Movement — H222

4th Movement Sarabande — H223

5th Movement Gigue — H224

6th Movement — H225

Suite No. 8 in F Minor Pft.
1st Movement — H226

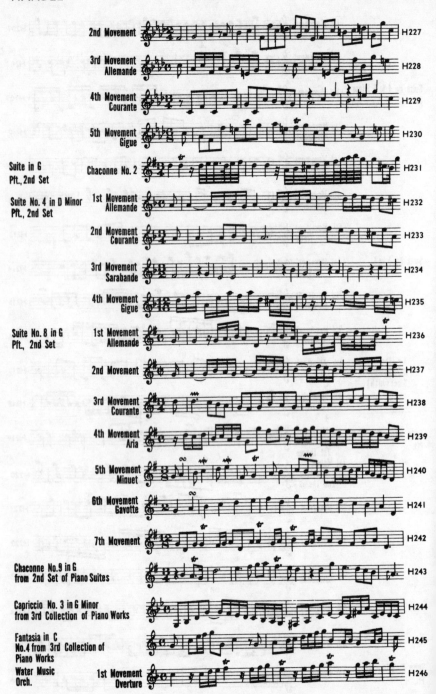

2nd Movement — H227

3rd Movement Allemande — H228

4th Movement Courante — H229

5th Movement Gigue — H230

Suite in G Pft., 2nd Set — Chaconne No. 2 — H231

Suite No. 4 in D Minor Pft., 2nd Set — 1st Movement Allemande — H232

2nd Movement Courante — H233

3rd Movement Sarabande — H234

4th Movement Gigue — H235

Suite No. 8 in G Pft., 2nd Set — 1st Movement Allemande — H236

2nd Movement — H237

3rd Movement Courante — H238

4th Movement Aria — H239

5th Movement Minuet — H240

6th Movement Gavotte — H241

7th Movement — H242

Chaconne No.9 in G from 2nd Set of Piano Suites — H243

Capriccio No. 3 in G Minor from 3rd Collection of Piano Works — H244

Fantasia in C No.4 from 3rd Collection of Piano Works — H245

Water Music Orch. — 1st Movement Overture — H246

2nd Movement — H247

3rd Movement — H248

4th Movement — H249

5th Movement
Andante — H250

6th Movement — H251

7th Movement
Air — H252

8th Movement — H253

9th Movement
Bourée — H254

10th Movement
Hornpipe — H255

11th Movement — H256

12th Movement — H257

13th Movement
1st Theme — H258

13th Movement
2nd Theme — H259

14th Movement — H260

15th Movement
Aria — H261

16th Movement — H262

17th Movement
Air — H263

18th Movement
Minuet
1st Theme — H264

18th Movement
2nd Theme — H265

19th Movement — H266

20th Movement Core — H267

HANSON, Howard (1896-)

Merry Mount Suite
Copyright 1933 by Harms, Inc.
Reprinted by special permission.
Overture — H268

Children's Dance 1st Theme — H269

2nd Theme — H270

Prelude to Act II & Maypole Dances 1st Theme — H271

2nd Theme — H272

3rd Theme — H273

Symphony No. 2
"Romantic"
Copyright 1934 by
Harold Flammer, Inc.
Used by permission.
1st Movement Intro. — H274

1st Movement 1st Theme — H275

1st Movement 2nd Theme — H276

1st Movement 3rd Theme, A — H277

1st Movement 3rd Theme, B — H278

2nd Movement — H279

3rd Movement 1st Theme — H280

3rd Movement 2nd Theme — H281

HARRIS, Roy (1898-)

Chorale for Strings, Op. 3
Copyright 1932 by
Eastman School of Music,
Rochester, N. Y.
— H282

Sonata Op. 1, Pft.
Copyright 1931
Cos Cob Press, Inc.
1st Movement Prelude — H283

2nd Movement Andante Ostinato — H284

3rd Movement Scherzo — H285

Symphony No. 3 — 1st Theme — H286

2nd Theme — H287

3rd Theme — H288

4th Theme — H289

5th Theme — H290

6th Theme, A — H291

6th Theme, B — H292

Three Variations on a Theme St. Quartet — H293

HAYDN, Franz Josef (1732-1809)

Andante & Variations, Pft. Op. 83, F. Minor — 1st Theme — H294

2nd Theme — H295

Arietta (Theme & Variations) E Flat Pft. — H296

Capriccio in G, Pft. — H297

Fantasia in C, Pft. — 1st Theme — H298

2nd Theme — H299

Concerto in D Cello & Orch. Op.101 — 1st Movement 1st Theme — H300

1st Movement 2nd Theme — H301

2nd Movement — H302

3rd Movement 1st Theme — H303

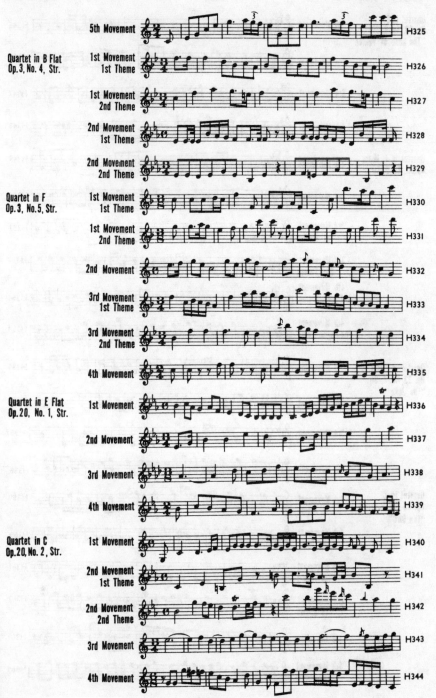

Quartet in D
Op. 20, No. 4, Str.
"The Rose of Venice"
1st Movement — H345
2nd Movement — H346
3rd Movement — H347
4th Movement — H348

Quartet in F Minor
Op. 20, No. 5, Str.
1st Movement — H349
2nd Movement — H350
3rd Movement 1st Theme — H351
3rd Movement 2nd Theme — H352
4th Movement 1st Fugue Theme — H353
4th Movement 2nd Fugue theme — H354

Quartet in E Flat
Op. 33, No. 2, Str.
"The Joke"
1st Movement — H355
2nd Movement — H356
.3rd Movement — H357
4th Movement — H358

Quartet in C
Op. 33, No. 3, Str.
"The Bird"
1st Movement 1st Theme — H359
1st Movement 2nd Theme — H360
2nd Movement 1st Theme — H361
2nd Movement 2nd Theme — H362
3rd Movement — H363
4th Movement 1st Theme — H364

4th Movement / 2nd Theme   H365

Quartet in D / Op. 33, No. 6, Str.   1st Movement   H366

2nd Movement   H367

3rd Movement   H368

4th Movement   H369

Quartet in E Flat / Op. 50, No. 3, Str.   1st Movement   H370

2nd Movement   H371

3rd Movement   H372

4th Movement   H373

Quartet in D / Op. 50, No. 6, Str. / "The Frog"   1st Movement   H374

2nd Movement   H375

3rd Movement / 1st Theme   H376

3rd Movement / 2nd Theme   H377

4th Movement / 1st Theme   H378

4th Movement / 2nd Theme   H379

Quartet in G / Op. 54, No. 1, Str.   1st Movement   H380

2nd Movement   H381

3rd Movement   H382

4th Movement   H383

Quartet in C / Op. 54, No. 2, Str.   1st Movement / 1st Theme   H384

Quartet in B Flat
Op.64, No.3, Str.

1st Movement 1st Theme — H405
1st Movement 2nd Theme — H406
2nd Movement — H407
3rd Movement 1st Theme — H408
3rd Movement 2nd Theme — H409
4th Movement 1st Theme — H410
4th Movement 2nd Theme — H411

Quartet in G
Op.64, No.4, Str.

1st Movement 1st Theme — H412
1st Movement 2nd Theme — H413
1st Movement 3rd Theme — H414
2nd Movement — H415
3rd Movement — H416
4th Movement — H417

Quartet in D
Op.64 No.5, Str.
"The Lark"

1st Movement 1st Theme — H418
1st Movement 2nd Theme — H419
1st Movement 3rd Theme — H420
2nd Movement — H421
3rd Movement 1st Theme — H422
3rd Movement 2nd Theme — H423
4th Movement — H424

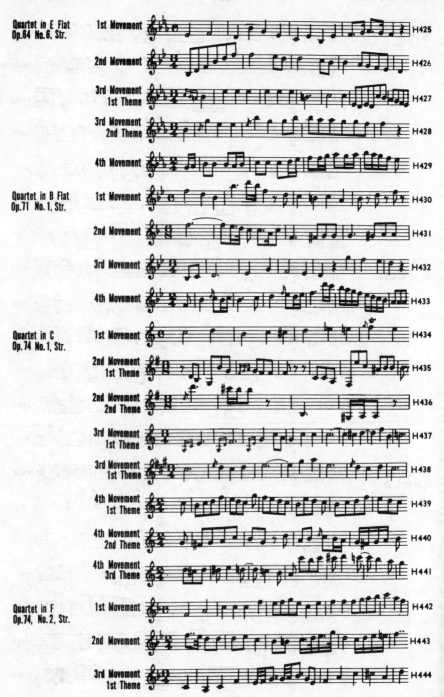

Quartet in E Flat
Op.64 No.6, Str.　1st Movement　H425

2nd Movement　H426

3rd Movement
1st Theme　H427

3rd Movement
2nd Theme　H428

4th Movement　H429

Quartet in B Flat
Op.71 No.1, Str.　1st Movement　H430

2nd Movement　H431

3rd Movement　H432

4th Movement　H433

Quartet in C
Op.74 No.1, Str.　1st Movement　H434

2nd Movement
1st Theme　H435

2nd Movement
2nd Theme　H436

3rd Movement
1st Theme　H437

3rd Movement
1st Theme　H438

4th Movement
1st Theme　H439

4th Movement
2nd Theme　H440

4th Movement
3rd Theme　H441

Quartet in F
Op.74, No.2, Str.　1st Movement　H442

2nd Movement　H443

3rd Movement
1st Theme　H444

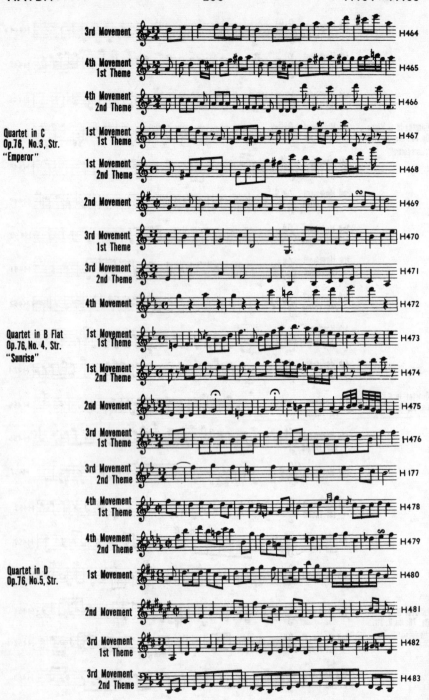

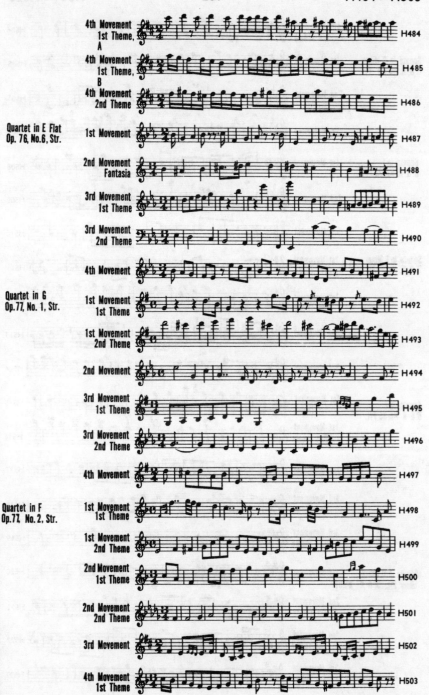

Quartet in E Flat
Op. 76, No.6, Str.

Quartet in G
Op.77, No. 1, Str.

Quartet in F
Op.77, No. 2, Str.

4th Movement 1st Theme, A — H484
4th Movement 1st Theme, B — H485
4th Movement 2nd Theme — H486
1st Movement — H487
2nd Movement Fantasia — H488
3rd Movement 1st Theme — H489
3rd Movement 2nd Theme — H490
4th Movement — H491
1st Movement 1st Theme — H492
1st Movement 2nd Theme — H493
2nd Movement — H494
3rd Movement 1st Theme — H495
3rd Movement 2nd Theme — H496
4th Movement — H497
1st Movement 1st Theme — H498
1st Movement 2nd Theme — H499
2nd Movement 1st Theme — H500
2nd Movement 2nd Theme — H501
3rd Movement — H502
4th Movement 1st Theme — H503

	4th Movement 2nd Theme	H504
Sonata in C Minor B. & H. No. 20, Pft.	1st Movement	H505
	2nd Movement	H506
	3rd Movement	H507
Sonata in F B. & H. No. 23, Pft.	1st Movement	H508
	2nd Movement	H509
	3rd Movement	H510
Sonata in E Minor B. & H. No. 34, Pft.	1st Movement 1st Theme	H511
	1st Movement 2nd Theme	H512
	2nd Movement	H513
	3rd Movement	H514
Sonata in C B. & H. No. 35, Pft.	1st Movement 1st Theme	H515
	1st Movement 2nd Theme	H516
	2nd Movement	H517
	3rd Movement 1st Theme	H518
	3rd Movement 2nd Theme	H519
Sonata in C Sharp Minor Pft. B. & H. No. 36	1st Movement	H520
	2nd Movement 1st Theme	H521
	2nd Movement 2nd Theme	H522
	3rd Movement 1st Theme	H523

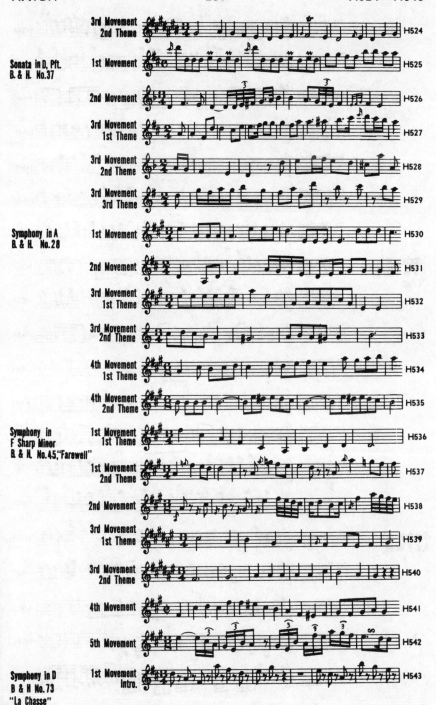

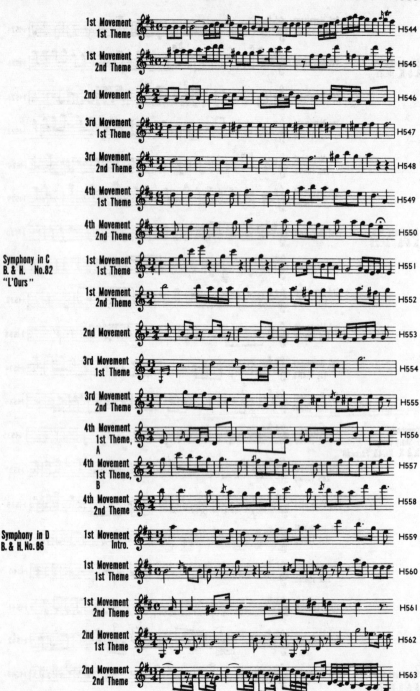

Symphony in C
B. & H.   No.82
"L'Ours"

Symphony in D
B. & H. No. 86

3rd Movement / 2nd Theme — H604
4th Movement / 1st Theme — H605
4th Movement / 2nd Theme — H606

Symphony in C Minor / B. & H. No.95 / London 5

1st Movement / 1st Theme — H607
1st Movement / 2nd Theme — H608
2nd Movement — H609
3rd Movement / 1st Theme — H610
3rd Movement / 2nd Theme — H611
4th Movement — H612

Symphony in C / B. & H. No. 97 / London 1

1st Movement / Intro. — H613
1st Movement / 1st Theme — H614
1st Movement / 2nd Theme — H615
2nd Movement — H616
3rd Movement / 1st Theme — H617
3rd Movement / 2nd Theme — H618
4th Movement / 1st Theme — H619
4th Movement / 2nd Theme — H620

Symphony in B Flat / B. & H. No.98 / London 4

1st Movement / Intro. — H621
1st Movement / 1st Theme — H622
1st Movement / 2nd Theme — H623

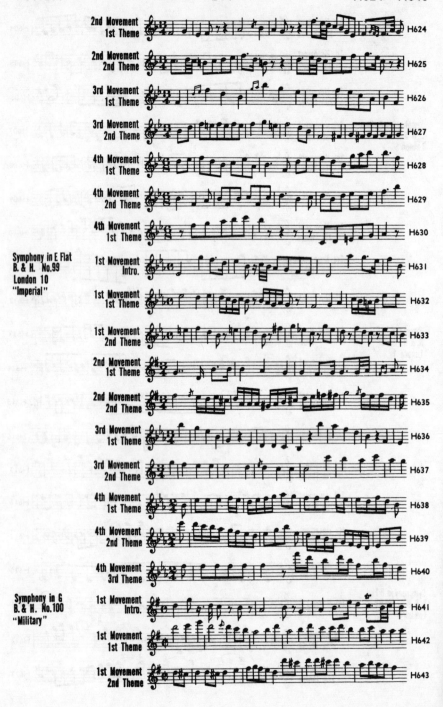

2nd Movement / 1st Theme — H624
2nd Movement / 2nd Theme — H625
3rd Movement / 1st Theme — H626
3rd Movement / 2nd Theme — H627
4th Movement / 1st Theme — H628
4th Movement / 2nd Theme — H629
4th Movement / 1st Theme — H630

Symphony in E Flat
B. & H. No.99
London 10
"Imperial"

1st Movement / Intro. — H631
1st Movement / 1st Theme — H632
1st Movement / 2nd Theme — H633
2nd Movement / 1st Theme — H634
2nd Movement / 2nd Theme — H635
3rd Movement / 1st Theme — H636
3rd Movement / 2nd Theme — H637
4th Movement / 1st Theme — H638
4th Movement / 2nd Theme — H639
4th Movement / 3rd Theme — H640

Symphony in G
B. & H. No.100
"Military"

1st Movement / Intro. — H641
1st Movement / 1st Theme — H642
1st Movement / 2nd Theme — H643

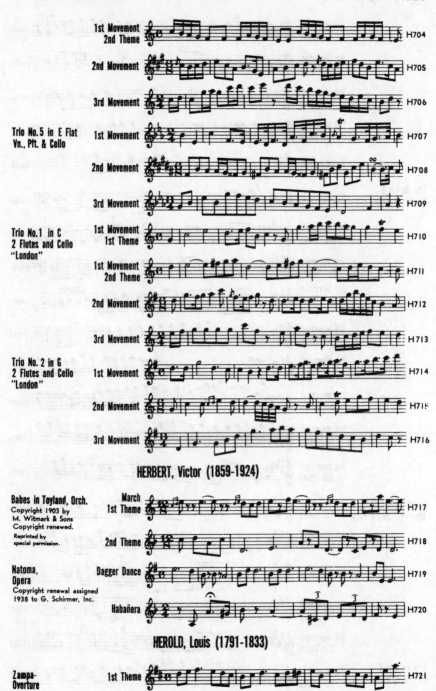

HERBERT, Victor (1859-1924)

HEROLD, Louis (1791-1833)

1st Movement
2nd Theme — H704

2nd Movement — H705

3rd Movement — H706

Trio No.5 in E Flat
Vn., Pft. & Cello — 1st Movement — H707

2nd Movement — H708

3rd Movement — H709

Trio No.1 in C
2 Flutes and Cello
"London" — 1st Movement 1st Theme — H710

1st Movement 2nd Theme — H711

2nd Movement — H712

3rd Movement — H713

Trio No. 2 in G
2 Flutes and Cello
"London" — 1st Movement — H714

2nd Movement — H715

3rd Movement — H716

Babes in Toyland, Orch.
Copyright 1903 by
M. Witmark & Sons
Copyright renewed.
Reprinted by
special permission. — March 1st Theme — H717

2nd Theme — H718

Natoma,
Opera
Copyright renewal assigned
1938 to G. Schirmer, Inc. — Dagger Dance — H719

Habañera — H720

Zampa-
Overture — 1st Theme — H721

2nd Theme  H722

HINDEMITH, Paul (1895-   )

Kleine Kammermusik Op. 24 No. 2
Ob., Fl., Cl., Hn., Fag.
By permission of
Associated Music
Publishers, Inc.

1st Movement / 1st Theme — H723
1st Movement / 2nd Theme — H724
2nd Movement / Waltz / 1st Theme — H725
2nd Movement / 2nd Theme — H726
2nd Movement / 3rd Theme — H727
3rd Movement / 1st Theme — H728
3rd Movement / 2nd Theme — H729
4th Movement — H730
5th Movement / 1st Theme — H731
5th Movement / 2nd Theme — H732
5th Movement / 3rd Theme — H733
5th Movement / 4th Theme — H734

Mathis der Mahler Symphony
By permission of
Associated Music
Publishers, Inc.

1st Movement / Concert of Angels / Intro. — H735
1st Movement / 1st Theme, A — H736
1st Movement / 1st Theme, B — H737
1st Movement / 2nd Theme — H738
1st Movement / 3rd Theme — H739
1st Movement / 4th Theme — H740

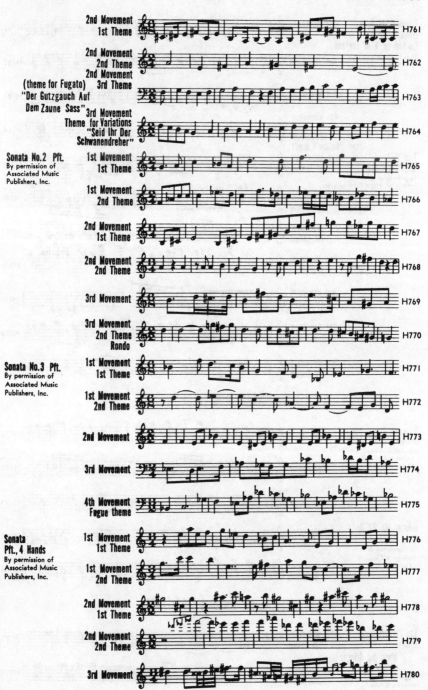

2nd Movement
1st Theme — H761

2nd Movement
2nd Theme — H762

2nd Movement
(theme for Fugato) 3rd Theme
"Der Gutzgauch Auf
Dem Zaune Sass" 3rd Movement — H763

Theme for Variations
"Seid Ihr Der
Schwanendreher" — H764

Sonata No.2 Pft.
By permission of
Associated Music
Publishers, Inc.

1st Movement
1st Theme — H765

1st Movement
2nd Theme — H766

2nd Movement
1st Theme — H767

2nd Movement
2nd Theme — H768

3rd Movement — H769

3rd Movement
2nd Theme
Rondo — H770

Sonata No.3 Pft.
By permission of
Associated Music
Publishers, Inc.

1st Movement
1st Theme — H771

1st Movement
2nd Theme — H772

2nd Movement — H773

3rd Movement — H774

4th Movement
Fugue theme — H775

**Sonata
Pft., 4 Hands**
By permission of
Associated Music
Publishers, Inc.

1st Movement
1st Theme — H776

1st Movement
2nd Theme — H777

2nd Movement
1st Theme — H778

2nd Movement
2nd Theme — H779

3rd Movement — H780

3rd Movement 2nd Theme — H819

4th Movement The Dargason Finale — H820

Two Songs without Words
Op. 22, Orch.
Copyright 1925
by E.C. Schirmer, Boston.

I Country Song 1st Theme — H821

2nd Theme — H822

II Marching Song 1st Theme — H823

2nd Theme — H824

3rd Theme — H825

HONEGGER, Arthur (1892-   )

Chant de Nigamon
Orch.
Copyright by Editions Salabert
Editions Salabert,
22 Rue Chaucat, Paris
Salabert, Inc.,
1 East 57 St., N. Y.

1st Theme — H826

2nd Theme — H827

3rd Theme — H828

4th Theme — H829

Concertino
Pft. & Orch.
Copyright by Editions
Salabert Editions Salabert,
22 Rue Chaucat, Paris
Salabert, Inc.,
1 East 57 St., N. Y.

1st Movement 1st Theme — H830

1st Movement 2nd Theme — H831

1st Movement 3rd Theme — H832

2nd Movement — H833

3rd Movement 1st Theme — H834

3rd Movement 2nd Theme — H835

King David
Symphonic Psalm

1st Movement Intro. — H836

Cortège
By permission of
Novello & Co.,
Ltd., London.

1st Theme — H837

2nd Theme — H838

March of the Philistines — H839

March of the Israelites — H840

Pastorale D'Été Orch.
Copyright by Editions Salabert
Editions Salabert,
22 Rue Chaucat, Paris
Salabert, Inc.,
I East 57 St., N. Y.

1st Theme — H841

2nd Theme — H842

3rd Theme — H843

4th Theme — H844

Rugby, Orch.
Copyright by Editions Salabert
Editions Salabert,
22 Rue Chaucat, Paris
Salabert, Inc.,
I East 57 St., N. Y.

1st Theme — H845

2nd Theme — H846

HOWELLS, Herbert (1892-   )

Puck's Minuet, Op. 20, No. 1, Orch.
Copyright 1919 by
Goodwin & Tabb,
Ltd., London.

1st Theme — H847

2nd Theme — H848

HUBAY, Jeno (1858-1937)

Hejre Kati, Op. 32, No. 4, Vn. & Orch., from Hungarian Czardas Scenes
Copyright 1901
by Carl Fischer, Inc., N. Y.

1st Theme — H849

2nd Theme — H850

3rd Theme — H851

Poème Hongrois, Op. 27, No. 1 Vn. & Orch. — H852

Poème Hongrois, Op. 27, No. 9 Vn. & Orch.
By permission of J. Hamelle
Music Publishers, Paris.

1st Theme — H853

2nd Theme — H854

HUMMEL, Johann (1778-1837)

Rondo in E Flat , Op. 11 — H855

HUMPERDINCK, Engelbert (1854-1921)

Hansel & Gretel, Opera
Prelude to Act 1
Copyright 1895
by B. Schott's Söhne

1st Theme — H856

2nd Theme — H857

Prelude to Act 2 "Witch's Ride" — H858

Pantomine — H859

Prelude "The Gingerbread House"
to Act 3   1st Theme — H860

2nd Theme — H861

"Gingerbread Waltz" — H862

Königskinder, Opera
Prelude   1st Theme, A — H863

1st Theme, B — H864

Prelude
to Act 2   "Children's Rounds"
1st Theme — H865

2nd Theme — H866

3rd Theme — H867

IBERT, Jacques (1890-   )

Concerto, Alto Sax
& Small Orch.
Copyright by A. Leduc
Music Publishers, Paris

1st Movement
1st Theme — I1

1st Movement
2nd Theme — I2

2nd Movement — I3

3rd Movement
1st Theme — I4

No. 4
A Giddy Girl

No. 8
Le Cage de Crystal
(The Crystal Cage)

Pièce, flute alone

Copyright by A. Leduc
Music Publishers, Paris

ILYINSKY, Alexander (1859-1919)

Berceuse, Pft.

D'INDY, Vincent (1851-1931)

Le Camp de Wallenstein,
Op. 12, Orch.

Permission for reprint
granted by Durand & Cie,
Paris. Elkan-Vogel Co., Inc.
Philadelphia, Copyright
Owners.

1st Theme

2nd Theme

3rd Theme

4th Theme

5th Theme

Istar, Op. 42,
Symphonic Variations

Permission for reprint granted
by Durand & Cie, Paris.
Elkan-Vogel Co., Philadelphia,
Inc. Copyright Owners.

1st Theme

2nd Theme

3rd Theme

4th Theme

5th Theme

6th Theme

Sonata in C,
Op. 59, Vn. &, Pft.

Permission for reprint
granted by Durand & Cie,
Paris. Elkan-Vogel Co., Inc.
Philadelphia, Copyright
Owners.

1st Movement
1st Theme

1st Movement
2nd Theme

1st Movement
3rd Theme

2nd Movement 1st Theme i43

2nd Movement 2nd Theme i44

3rd Movement 1st Theme, A i45

3rd Movement 1st Theme, B i46

3rd Movement 2nd Theme i47

4th Movement i48

Suite en Parties, Op. 91, 1st Movement
Fl., Vn., Viola, Cello, Entrée en Sonate i49
Harp

By permission of the copyright owner, Heugel Ltd., London.

2nd Movement Air Désuet i50

3rd Movement Sarabande 1st Theme i51

3rd Movement 2nd Theme i52

3rd Movement 3rd Theme i53

4th Movement Farandole i54

Symphony on a French 1st Movement 1st Theme i55
Mountain Theme, Op. 25

By permission of J. Hamelle Music Publishers, Paris.

1st Movement 2nd Theme i56

2nd Movement i57

3rd Movement 1st Theme i58

3rd Movement 2nd Theme i59

INFANTE, Manuel (1883-   )

Pochades Andalouses, No. 1
Pft. Canto Flamenco i60

No. 2 Danse Gitane i61

No. 3
Aniers sur la Route de Seville — 162

No. 4
Tientos — 163

INGHELBRECHT, D. E. (1880-   )

Four Fanfares, Brass   No. 1   Pour une Fête — 164
Copyright by Editions
Salabert Editions Salabert,
22 Rue Chaucat, Paris
Salabert, Inc.,
I East 57 St., N. Y.

No. 2   Pour le Président — 165

No. 3
Funèbre Pour des Mineurs Ensevelis — 166

No. 4
Dédicatoire — 167

Nurseries (3rd Set),   No. 1
Orch.   Nous N'irons Plus au Bois — 168
Copyright by A. Leduc
Music Publishers, Paris

No. 2
Le Tour Prends Garde ! — 169

No. 3
Bon Voyage Monsieur Dumollet — 170

No. 4
Sur le Pont d'Avignon — 171

No. 5
Où est la Marguerite? — 172

No. 6
Arlequin marie sa Fille — 173

IPPOLITOFF-IVANOFF, Michael (1859-1935)

Caucasian Sketches,   1st Movement
Op. 10, Orch.   In the Mountain Pass — 174
By permission of   1st Theme
International Music Co.

1st Movement
2nd Theme — 175

1st Movement
3rd Theme — 176

2nd Movement
In the Village
Intro. — 177

2nd Movement
1st Theme — 178

2nd Movement
2nd Theme — 179

3rd Movement
In the Mosque   180

4th Movement
Procession of the Sardar
1st Theme   181

4th Movement
2nd Theme   182

Quartet, Op. 13, Str.   1st Movement
Intro.   183

1st Movement
1st Theme   184

1st Movement
2nd Theme   185

2nd Movement
(Humoresca—Scherzando)
1st Theme   186

2nd Movement
2nd Theme   187

3rd Movement
Intermezzo   188

4th Movement
1st Theme   189

4th Movement
2nd Theme   190

4th Movement
3rd Theme   191

IRELAND, John (1879-   )

April, Pft.   192

Concertino Pastorale,
Str. Orch.
By permission of the
copyright owner, Boosey
and Hawkes, Inc.   1st Movement
Eclogue
1st Theme   193

1st Movement
2nd Theme   194

2nd Movement
Threnody   195

Concerto in E Flat
Pft. & Orch.
By permission of the
copyright holders,
J. & W. Chester, Ltd.,
11 Great Marlborough
Street, London, W. 1.   1st Movement
1st Theme   196

1st Movement
2nd Theme   197

2nd Movement
1st Theme   198

IRELAND

2nd Movement / 2nd Theme — i99

3rd Movement / 1st Theme — i100

3rd Movement / 2nd Theme — i101

The Holy Boy, Pft. — i102

A London Overture, Orch. / 1st Theme — i103
By permission of the copyright owner, Boosey and Hawkes, Inc.

2nd Theme — i104

3rd Theme — i105

Phantasy in A Minor, Vn., Pft. & Cello / 1st Theme — i106
By permission of Augener, Ltd., London

2nd Theme — i107

3rd Theme — i108

Sonata in G Minor, Cello & Pft. / 1st Movement / 1st Theme — i109
By permission of Augener, Ltd., London

1st Movement / 2nd Theme — i110

2nd Movement / 1st Theme — i111

2nd Movement / 2nd Theme — i112

3rd Movement / 1st Theme — i113

3rd Movement / 2nd Theme — i114

Trio No. 3 in E Minor & Major, Vn., Cello & Pft. / 1st Movement / 1st Theme — i115

1st Movement / 2nd Theme — i116

2nd Movement / 1st Theme — i117

2nd Movement / 2nd Theme, A — i118

2nd Movement 2nd Theme, B — 1119

3rd Movement 1st Theme — 1120

3rd Movement 2nd Theme — 1121

4th Movement 1st Theme — 1122

4th Movement 2nd Theme — 1123

IVANOVICI, J. (-1902)

Waves of the Danube, Waltzes, Orch.

No. 1 1st Theme — 1124

No. 1 2nd Theme — 1125

No. 2 1st Theme — 1126

No. 2 2nd Theme — 1127

No. 3 — 1128

No. 4 — 1129

IVES, Charles (1874-)

New England Holidays, Orch. Washington's Birthday (Barn Dance) 1st Theme — 1130

2nd Theme — 1131

JACOBI, Frederick (1891-)

Indian Dances, Orch.

Buffalo Dance Intro. — J1

Theme — J2

Butterfly Dance — J3

War Dance 1st Theme — J4

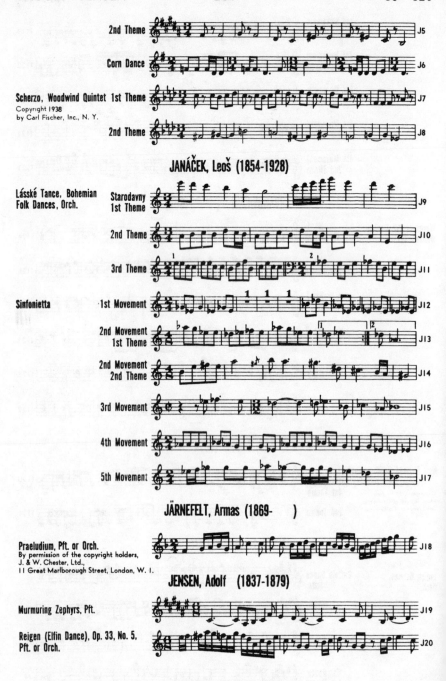

2nd Theme — J5

Corn Dance — J6

Scherzo, Woodwind Quintet 1st Theme — J7
Copyright 1938
by Carl Fischer, Inc., N. Y.

2nd Theme — J8

JANÁČEK, Leoš (1854-1928)

Lásské Tance, Bohemian
Folk Dances, Orch.

Starodavny
1st Theme — J9

2nd Theme — J10

3rd Theme — J11

Sinfonietta

1st Movement — J12

2nd Movement
1st Theme — J13

2nd Movement
2nd Theme — J14

3rd Movement — J15

4th Movement — J16

5th Movement — J17

JÄRNEFELT, Armas (1869-   )

Praeludium, Pft. or Orch.
By permission of the copyright holders,
J. & W. Chester, Ltd.,
11 Great Marlborough Street, London, W. I. — J18

JENSEN, Adolf (1837-1879)

Murmuring Zephyrs, Pft. — J19

Reigen (Elfin Dance), Op. 33, No. 5,
Pft. or Orch. — J20

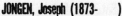

JONGEN, Joseph (1873-   )

Légende Naïve, Op. 59, No. 1,
Vn. & Pft.
By permission of the copyright holders,
J. & W. Chester, Ltd., 11 Great Marlborough
Street, London, W. 1.

Petite Suite, Pft.

1st Movement
Petite Marche
Militaire

2nd Movement
Conte Plaisant

3rd Movement
Nostalgie

4th Movement
Valse Gracieuse

5th Movement
Tambourin
1st Theme

5th Movement
2nd Theme

JUON, Paul (1872-1940)

Arva (Valse Mignonne),
Op. 52, No. 2, Vn. & Pft.
Copyright by Lienau, Licensed
by SESAC, Inc., N. Y.

1st Theme

2nd Theme

Berceuse, Op. 28, No. 3, Vn. & Pft.
Copyright by Lienau, Licensed
by SESAC, Inc., N. Y.

Chamber Symphony in
B Flat, Op. 27
Copyright by Lienau, Licensed
by SESAC, Inc., N. Y.

1st Movement
1st Theme

1st Movement
2nd Theme

2nd Movement

3rd Movement
1st Theme,
A

3rd Movement
1st Theme,
B

3rd Movement
2nd Theme

4th Movement

KABALEVSKY, Dmitri (1904-   )

Colas Breugnon, Op. 24, Overture
Copyright 1946 by Leeds Music Corp., N. Y. Reprinted here by permission of the copyright owner.

Symphony No. 2 in C Minor, Op. 19
Copyright 1945 by Leeds Music Corp., N. Y. Reprinted here by permisssion of the copyright owner.

KALINNIKOFF, Basil (1866-1901)

Symphony No. 1 in G Minor

4th Movement
2nd Theme
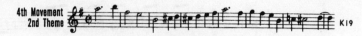
K19

KETELBEY, Albert W. (1880-   )

In a Chinese Temple
Garden, Pft. or Orch.
By permission of Belwin, Inc.,
Sole Selling Agents for
the copyright owner,
Bosworth & Co.,
Ltd., Copyright 1920
renewal copyright secured.

1st Theme

K19a

2nd Theme
K19b

3rd Theme
K19c

4th Theme

K19d

In a Monastery Garden,
Pft. or Orch.
Copyright 1915
by J. H. Larway.

Copyright renewed and
assigned to Harms, Inc. N. Y.

1st Theme
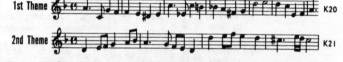
K20

2nd Theme
K21

3rd Theme

K22

In a Persian Market,
Pft. or Orch.
By permission of Belwin, Inc.,
Sole Selling Agents for
the copyright owner,
Bosworth & Co., Ltd.,
Copyright 1923.

1st Theme

K22a

2nd Theme

K22b

3rd Theme
K22c

4th Theme
K22d

5th Theme
K22e

6th Theme
K22f

KHACHATURIAN, Aram (1903-   )

Concerto, Pft. & Orch.
Copyright 1945 by Leeds
Music Corp., N. Y.
Reprinted here by
permisssion of the
copyright owner.

1st Movement
1st Theme

K23

1st Movement
2nd Theme
K24

2nd Movement
Intro.
K25

2nd Movement
Theme
K26

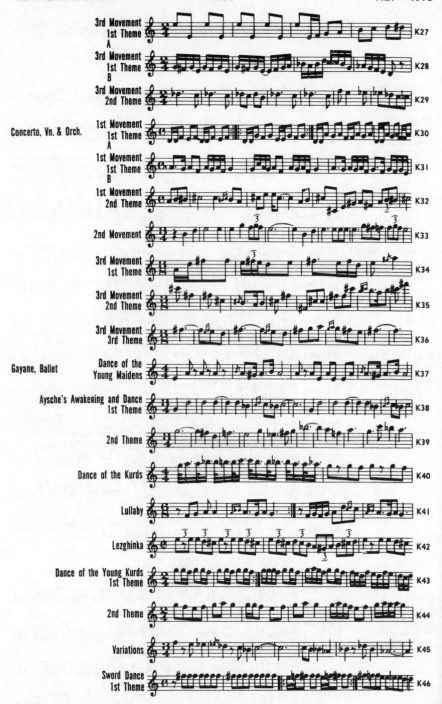

Concerto, Vn. & Orch.

3rd Movement 1st Theme A — K27
3rd Movement 1st Theme B — K28
3rd Movement 2nd Theme — K29
1st Movement 1st Theme A — K30
1st Movement 1st Theme B — K31
1st Movement 2nd Theme — K32
2nd Movement — K33
3rd Movement 1st Theme — K34
3rd Movement 2nd Theme — K35
3rd Movement 3rd Theme — K36

Gayane, Ballet

Dance of the Young Maidens — K37
Aysche's Awakening and Dance 1st Theme — K38
2nd Theme — K39
Dance of the Kurds — K40
Lullaby — K41
Lezghinka — K42
Dance of the Young Kurds 1st Theme — K43
2nd Theme — K44
Variations — K45
Sword Dance 1st Theme — K46

Masquerade Suite for Orch.

2nd Theme — K47

1st Movement Waltz 1st Theme — K48

1st Movement 2nd Theme — K49

2nd Movement Nocturne — K50

3rd Movement Mazurka — K51

4th Movement Romance — K52

5th Movement Galop — K53

Toccata, Pft.

1st Theme — K54

2nd Theme — K55

KHRENNIKOFF, Tikhon (1913-   )

Symphony No. 1, Op. 4
Copyright 1945 by Leeds Music Corp., N. Y. Reprinted here by permisssion of the copyright owner.

1st Movement 1st Theme — K56

1st Movement 2nd Theme — K57

1st Movement 3rd Theme — K58

2nd Movement 1st Theme — K59

2nd Movement 2nd Theme — K60

3rd Movement 1st Theme — K61

3rd Movement 2nd Theme — K62

KODÁLY, Zoltán (1882-   )

Galanta Dances Orch.
By permission of the copyright owner, Boosey and Hawkes, Inc.

Intro. — K63

1st Movement — K64

2nd Movement — K65

3rd Movement — K66

4th Movement
1st Theme — K67

4th Movement
2nd Theme — K68

5th Movement
1st Theme — K69

5th Movement
2nd Theme — K70

Háry János, Op. 15,
Suite from Opera
By permission of the
copyright owner,
Boosey and Hawkes, Inc.

Kezdodik a Mese
(The Fairy Tale
Begins) — K71

Bécsi Harangjáték
(Viennese Musical Clock) — K72

Dal (Song) — K73

(Battle and Defeat of Napoleon)
1st Theme
Franciak Indulója — K74

2nd Theme
Napoleon Bevonulása — K75

3rd Theme
Gyászinduló — K76

Kőzjáték
1st Theme — K77

2nd Theme — K78

3rd Theme — K79

Piros Alma — K80

Bordal-Ő Melysok Hal — K81

Hogyan Tudtal Rozsám — K82

Hej Két Tikom — K83

Toborzó
1st Theme — K84

2nd Theme — K85

A Császári Udvar Bevonulása
1st Theme — K86

2nd Theme — K87

Szegény Vagyok — K88

Felszántóm A Császár Udvarát — K89

KORNGOLD, Erich Wolfgang (1897-   )

Much Ado About Nothing,
Suite, Op. 11
Vn. & Pft.
By permission of
Associated Music
Publishers, Inc.

1st Movement
Mädchen im
Brautgemach
1st Theme — K90

1st Movement
2nd Theme — K91

2nd Movement
Holzapfel und Schlehwein
1st Theme — K92

2nd Movement
2nd Theme — K93

3rd Movement
Mummenschantz — K94

KREISLER, Fritz (1875-   )

Andantino, (Style of Padre Martini)
Vn. & Pft.
Copyright by Charles Foley, New York — K95

Caprice Viennois, Op. 2,
Vn. & Pft.
Copyright by
Charles Foley, New York

1st Theme,
A — K96

1st Theme,
B — K97

2nd Theme — K98

Chanson Louis XIII et
Pavane, (Style of
Couperin), Vn. & Pft.
Copyright by Charles Foley,
New York

1st Theme
Chanson — K99

2nd Theme
Pavane — K100

La Chasse, Caprice (Style of
Jean-Baptiste Cartier), Vn. & Pft.
Copyright by Charles Foley, New York — K101

Liebesfreud,
Old Viennese Song
Vn. & Pft.
Copyright by Charles Foley, New York

1st Theme — K102

2nd Theme   K103

3rd Theme   K104

Liebesleid,
Old Viennese Song
Vn. & Pft
Copyright by Charles Foley,
New York

1st Theme   K105

2nd Theme   K106

The Old Refrain
Viennese Popular Song
Vn. & Pft.
Copyright by Charles Foley, New York   K107

Polichinelle, Serenade
Vn. & Pft.
Copyright by Charles Foley, New York   K108

Praeludium and Allegro
(Style of Pugnani)
Vn. & Pft.
Copyright by Charles Foley, New York

Praeludium   K109

Allegro   K110

La Précieuse
(Style of Couperin)
Vn. & Pft.
Copyright by Charles Foley,
New York

1st Theme   K111

2nd Theme   K112

Rondino on a Theme by Beethoven
Vn. & Pft.
Copyright by Charles Foley, New York   K113

Schön Rosmarin
Vn. & Pft.
Copyright by Charles Foley, New York

1st Theme   K114

2nd Theme   K115

Tambourin Chinois, Op. 3
Vn. & Pft.
Copyright by Charles Foley, New York

1st Theme   K116

2nd Theme   K117

Tempo di Minuetto
(Style of Pugnani), Vn. & Pft.
Copyright by Charles Foley, New York   K118

KREUTZER, Conradin (1780-1849)

Das Nachtlager in Granada,
Overture

1st Theme   K119

2nd Theme   K120

3rd Theme   K121

KUHNAU, Johann (1660-1722)

Sonata, The Combat
Between David and
Goliath, Pft.

1st Theme
The Bravado of Goliath — K122

2nd Theme
The Prayer of the Israelites — K123

3rd Theme
The Courage of David — K124

4th Theme
The Contest — K125

5th Theme
Joy of the Israelites Over the Victory — K126

LACK, Théodore (1846-1921)

Idilio, Op. 134, Pft. — L1

Arlequin, Vn. & Orch.   1st Theme — L2

2nd Theme — L3

LALO, Edouard (1823-1892)

Concerto in D Minor,
Vcl. & Orch.

1st Movement
1st Theme — L4

1st Movement
2nd Theme — L5

2nd Movement
Intermezzo
1st Theme — L6

2nd Movement
2nd Theme — L7

3rd Movement — L8

Concerto Russe, Op. 29,
Vn. & Orch.

1st Movement
Intro. — L9

1st Movement
1st Theme — L10

1st Movement
2nd Theme — L11

2nd Movement
Chant Russe — L12

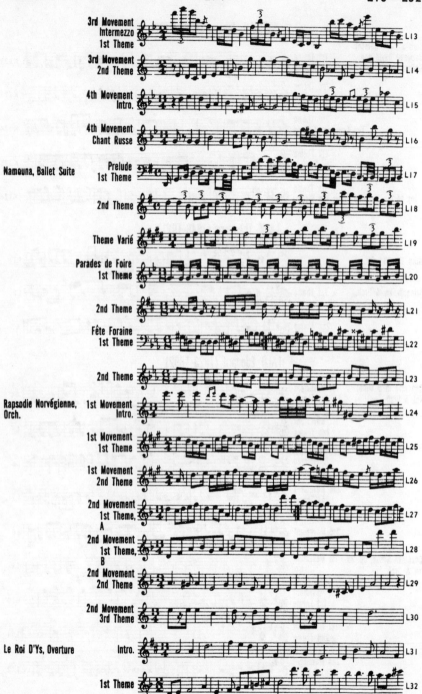

Namouna, Ballet Suite

Rapsodie Norvégienne, Orch.

Le Roi D'Ys, Overture

3rd Movement Intermezzo 1st Theme — L13
3rd Movement 2nd Theme — L14
4th Movement Intro. — L15
4th Movement Chant Russe — L16
Prelude 1st Theme — L17
2nd Theme — L18
Theme Varié — L19
Parades de Foire 1st Theme — L20
2nd Theme — L21
Fête Foraine 1st Theme — L22
2nd Theme — L23
1st Movement Intro. — L24
1st Movement 1st Theme — L25
1st Movement 2nd Theme — L26
2nd Movement 1st Theme, A — L27
2nd Movement 1st Theme, B — L28
2nd Movement 2nd Theme — L29
2nd Movement 3rd Theme — L30
Intro. — L31
1st Theme — L32

2nd Theme — L33

Symphonie Espagnole, Op. 21, Vn. & Orch.

1st Movement 1st Theme, A — L34

1st Movement 1st Theme, B — L35

1st Movement 2nd Theme — L36

2nd Movement 1st Theme — L37

2nd Movement 2nd Theme — L38

3rd Movement Intermezzo Intro. — L39

3rd Movement Intermezzo 1st Theme — L40

3rd Movement 2nd Theme — L41

4th Movement Intro. — L42

4th Movement — L43

5th Movement Intro. — L44

5th Movement 1st Theme — L45

5th Movement 2nd Theme — L46

LANGE, Gustav (1830-1889)

Flower Song, Pft. — L47

LASSEN, Eduard (1830-1904)

Fest-Overtüre Op. 51, Orch.
By permission of Associated Music Publishers, Inc.

Intro. — L48

1st Theme — L49

2nd Theme — L50

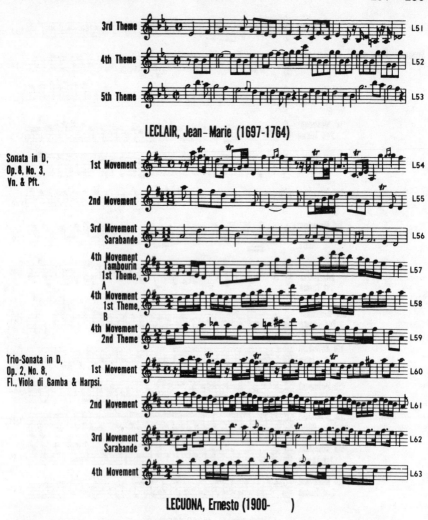

3rd Theme — L51

4th Theme — L52

5th Theme — L53

LECLAIR, Jean-Marie (1697-1764)

Sonata in D,
Op. 8, No. 3,
Vn. & Pft.

1st Movement — L54

2nd Movement — L55

**3rd Movement
Sarabande** — L56

**4th Movement
Tambourin
1st Theme,
A** — L57

**4th Movement
1st Theme,
B** — L58

**4th Movement
2nd Theme** — L59

Trio-Sonata in D,
Op. 2, No. 8,
Fl., Viola di Gamba & Harpsi.

1st Movement — L60

2nd Movement — L61

**3rd Movement
Sarabande** — L62

4th Movement — L63

LECUONA, Ernesto (1900-   )

Suite Andalucia, Pft.
Copyright 1929 by
Ernesto Lecuono
Copyright assigned 1931
to Edward B. Marks Co.
Copyright Assigned 1932
to Edward B. Marks Corp.
Used by Permission

**Andalucia
1st Theme** — L64

2nd Theme — L65

**Gitanerias
1st Theme** — L66

2nd Theme — L67

**Malaguena
1st Theme** — L68

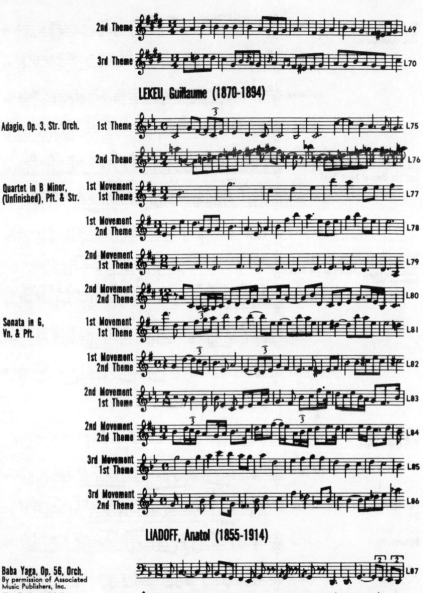

2nd Theme L69

3rd Theme L70

LEKEU, Guillaume (1870-1894)

Adagio, Op. 3, Str. Orch.   1st Theme L75

                             2nd Theme L76

Quartet in B Minor,   1st Movement
(Unfinished), Pft. & Str.   1st Theme L77

                       1st Movement
                       2nd Theme L78

                       2nd Movement
                       1st Theme L79

                       2nd Movement
                       2nd Theme L80

Sonata in G,   1st Movement
Vn. & Pft.   1st Theme L81

                1st Movement
                2nd Theme L82

                2nd Movement
                1st Theme L83

                2nd Movement
                2nd Theme L84

                3rd Movement
                1st Theme L85

                3rd Movement
                2nd Theme L86

LIADOFF, Anatol (1855-1914)

Baba Yaga, Op. 56, Orch.
By permission of Associated
Music Publishers, Inc. L87

The Enchanted Lake
Op. 62, Orch.   1st Theme L88
By permission of Associated
Music Publishers, Inc.

                 2nd Theme L89

Kikimora, Op. 63, Orch.
By permission of Associated
Music Publishers, Inc.
1st Theme, A — L90

1st Theme, B — L91

2nd Theme — L92

3rd Theme — L93

The Music Box, Op. 32, Pft.
(or The Musical Snuff Box)
By permission of Associated
Music Publishers, Inc.
1st Theme — L94

2nd Theme — L95

3rd Theme — L96

Russian Folk Dances, Op. 58, Orch.
By permission of Associated Music Publishers, Inc.
Legend of the Birds — L97

I Danced With a Mosquito — L98

Cradle Song — L99

Village Dance — L100

LISZT, Franz (1811-1886)

Ballade No. 2, in B Minor, Pft.
1st Theme — L101

2nd Theme — L102

Bénédiction de Dieu Dans la Solitude Pft. — L103

Berceuse, Pft. — L104

Concerto No. 1 in E Flat Pft. & Orch.
1st Theme — L105

2nd Theme — L106

3rd Theme — L107

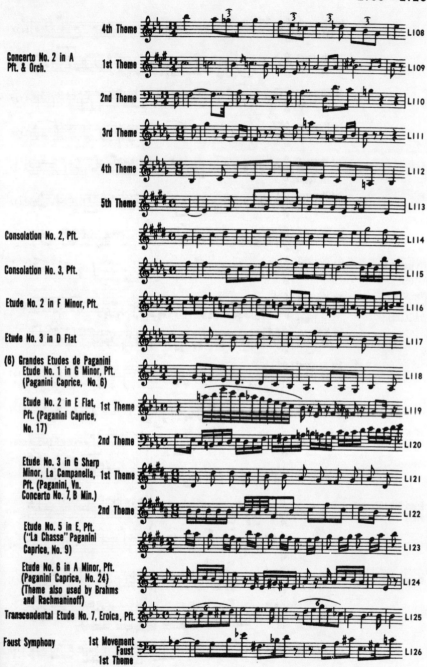

4th Theme — L108

Concerto No. 2 in A
Pft. & Orch.   1st Theme — L109

2nd Theme — L110

3rd Theme — L111

4th Theme — L112

5th Theme — L113

Consolation No. 2, Pft. — L114

Consolation No. 3, Pft. — L115

Etude No. 2 in F Minor, Pft. — L116

Etude No. 3 in D Flat — L117

(6) Grandes Etudes de Paganini
Etude No. 1 in G Minor, Pft.
(Paganini Caprice, No. 6) — L118

Etude No. 2 in E Flat, 1st Theme
Pft. (Paganini Caprice,
No. 17) — L119

2nd Theme — L120

Etude No. 3 in G Sharp
Minor, La Campanella, 1st Theme
Pft. (Paganini, Vn.
Concerto No. 7, B Min.) — L121

2nd Theme — L122

Etude No. 5 in E, Pft.
("La Chasse" Paganini
Caprice, No. 9) — L123

Etude No. 6 in A Minor, Pft.
(Paganini Caprice, No. 24)
(Theme also used by Brahms
and Rachmaninoff) — L124

Transcendental Etude No. 7, Eroica, Pft. — L125

Faust Symphony   1st Movement
Faust
1st Theme — L126

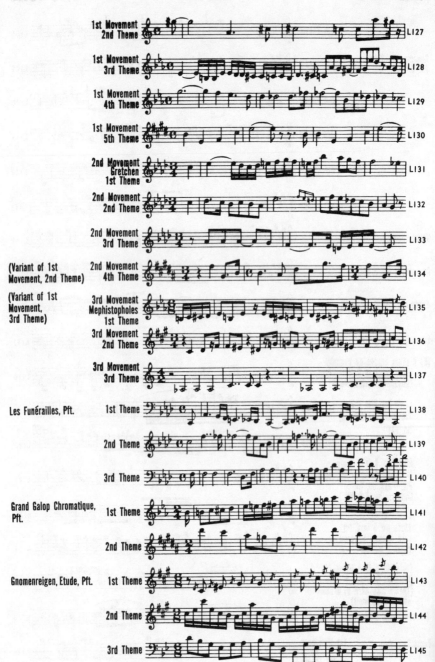

1st Movement 2nd Theme — L127
1st Movement 3rd Theme — L128
1st Movement 4th Theme — L129
1st Movement 5th Theme — L130
2nd Movement Gretchen 1st Theme — L131
2nd Movement 2nd Theme — L132
2nd Movement 3rd Theme — L133
(Variant of 1st Movement, 2nd Theme) 2nd Movement 4th Theme — L134
(Variant of 1st Movement, 3rd Theme) 3rd Movement Mephistopholes 1st Theme — L135
3rd Movement 2nd Theme — L136
3rd Movement 3rd Theme — L137
Les Funérailles, Pft. 1st Theme — L138
2nd Theme — L139
3rd Theme — L140
Grand Galop Chromatique, Pft. 1st Theme — L141
2nd Theme — L142
Gnomenreigen, Etude, Pft. 1st Theme — L143
2nd Theme — L144
3rd Theme — L145

**Hungarian Rhapsody No. 1
in E, Pft.**

1st Theme  L146

2nd Theme L147

3rd Theme L148

**Hungarian Rhapsody No. 2
in C Sharp Minor, Pft.**

1st Theme L149

2nd Theme L150

3rd Theme L151

4th Theme L152

5th Theme L153

6th Theme L154

7th Theme L155

**Hungarian Rhapsody No. 4
in E Flat, Pft.**

1st Theme L156

2nd Theme L157

**Hungarian Rhapsody No. 5
in E Minor, Pft.**

1st Theme L158

2nd Theme L159

3rd Theme L160

**Hungarian Rhapsody No. 6
in D Flat, Pft.**

1st Theme L161

2nd Theme L162

3rd Theme L163

4th Theme L164

LISZT

282

L165—L184

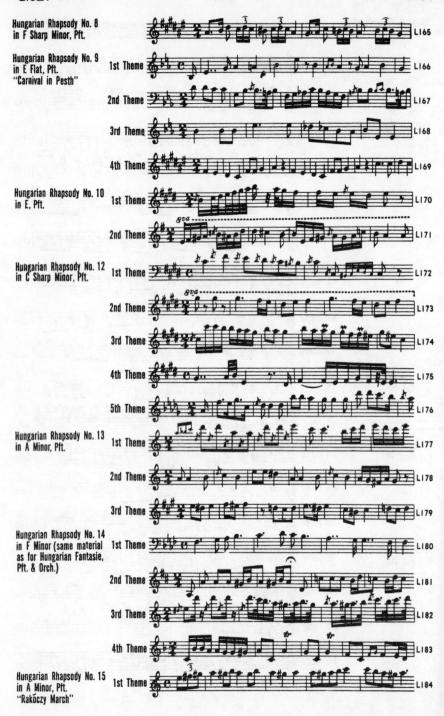

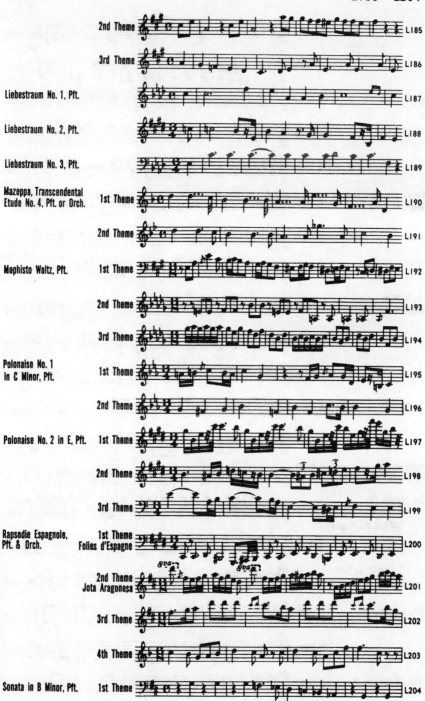

2nd Theme   L185

3rd Theme   L186

Liebestraum No. 1, Pft.   L187

Liebestraum No. 2, Pft.   L188

Liebestraum No. 3, Pft.   L189

Mazeppa, Transcendental Etude No. 4, Pft. or Orch.   1st Theme   L190

2nd Theme   L191

Mephisto Waltz, Pft.   1st Theme   L192

2nd Theme   L193

3rd Theme   L194

Polonaise No. 1 in C Minor, Pft.   1st Theme   L195

2nd Theme   L196

Polonaise No. 2 in E, Pft.   1st Theme   L197

2nd Theme   L198

3rd Theme   L199

Rapsodie Espagnole, Pft. & Orch.   1st Theme Folies d'Espagne   L200

2nd Theme Jota Aragonesa   L201

3rd Theme   L202

4th Theme   L203

Sonata in B Minor, Pft.   1st Theme   L204

2nd Theme ... L205

3rd Theme ... L206

4th Theme ... L207

5th Theme ... L208

6th Theme ... L209

Funeral Triumph of Tasso,
Symphonic Poem No. 2A   1st Theme ... L210

2nd Theme ... L211

3rd Theme ... L212

Les Préludes,
Symphonic Poem No. 3   1st Theme ... L213

2nd Theme ... L214

3rd Theme ... L215

4th Theme ... L216

5th Theme ... L217

Totentanz, (paraphrase on "Dies Irae"),
Pft. & Orch. ... L218

Two Legends, Pft.
  St. François d'Assise   1st Theme ... L219
  Prédicant aux Oiseaux

2nd Theme ... L220

  St. François De Paule
  Marchant Sur Les Flots ... L221

Valse-Impromptu, Pft.   1st Theme ... L222

2nd Theme ... L223

Valse Mélancolique, Pft.   1st Theme ... L224

2nd Theme — L225

Valse Oubliée, Pft. 1st Theme — L226

2nd Theme — L227

Waldesrauschen, (Etude), Pft. — L228

Years of Travel, Pft.
First Year — At the Spring, (Au Bord d'Une Source) — L229

Au Lac De Wallenstadt — L230

Second Year
Sonnet 47 of Petrarch — L231

Sonnet 104 of Petrarch — L232

Sonnet 123 of Petrarch — L233

Sposalizio, Pft. 1st Theme — L234

2nd Theme — L235

Tarantella, Pft. 1st Theme — L236

Fountains at the Villa D'Este Pft. 2nd Theme — L237

1st Theme — L238

2nd Theme — L239

Venice and Naples, "Gondoliera" Pft. — L240

LOCATELLI, Pietro (1695-1764)

Concerto Grosso, Op. 1, No. 2, Str. Orch. & Pft. 1st Movement — L241

2nd Movement — L242

3rd Movement — L243

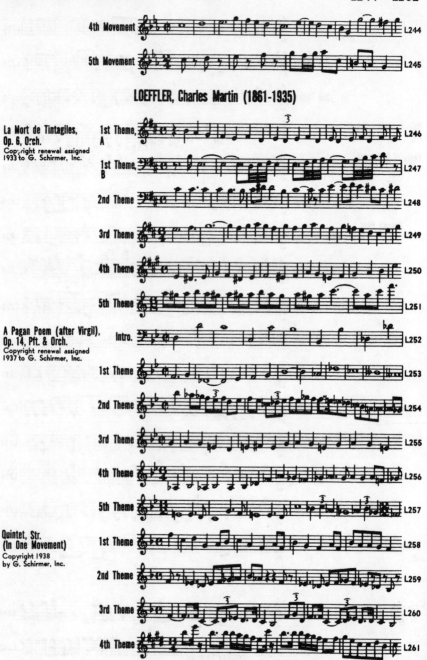

4th Movement — L244

5th Movement — L245

LOEFFLER, Charles Martin (1861-1935)

La Mort de Tintagiles, Op. 6, Orch.
Copyright renewal assigned 1933 to G. Schirmer, Inc.

1st Theme, A — L246

1st Theme, B — L247

2nd Theme — L248

3rd Theme — L249

4th Theme — L250

5th Theme — L251

A Pagan Poem (after Virgil), Op. 14, Pft. & Orch.
Copyright renewal assigned 1937 to G. Schirmer, Inc.

Intro. — L252

1st Theme — L253

2nd Theme — L254

3rd Theme — L255

4th Theme — L256

5th Theme — L257

Quintet, Str. (In One Movement)
Copyright 1938 by G. Schirmer, Inc.

1st Theme — L258

2nd Theme — L259

3rd Theme — L260

4th Theme — L261

5th Theme — L262

Two Rhapsodies,
Oboe, Vla. & Pft. L'Étang,(The Pool)
Copyright renewal assigned
1932 to G. Schirmer, Inc.
L263

La Cornemuse,(The Bagpipe)
1st Theme
L264

2nd Theme
L265

LOEILLET, Jean Baptiste (1653-1728)

Sonata No. 7 in
F, Fl. & Pft.

1st Movement
L266

2nd Movement
L267

3rd Movement
L268

4th Movement
Gavotte
L269

5th Movement
Aria
L270

6th Movement
L271

Suite No. 1 in
G Minor, Harpsi.

1st Movement
Allemande
L272

2nd Movement
Minuet
L273

3rd Movement
Sarabande
L274

4th Movement
L275

LORTZING, Gustav Albert (1801-1851)

Czar und Zimmerman,
Overture

1st Theme
L276

2nd Theme
L277

3rd Theme
L278

4th Theme, A
Clog Dance
L279

4th Theme,
B
L280

Undine, Overture — 1st Theme — L281

2nd Theme — L282

3rd Theme — L283

LOUIS XIII (1601-1643)

Amaryllis, Pft. — 1st Theme — L284

2nd Theme — L285

3rd Theme — L286

LUIGINI, Alexandre (1850-1906)

Ballet Egyptien, Orch.
By permission of
The Boston Music Co.,
copyright owner. — 1st Movement — L287

2nd Movement — L288

LULLY, Jean Baptiste (1632-1687)

Alceste,
Opera — Overture 1st Theme — L289

2nd Theme — L290

Amadis de Gaule
Opera — Minuet — L291

L'Amour Médecin,
(Comedy-Ballet),
Opera — Overture — L292

Atys
Opera — Entrée des Songes Agréables — L293

Les Songes Agréables — L294

Gavotte
Air Pour la Suite de Flore — L295

Le Bourgeois Gentilhomme,
Opera — Overture 1st Theme — L296

2nd Theme — L297

Ballet, Act 1 / 1st Theme — L298
2nd Theme / Sarabande — L299
3rd Theme / Gaillarde — L300
4th Theme — L301
Act IV / Cérémonie Turque — L302
Proserpine, Menuet des Ombres Heureuses Opera / 1st Movement — L303
2nd Movement — L304
Le Temple de la Paix Orch. / Intro. 1st Theme — L305
Intro. 2nd Theme — L306
Minuet 1st Theme — L307
2nd Theme — L308
Thésée Opera / Overture 1st Theme — L309
2nd Theme — L310
Marche des Sacrificateurs — L311
Le Triomphe de L'Amour, Ballet / Nocturne — L312

MacDOWELL, Edward (1861-1908)

Concerto No. 1, in A Minor, Op. 15, Pft. & Orch.
By permission of Associated Music Publishers, Inc.

1st Movement / 1st Theme — M1
1st Movement / 2nd Theme — M2
2nd Movement — M3
3rd Movement / 1st Theme — M4

3rd Movement / 2nd Theme — M5

3rd Movement / 3rd Theme — M6

3rd Movement / 4th Theme — M7

Concerto No. 2. in D Minor, Op. 23, Pft. & Orch.
Copyright 1922 by G. Schirmer, Inc.

1st Movement / 1st Theme — M8

1st Movement / 2nd Theme — M9

2nd Movement / 1st Theme — M10

2nd Movement / 2nd Theme — M11

2nd Movement / 3rd Theme — M12

3rd Movement / 1st Theme — M13

3rd Movement / 2nd Theme — M14

Marionettes, Pft. Witch. Op. 38. No. 4
Revised and Augmented Edition, Copyright 1929 by The Arthur P. Schmidt Co. Used by Permission. — M15

Clown, Op. 38, No. 5
Revised and Augmented Edition, Copyright 1929 by The Arthur P. Schmidt Co. Used by Permission. — M16

Villain, Op. 38, No. 6
Revised and Augmented Edition, Copyright 1929 by The Arthur P. Schmidt Co. Used by Permission — M17

Of Br'er Rabbit, Op. 61, No. 2, Pft.
Copyright 1930 by The Arthur P. Schmidt Co. Used by Permission — M18

Of a Tailor and a Bear, Pft.
Copyright 1925 and 1942 by The Arthur P. Schmidt Co. Used by Permission. — M19

An Old Garden. Op. 62. No. 1. Pft.,
Copyright 1930 by The Arthur P. Schmidt Co. Used by Permission. — M20

Polonaise, Op. 46, No. 12, Pft. — M21

Scotch Poem, Op. 31, No. 2, Pft.
Revised Edition, Copyright 1923 by The Arthur P. Schmidt Co. Used by Permission — M22

Sea Pieces, Pft.
To the Sea. Op. 55, No. 1
Copyright 1926 by The Arthur P. Schmidt Co. Used by Permission. — M23

A. D. 1620, Op. 55, No. 3
Copyright 1926 by The Arthur P. Schmidt Co. Used by Permission. — M24

Starlight, Op. 55, No. 4
Copyright 1926 by The Arthur P.
Schmidt Co. Used by Permission.
M25

Nautilus, Op. 55, No. 7
Copyright 1926 by The Arthur P.
Schmidt Co. Used by Permission.
M26

Suite No. 2, (Indian)   I. Legend,
Orch.   Intro.
By permission of Associated
Music Publishers, Inc.
M27

1st Theme
M28

2nd Theme
M29

II. Love Song
1st Theme
M30

2nd Theme
M31

III. In War-Time
M32

IV. Elegy
M33

V. Village Festival
1st Theme
M34

2nd Theme
M35

Witches' Dance, Op. 17, No. 2, Pft.
Revised Edition, Copyright 1918 by The
Arthur P. Schmidt Co. Used by Permission.
M36

Woodland Sketches, Pft. To a Wild Rose,
Copyright 1924 by   Op. 51, No. 1
The Arthur P. Schmidt Co.
Used by Permission.
M37

Will O'the Wisp, Op. 51, No. 2
Copyright 1924 by The Arthur P. Schmidt
Co. Used by Permission.
M38

In Autumn, Op. 51, No. 4
Copyright 1924 by The Arthur P. Schmidt
Co. Used by Permission.
M39

From an Indian Lodge, Op. 51, No. 5
Copyright 1924 by   1st Theme
The Arthur P. Schmidt Co.
Used by Permission.
M40

2nd Theme
M41

To a Water Lily, Op. 51, No. 6
Copyright 1924 by 1st Theme
The Arthur P. Schmidt Co.
Used by Permission.
M42

2nd Theme
M43

From Uncle Remus, Op. 51, No. 7
Copyright 1924 by The Arthur P.
Schmidt Co. Used by Permission.
M44

Op. 51, No. 8   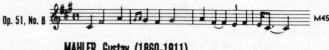   M45

MAHLER, Gustav (1860-1911)

Symphony No. 1
in D

1st Movement / Intro.   M46

1st Movement / 1st Theme   M47

1st Movement / 2nd Theme   M48

1st Movement / 3rd Theme   M49

2nd Movement / 1st Theme   M50

2nd Movement / 2nd Theme   M51

3rd Movement / 1st Theme   M52

3rd Movement / 2nd Theme   M53

4th Movement / 1st Theme, A   M54

4th Movement / 1st Theme, B   M55

4th Movement / 2nd Theme   M56

Symphony No. 2
in C Minor
"Resurrection"

1st Movement / 1st Theme, A   M57

1st Movement / 1st Theme, B   M58

1st Movement / 2nd Theme   M59

1st Movement / 3rd Theme   M60

2nd Movement / 1st Theme   M61

2nd Movement / 2nd Theme   M62

2nd Movement / 3rd Theme   M63

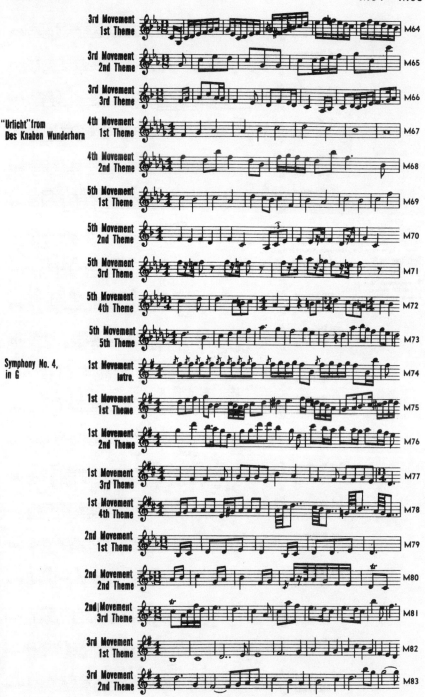

"Urlicht" from
Des Knaben Wunderhorn

Symphony No. 4,
in G

3rd Movement 3rd Theme   M84

3rd Movement 4th Theme   M85

3rd Movement 5th Theme   M86

4th Movement 1st Theme   M87

4th Movement 2nd Theme   M88

4th Movement 3rd Theme   M89

Symphony No. 5
By Permission of C. F. Peters,
Clayton F. Summy Co., Chicago, Agents in the U. S.

Adagietto   M90

Symphony No.9
in D
By permission of the
copyright owner,
Boosey and Hawkes, Inc.

1st Movement 1st Theme   M91

1st Movement 2nd Theme   M92

1st Movement 3rd Theme   M93

1st Movement 4th Theme   M94

1st Movement 5th Theme   M95

2nd Movement 1st Theme   M96

2nd Movement 2nd Theme   M97

2nd Movement 3rd Theme   M98

2nd Movement 4th Theme   M99

2nd Movement 5th Theme   M100

3rd Movement 1st Theme   M101

3rd Movement 2nd Theme   M102

3rd Movement 3rd Theme   M103

3rd Movement
4th Theme — M104

3rd Movement
5th Theme — M105

4th Movement
Intro. — M106

4th Movement
1st Theme — M107

4th Movement
2nd Theme — M108

4th Movement
3rd Theme — M109

MAILLART, Louis (1817-1871)

Les Dragons De Villars
Overture

1st Theme — M110

2nd Theme — M111

3rd Theme — M112

MALIPIERO, Francesco (1882-   )

Cantari Alla Madrigalesca,
Str. Quartet

1st Theme — M113

2nd Theme — M114

3rd Theme — M115

4th Theme — M116

La Cimarosiana, Orch.
By permission of the
copyright holders,
J. & W. Chester, Ltd.,
11 Great Marlborough
Street, London, W. 1.

1st Movement — M117

2nd Movement — M118

3rd Movement
1st Theme — M119

3rd Movement
2nd Theme — M120

4th Movement
1st Theme — M121

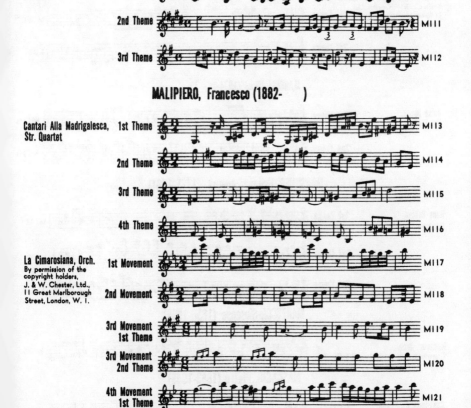

4th Movement
2nd Theme   M122

5th Movement   M123

Impressioni Dal Vero
Orch.
By permission of the copyright
holders, J. & W. Chester, Ltd.,
11 Great Marlborough Street,
London, W. 1.

Il Capinero
1st Theme   M124

2nd Theme   M125

Il Picchio
1st Theme   M126

2nd Theme   M127

Il Chiù   M128

Rispetti E Strambotti
Quartet, Str.
By permission of the copyright
holders, J. & W. Chester, Ltd.,
11 Great Marlborough Street,
London, W. 1.

1st Theme   M129

2nd Theme   M130

3rd Theme   M131

MARGIS, Alfred (1874-)

Valse Bleue,
Vn. & Pft.

1st Theme   M131a

2nd Theme   M131b

MARSHNER, Heinrich August (1795-1861)

Hans Heiling
Overture

1st Theme   M132

2nd Theme   M133

3rd Theme   M134

MARTUCCI, Giuseppe (1856-1909)

Notturno, Orch.
Copyright 1922 by G. Ricordi & Co., Inc.

M135

MASCAGNI, Pietro (1863-1945)

Cavalleria Rusticana,
Opera

Prelude
1st Theme   M136

2nd Theme   M137

Intermezzo
1st Theme   M138

2nd Theme   M139

MASSENET, Jules (1842-1912)

Le Cid, Ballet
By permission of
the copyright owner,
Heugel Ltd., London.

1st Movement
Castillane   M140

2nd Movement
Andalouse   M141

3rd Movement
Aragonaise   M142

4th Movement
Aubade   M143

5th Movement
Catalane
1st Theme   M144

5th Movement
2nd Theme   M145

6th Movement
Madrilène
1st Theme   M146

6th Movement
2nd Theme   M147

7th Movement
Navarraise   M148

**Les Erinnyes
(Incidental Music)
Orch.**
By permission of the
copyright owner,
Heugel Ltd., London.

Prelude   M149

Danse Grecque
1st Theme   M150

2nd Theme   M151

Entr'acte   M152

Scène Religieuse   M153

Invocation, Elegy   M154

Finale, Saturnales
1st Theme   M155

2nd Theme M156

Meditation from Opera
Thais
By permission of
the copyright owner,
Heugel Ltd., London.

1st Theme M157

2nd Theme M158

Phedre
Overture
By permission of the
copyright owner,
Heugel Ltd., London.

1st Theme M159

2nd Theme M160

3rd Theme M161

Le Roi De Lahore
Overture
By permission of the
copyright owner,
Heugel Ltd., London.

1st Theme M162

2nd Theme M163

Scènes Alsaciennes,
Suite No. 7,
By permission of the
copyright owner,
Heugel Ltd., London.

I--Sunday Morning
1st Theme M164

2nd Theme M165

II--Cabaret
1st Theme M166

2nd Theme M167

3rd Theme M168

III--Under the Lindens M169

IV--Sunday Evening
1st Theme M170

2nd Theme
Alsatian Folk Tune M171

3rd Theme
Alsatian Tune M172

Scènes Pittoresques,
Suite No. 4,
By permission of the
copyright owner,
Heugel Ltd., London.

I--March
1st Theme M173

2nd Theme M174

3rd Theme M175

4th Theme — M176

H--Air De Ballet
1st Theme — M177

2nd Theme — M178

III--Angelus
1st Theme — M179

2nd Theme — M180

IV--Fête Bohême
1st Theme — M181

2nd Theme — M182

McDONALD, Harl (1899-)

Rhumba, from
Symphony No. 2
Permission granted by
Elkan-Vogel Co., Inc.,
Philadelphia, Pa.
Copyright 1936

1st Theme — M183

2nd Theme — M184

3rd Theme — M185

4th Theme — M186

MEDTNER, Nicolas (1880-)

Arabesque, "Tragedie-Fragment",
Op. 7, No. 3, Pft.
By permission of International Music Co. — M187

Fairy Tales, Pft.
Op. 14, No. 2
By permission of International Music Co.

1st Theme — M188

2nd Theme — M189

Op. 20, No. 1 — M190

Op. 26, No. 3 — M191

Op. 34, No. 2 — M192

Op. 51, No. 1 — M193

Op. 51, No. 2 — M194

Novelette, Op. 17, No. 1, Pft.
By permission of International Music Co. — M195

MENDELSSOHN, Felix (1809-1847)

Capriccio Brilliant,
Op. 22, Pft. & Orch. — 1st Theme Intro. — M196

2nd Theme — M197

3rd Theme — M198

4th Theme — M199

Concerto No. 1,
in G Minor, Op. 25,
Pft. & Orch. — 1st Movement Intro. — M200

1st Movement 1st Theme — M201

1st Movement 2nd Theme — M202

1st Movement 3rd Theme — M203

2nd Movement — M204

3rd Movement — M205

Concerto No. 2,
in D Minor, Op. 40,
Pft. & Orch. — 1st Movement Intro. — M206

1st Movement 1st Theme — M207

1st Movement 2nd Theme — M208

2nd Movement — M209

3rd Movement — M210

Concerto in E Minor,
Op. 64, Vn. & Orch. — 1st Movement 1st Theme — M211

1st Movement 2nd Theme — M212
1st Movement 3rd Theme — M213
2nd Movement 1st Theme — M214
2nd Movement 2nd Theme — M215
3rd Movement Intro. — M216
3rd Movement 1st Theme — M217
3rd Movement 2nd Theme — M218
3rd Movement 3rd Theme — M219

Midsummer Night's Dream
Orch.
Overture, Op. 21 1st Theme — M220
2nd Theme — M221
3rd Theme — M222
4th Theme, A — M223
4th Theme, B — M224

Scherzo, Op. 61, No. 1 1st Theme — M225
2nd Theme — M226

Intermezzo, Op. 61, No. 5 1st Theme — M227
2nd Theme — M228
3rd Theme — M229
4th Theme — M230

Nocturne, Op. 61, No. 7 — M231

Wedding March, Op. 61, No. 9 1st Theme — M232

2nd Theme — M233

3rd Theme — M234

4th Theme — M235

Octet, in E Flat, Op. 20, Str. 1st Movement 1st Theme — M236

1st Movement 2nd Theme — M237

2nd Movement 1st Theme — M238

2nd Movement 2nd Theme — M239

3rd Movement 1st Theme — M240

3rd Movement 2nd Theme — M241

3rd Movement 3rd Theme — M242

4th Movement 1st Theme — M243

4th Movement 2nd Theme — M244

Meeresstille und Glückliche Fahrt, Op. 27 Overture, (Calm Sea and Prosperous Voyage) Meeresstille — M245

Glückliche Fahrt 1st Theme — M246

2nd Theme — M247

3rd Theme — M248

Fingal's Cave (or The Hebrides), Op. 26 Overture 1st Theme — M249

2nd Theme — M250

3rd Theme — M251

Ruy Blas, Overture, Op. 95 — Intro. — M252

1st Theme — M253

2nd Theme, A — M254

2nd Theme, B — M255

3rd Theme — M256

Quartet No. 1, in E Flat, Op. 12, Str. — 1st Movement Intro. — M257

1st Movement 1st Theme — M258

1st Movement 2nd Theme — M259

1st Movement 3rd Theme — M260

2nd Movement — M261

3rd Movement — M262

4th Movement 1st Theme — M263

4th Movement 2nd Theme — M264

Quartet, No. 3 in D, Op. 44, No. 1, Str. — 1st Movement 1st Theme — M265

1st Movement 2nd Theme — M266

1st Movement 3rd Theme — M267

2nd Movement 1st Theme — M268

2nd Movement 2nd Theme — M269

3rd Movement 1st Theme, A — M270

3rd Movement 1st Theme, B — M271

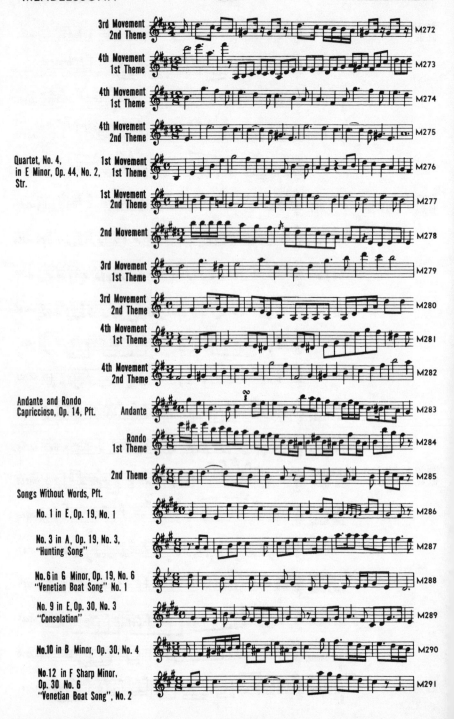

	3rd Movement, 2nd Theme	M272
	4th Movement, 1st Theme	M273
	4th Movement, 1st Theme	M274
	4th Movement, 2nd Theme	M275
Quartet, No. 4, in E Minor, Op. 44, No. 2, Str.	1st Movement, 1st Theme	M276
	1st Movement, 2nd Theme	M277
	2nd Movement	M278
	3rd Movement, 1st Theme	M279
	3rd Movement, 2nd Theme	M280
	4th Movement, 1st Theme	M281
	4th Movement, 2nd Theme	M282
Andante and Rondo Capriccioso, Op. 14, Pft.	Andante	M283
	Rondo, 1st Theme	M284
	2nd Theme	M285
Songs Without Words, Pft.		
No. 1 in E, Op. 19, No. 1		M286
No. 3 in A, Op. 19, No. 3, "Hunting Song"		M287
No. 6 in G Minor, Op. 19, No. 6 "Venetian Boat Song" No. 1		M288
No. 9 in E, Op. 30, No. 3 "Consolation"		M289
No. 10 in B Minor, Op. 30, No. 4		M290
No. 12 in F Sharp Minor, Op. 30 No. 6 "Venetian Boat Song", No. 2		M291

No.14 in C Minor, Op. 38, No. 2, "Lost Happiness" — M292

No.18 in A Flat, Op. 38, No. 6, "Duet" — M293

No.20 in E Flat, Op. 53, No. 2, "The Fleecy Cloud" — M294

No.22 in F, Op. 53, No. 4, "Sadness of Soul" — M295

No.23 in A, Op. 53, No. 5, "Folk Song" 1st Theme — M296

2nd Theme — M297

No.25 in G, Op. 62, No. 1, "May Breezes" — M298

No. 27, in E Minor Op. 62, No. 3, "Funeral March" — M299

No. 28, in G Op. 62, No. 4, "Morning Song" — M300

No.29, in A Minor, Op.62, No. 5 "Venetian Boat Song", No. 3 — M301

No. 30, in A, Op.62, No. 6 "Spring Song" — M302

No. 34, in C, Op.67, No.4 "Spinning Song" — M303

No.35, in B Minor, Op.67, No. 5 "Song of the Heather" — M304

No. 45, in C, "Tarantella" — M305

No.47, in A, Op.102 No. 5 "The Joyous Peasant" — M306

No.48, in C, Op. 102, No. 6 "Faith" — M307

No. 49, in A, Op.102, No. 7 "Boat-Song" — M308

Scherzo, Op. 16, No. 2, Pft. 1st Theme — M309

2nd Theme — M310

Symphony No. 3, in A Minor, Op.56 "Scotch" 1st Movement Intro. — M311

1st Movement 1st Theme   M312

1st Movement 2nd Theme   M313

1st Movement 3rd Theme   M314

1st Movement 4th Theme   M315

2nd Movement 1st Theme   M316

2nd Movement 2nd Theme   M317

3rd Movement 1st Theme   M318

3rd Movement 2nd Theme   M319

4th Movement 1st Theme   M320

4th Movement 2nd Theme   M321

4th Movement 3rd Theme   M322

4th Movement 4th Theme   M323

Symphony No. 4, in A, Op. 90, "Italian"

1st Movement 1st Theme   M324

1st Movement 2nd Theme   M325

1st Movement 3rd Theme   M326

2nd Movement Intro.   M327

2nd Movement 1st Theme   M328

2nd Movement 2nd Theme   M329

2nd Movement 3rd Theme   M330

3rd Movement 1st Theme   M331

3rd Movement / 2nd Theme   M332
4th Movement / 1st Theme   M333
4th Movement / 2nd Theme   M334
4th Movement / 3rd Theme   M335
4th Movement / 4th Theme   M336

Symphony No. 5, in D, Op. 107, "Reformation"

1st Movement / Intro.   M337
1st Movement / 1st Theme   M338
1st Movement / 2nd Theme   M339
2nd Movement / 1st Theme   M340
2nd Movement / 2nd Theme   M341
3rd Movement / 1st Theme   M342

Chorale, Ein Feste Burg ist unser Gott!

3rd Movement / 2nd Theme   M343
3rd Movement / 3rd Theme   M344
3rd Movement / 4th Theme   M345
3rd Movement / 5th Theme   M346
3rd Movement / 6th Theme   M347

Trio No. 1, in D Minor, Op. 49, Vn, Cello, Pft.

1st Movement / 1st Theme A   M348
1st Movement / 1st Theme B   M349
2nd Movement / 1st Theme   M350
2nd Movement / 2nd Theme   M351

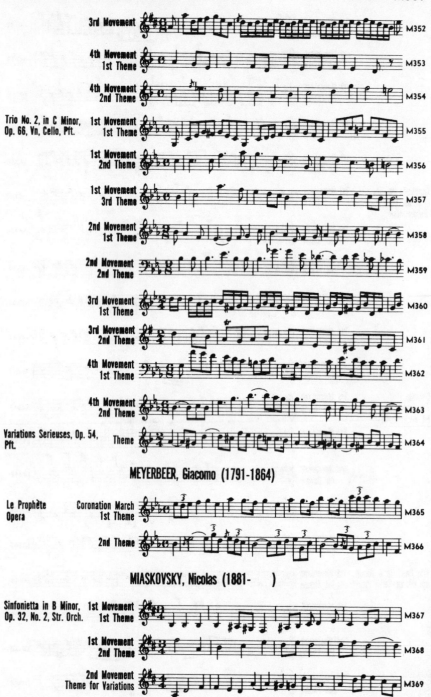

3rd Movement — M352

4th Movement
1st Theme — M353

4th Movement
2nd Theme — M354

Trio No. 2, in C Minor,
Op. 66, Vn, Cello, Pft.

1st Movement
1st Theme — M355

1st Movement
2nd Theme — M356

1st Movement
3rd Theme — M357

2nd Movement
1st Theme — M358

2nd Movement
2nd Theme — M359

3rd Movement
1st Theme — M360

3rd Movement
2nd Theme — M361

4th Movement
1st Theme — M362

4th Movement
2nd Theme — M363

Variations Serieuses, Op. 54,
Pft.

Theme — M364

MEYERBEER, Giacomo (1791-1864)

Le Prophète
Opera

Coronation March
1st Theme — M365

2nd Theme — M366

MIASKOVSKY, Nicolas (1881-   )

Sinfonietta in B Minor,
Op. 32, No. 2, Str. Orch.

1st Movement
1st Theme — M367

1st Movement
2nd Theme — M368

2nd Movement
Theme for Variations — M369

3rd Movement 1st Theme   M370

3rd Movement 2nd Theme   M371

3rd Movement 3rd Theme   M372

Symphony No. 21, in F Sharp Minor, Op. 51

1st Theme   M372a

2nd Theme   M372b

3rd Theme   M372c

4th Theme   M372d

5th Theme   M372e

6th Theme (Variant of 4th Theme Used as Fugue Theme)   M372 f

MILHAUD, Darius (1892-)

Le Boeuf Sur Le Toit, (The Nothing Doing Bar), Ballet based on South American Tunes
Copyright by Editions Salabert Editions Salabert, 22 Rue Chaucat, Paris Salabert, Inc., 1 East 57 St., N. Y.

1st Theme Barman Theme   M373

2nd Theme Entry of the Negroes   M374

3rd Theme Entry of the Women, A   M375

3rd Theme, B   M376

4th Theme Entry of the Men   M377

5th Theme Dance of the Bookmakers   M378

6th Theme Tango   M379

7th Theme Dance of the Policemen   M380

8th Theme Dance of the Negro   M381

Concerto, Pft. & Orch.
Copyright by Editions Salabert Editions Salabert, 22 Rue Chaucat, Paris Salabert, Inc., 1 East 57 St., N. Y.

1st Movement 1st Theme   M382

1st Movement 2nd Theme — M383
1st Movement 3rd Theme — M384
2nd Movement — M385
3rd Movement 1st Theme — M386
3rd Movement 2nd Theme — M387

Création Du Monde, Ballet
By permission of Associated Music Publishers, Inc.

Prelude — M388
1st Movement — M389
2nd Movement — M390
3rd Movement — M391
4th Movement 1st Theme — M392
4th Movement 2nd Theme — M393

Pastorale for Oboe, Cl., Bassoon
By permission of Associated Music Publishers, Inc.

1st Theme — M394
2nd Theme — M395

Saudades Do Brazil, Pft.
Copyright by Editions Salabert Editions Salabert, 22 Rue Chaucat, Paris Salabert, Inc., 1 East 57 St., N. Y.

I Sorocaba — M396
VII Corcovado — M397
VIII Tijuca — M398
IX Sumare — M399
XII Paysandu — M400

MONIUSZKO, Stanislaw (1819-1872)

Halka Overture

Intro. — M401

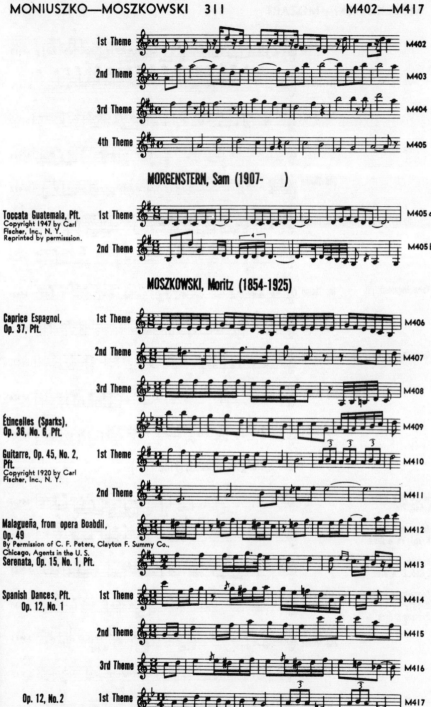

1st Theme — M402

2nd Theme — M403

3rd Theme — M404

4th Theme — M405

MORGENSTERN, Sam (1907-   )

Toccata Guatemala, Pft.
Copyright 1947 by Carl
Fischer, Inc., N. Y.
Reprinted by permisssion.

1st Theme — M405 a

2nd Theme — M405 b

MOSZKOWSKI, Moritz (1854-1925)

**Caprice Espagnol,
Op. 37, Pft.**

1st Theme — M406

2nd Theme — M407

3rd Theme — M408

**Étincelles (Sparks),
Op. 36, No. 6, Pft.** — M409

**Guitarre, Op. 45, No. 2,
Pft.**
Copyright 1920 by Carl
Fischer, Inc., N. Y.

1st Theme — M410

2nd Theme — M411

**Malagueña, from opera Boabdil,
Op. 49**
By Permission of C. F. Peters, Clayton F. Summy Co.,
Chicago, Agents in the U. S. — M412

Serenata, Op. 15, No. 1, Pft. — M413

**Spanish Dances, Pft.
Op. 12, No. 1**

1st Theme — M414

2nd Theme — M415

3rd Theme — M416

Op. 12, No. 2

1st Theme — M417

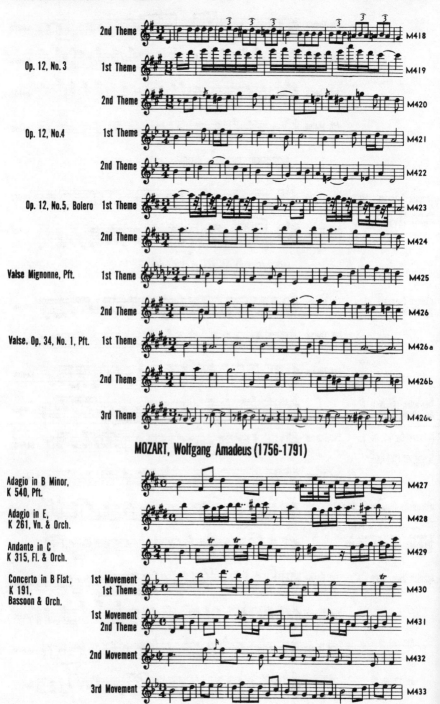

2nd Theme   M418

Op. 12, No. 3   1st Theme   M419

2nd Theme   M420

Op. 12, No.4   1st Theme   M421

2nd Theme   M422

Op. 12, No.5, Bolero   1st Theme   M423

2nd Theme   M424

Valse Mignonne, Pft.   1st Theme   M425

2nd Theme   M426

Valse, Op. 34, No. 1, Pft.   1st Theme   M426a

2nd Theme   M426b

3rd Theme   M426c

MOZART, Wolfgang Amadeus (1756-1791)

Adagio in B Minor,
K 540, Pft.   M427

Adagio in E,
K 261, Vn. & Orch.   M428

Andante in C
K 315, Fl. & Orch.   M429

Concerto in B Flat,
K 191,
Bassoon & Orch.   1st Movement
1st Theme   M430

1st Movement
2nd Theme   M431

2nd Movement   M432

3rd Movement   M433

Concerto in A, K 622, Cl. & Orch. — 1st Movement — M434
2nd Movement — M435
3rd Movement 1st Theme — M436
3rd Movement 2nd Theme — M437

Concerto in G, K 313, Fl. & Orch. — 1st Movement — M438
2nd Movement — M439
3rd Movement — M440

Concerto in C, K 299, Fl., Harp & Orch. — 1st Movement 1st Theme — M441
1st Movement 2nd Theme — M442
2nd Movement — M443
3rd Movement — M444

Concerto in E Flat K 447, Horn & Orch. — 1st Movement 1st Theme — M445
1st Movement 2nd Theme — M446
2nd Movement — M447
3rd Movement — M448

Concerto in E Flat, K 271, Pft. & Orch. — 1st Movement 1st Theme — M449
1st Movement 2nd Theme — M450
2nd Movement — M451
3rd Movement 1st Theme — M452
3rd Movement 2nd Theme — M453

Concerto in A, K 414, Pft. & Orch. — 1st Movement 1st Theme — M454
1st Movement 2nd Theme — M455
2nd Movement — M456
3rd Movement 1st Theme — M457
3rd Movement 2nd Theme — M458

Concerto in E Flat, K 449, Pft. & Orch. — 1st Movement 1st Theme — M459
2nd Movement — M460
3rd Movement — M461

Concerto in B Flat K 450, Pft. & Orch. — 1st Movement 1st Theme — M462
1st Movement 2nd Theme — M463
2nd Movement — M464
3rd Movement — M465

Concerto in G K 453, Pft. & Orch. — 1st Movement 1st Theme — M466
1st Movement 2nd Theme — M467
2nd Movement — M468
3rd Movement — M469

Concerto in F K 459, Pft. & Orch. — 1st Movement — M470
2nd Movement — M471
3rd Movement 1st Theme — M472
3rd Movement 2nd Theme — M473

Concerto in D Minor, K 466, Pft. & Orch.
1st Movement 1st Theme — M474
1st Movement 2nd Theme — M475
1st Movement 3rd Theme (Solo Theme) — M476
2nd Movement — M477
3rd Movement 1st Theme — M478
3rd Movement 2nd Theme — M479

Concerto in C K 467, Pft. & Orch.
1st Movement 1st Theme — M480
1st Movement 2nd Theme — M481
2nd Movement — M482
3rd Movement 1st Theme — M483
3rd Movement 2nd Theme — M484

Concerto in E Flat, K 482, Pft. & Orch.
1st Movement 1st Theme — M485
1st Movement 2nd Theme — M486
2nd Movement — M487
3rd Movement 1st Theme — M488
3rd Movement 2nd Theme — M489

Concerto in A, K 488, Pft. & Orch.
1st Movement 1st Theme — M490
1st Movement 2nd Theme — M491
2nd Movement 1st Theme — M492
2nd Movement 2nd Theme — M493

3rd Movement 1st Theme — M494
3rd Movement 2nd Theme — M495

Concerto in C Minor, K 491, Pft. & Orch.
1st Movement — M496
2nd Movement — M497
3rd Movement — M498

Concerto in C, K 503, Pft. & Orch.
1st Movement 1st Theme — M499
1st Movement 2nd Theme — M500
2nd Movement — M501
3rd Movement — M502

Concerto in D K 537, Pft. & Orch. "Coronation"
1st Movement 1st Theme — M503
1st Movement 2nd Theme — M504
2nd Movement — M505
3rd Movement 1st Theme — M506
3rd Movement 2nd Theme — M507

Concerto in B Flat, K 595, Pft. & Orch.
1st Movement — M508
2nd Movement — M509
3rd Movement 1st Theme — M510
3rd Movement 2nd Theme — M511

Concerto in G, K 216, Vn. & Orch.
1st Movement — M512
2nd Movement — M513

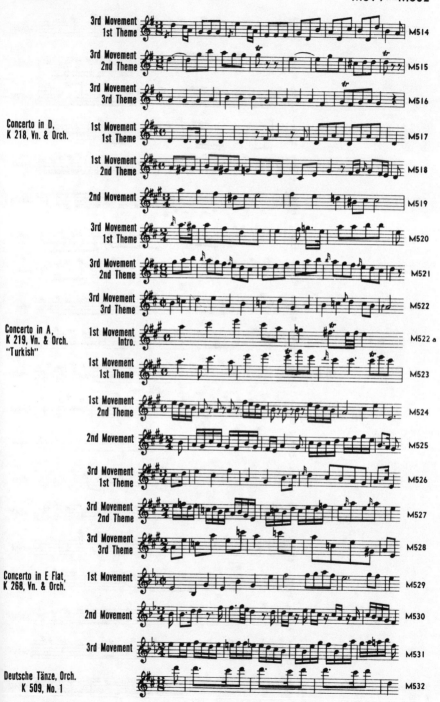

3rd Movement / 1st Theme   M514

3rd Movement / 2nd Theme   M515

3rd Movement / 3rd Theme   M516

Concerto in D, K 218, Vn. & Orch.

1st Movement / 1st Theme   M517

1st Movement / 2nd Theme   M518

2nd Movement   M519

3rd Movement / 1st Theme   M520

3rd Movement / 2nd Theme   M521

3rd Movement / 3rd Theme   M522

Concerto in A, K 219, Vn. & Orch. "Turkish"

1st Movement / Intro.   M522 a

1st Movement / 1st Theme   M523

1st Movement / 2nd Theme   M524

2nd Movement   M525

3rd Movement / 1st Theme   M526

3rd Movement / 2nd Theme   M527

3rd Movement / 3rd Theme   M528

Concerto in E Flat, K 268, Vn. & Orch.

1st Movement   M529

2nd Movement   M530

3rd Movement   M531

Deutsche Tänze, Orch. K 509, No. 1   M532

K 509, No. 2 — M533
K 509, No. 4 — M534
K 509, No. 5 — M535
K 509, No. 6 — M536
K 571, No. 4 — M537
K 571, No. 6 — M538
K 600, No. 1 — M539
K 600, No. 2 — M540
K 600, No. 3 — M541
K 600, No. 4 — M542
K 600, No. 5 1st Theme — M543
2nd Theme (Der Kanarienvogel) — M544
K 600, No. 6 — M545
K 602, No. 3 1st Theme — M546
2nd Theme (Der Leiermann) — M547
K 605, No. 1 — M548
K 605, No. 2 — M549
K 605, No. 3 1st Theme — M550
2nd Theme (Die Schlitten Fahrt) — M551
Divertimento in D, K 136 2 Vns., Viola & Bass 1st Movement — M552

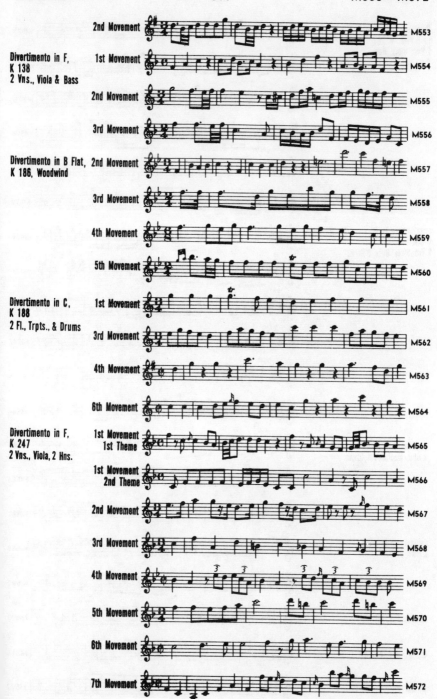

Divertimento in B Flat, K 287
2 Vns., Viola, Bass, 2 Horns

1st Movement    M573

2nd Movement 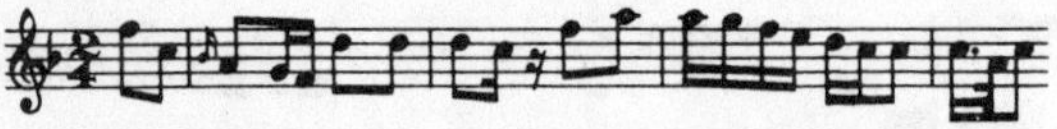   M574

3rd Movement 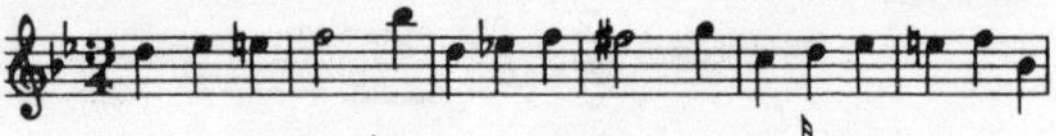   M575

4th Movement    M576

5th Movement    M577

6th Movement    M578

Divertimento in D, K 334
2 Vns., Viola, Bass, 2 Horns

1st Movement    M579

2nd Movement    M580

3rd Movement    M581

4th Movement    M582

5th Movement    M583

6th Movement    M584

Fantasia in F Minor, K 608, Mechanical Organ

1st Theme    M585

2nd Theme    M586

3rd Theme    M587

Fantasia in D Minor, K 397, Pft.

1st Theme 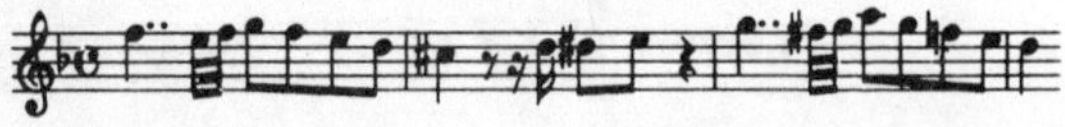   M588

2nd Theme    M589

Minuet, K 1, Pft.    M590

Minuet in F, K 2, Pft.    M591

Minuet in D, K 355, Pft.    M592

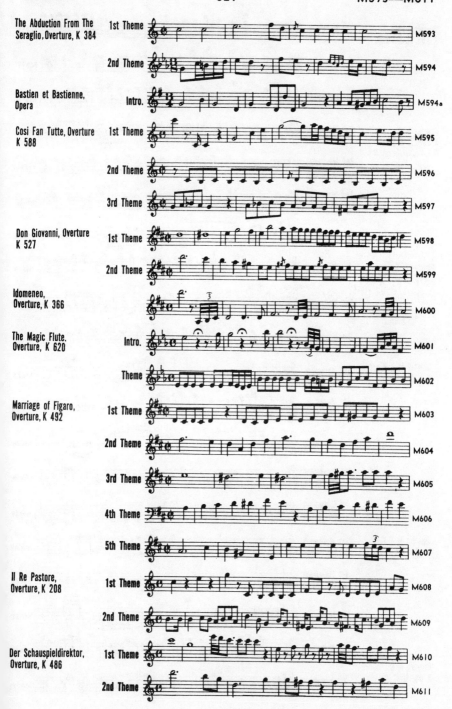

The Abduction From The Seraglio, Overture, K 384 — 1st Theme — M593

2nd Theme — M594

Bastien et Bastienne, Opera — Intro. — M594a

Cosi Fan Tutte, Overture K 588 — 1st Theme — M595

2nd Theme — M596

3rd Theme — M597

Don Giovanni, Overture K 527 — 1st Theme — M598

2nd Theme — M599

Idomeneo, Overture, K 366 — M600

The Magic Flute, Overture, K 620 — Intro. — M601

Theme — M602

Marriage of Figaro, Overture, K 492 — 1st Theme — M603

2nd Theme — M604

3rd Theme — M605

4th Theme — M606

5th Theme — M607

Il Re Pastore, Overture, K 208 — 1st Theme — M608

2nd Theme — M609

Der Schauspieldirektor, Overture, K 486 — 1st Theme — M610

2nd Theme — M611

Quartet in D,
K 285, Fl. & Str.

1st Movement   M612

2nd Movement   M613

3rd Movement   M614

Quartet in A,
K 298, Fl. & Str.

1st Movement   M615

2nd Movement
1st Theme   M616

2nd Movement
2nd Theme   M617

3rd Movement   M618

Quartet in F,
K 370, Oboe & Str.

1st Movement   M619

2nd Movement   M620

3rd Movement   M621

Quartet in G Minor
K 4, Pft. & Str.

1st Movement
1st Theme   M622

1st Movement
2nd Theme   M623

2nd Movement   M624

3rd Movement
1st Theme   M625

3rd Movement
2nd Theme   M626

Quartet in E Flat
K 493, Pft. & Str.

1st Movement
1st Theme   M627

1st Movement
2nd Theme   M628

2nd Movement   M629

3rd Movement   M630

Quartet in G
K 80, Str.

1st Movement   M631

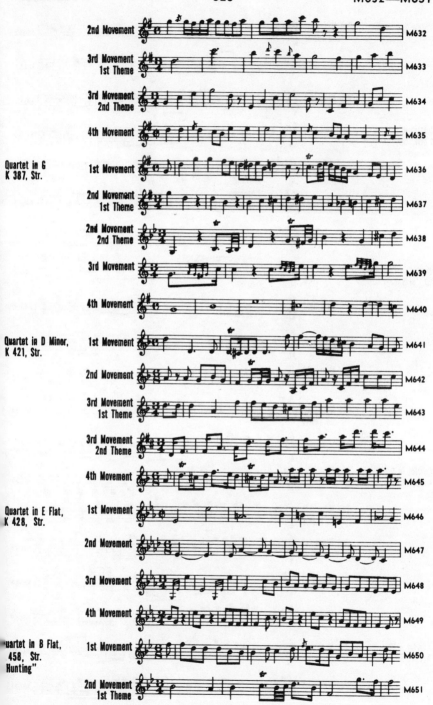

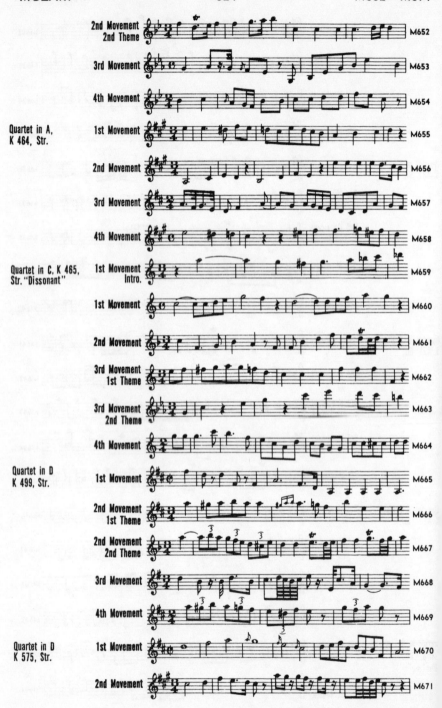

2nd Movement 2nd Theme — M652

3rd Movement — M653

4th Movement — M654

Quartet in A, K 464, Str. — 1st Movement — M655

2nd Movement — M656

3rd Movement — M657

4th Movement — M658

Quartet in C, K 465, Str. "Dissonant" — 1st Movement Intro. — M659

1st Movement — M660

2nd Movement — M661

3rd Movement 1st Theme — M662

3rd Movement 2nd Theme — M663

4th Movement — M664

Quartet in D K 499, Str. — 1st Movement — M665

2nd Movement 1st Theme — M666

2nd Movement 2nd Theme — M667

3rd Movement — M668

4th Movement — M669

Quartet in D K 575, Str. — 1st Movement — M670

2nd Movement — M671

3rd Movement — M672
4th Movement — M673
Quartet in B Flat K 589, Str. — 1st Movement — M674
2nd Movement — M675
3rd Movement — M676
4th Movement — M677
Quartet in F K 590, Str. — 1st Movement — M678
2nd Movement — M679
3rd Movement — M680
4th Movement — M681
Quintet in A, K 581, Cl. & Str. — 1st Movement — M682
2nd Movement — M683
3rd Movement 1st Theme — M684
3rd Movement 2nd Theme — M685
4th Movement — M686
Quintet in E Flat, K 452, Piano & Woodw. — 1st Movement Intro. — M687
1st Movement — M688
2nd Movement — M689
3rd Movement — M690
Quintet in C, K 515, Str. — 1st Movement — M691

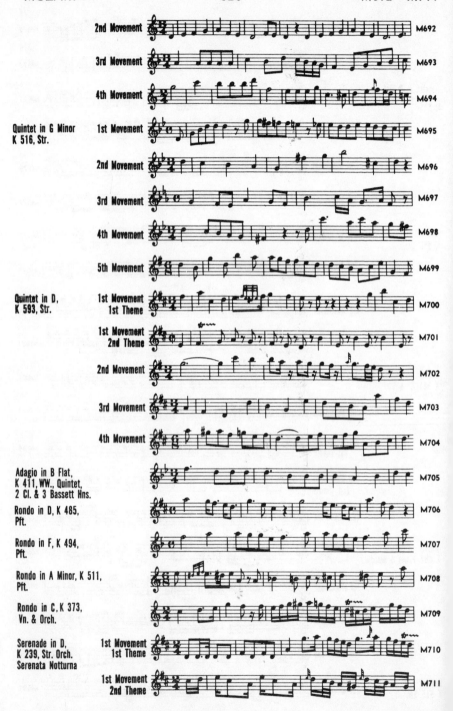

2nd Movement — M692

3rd Movement — M693

4th Movement — M694

Quintet in G Minor
K 516, Str.
1st Movement — M695

2nd Movement — M696

3rd Movement — M697

4th Movement — M698

5th Movement — M699

Quintet in D,
K 593, Str.
1st Movement
1st Theme — M700

1st Movement
2nd Theme — M701

2nd Movement — M702

3rd Movement — M703

4th Movement — M704

Adagio in B Flat,
K 411, WW., Quintet,
2 Cl. & 3 Bassett Hns. — M705

Rondo in D, K 485,
Pft. — M706

Rondo in F, K 494,
Pft. — M707

Rondo in A Minor, K 511,
Pft. — M708

Rondo in C, K 373,
Vn. & Orch. — M709

Serenade in D,
K 239, Str. Orch.
Serenata Notturna
1st Movement
1st Theme — M710

1st Movement
2nd Theme — M711

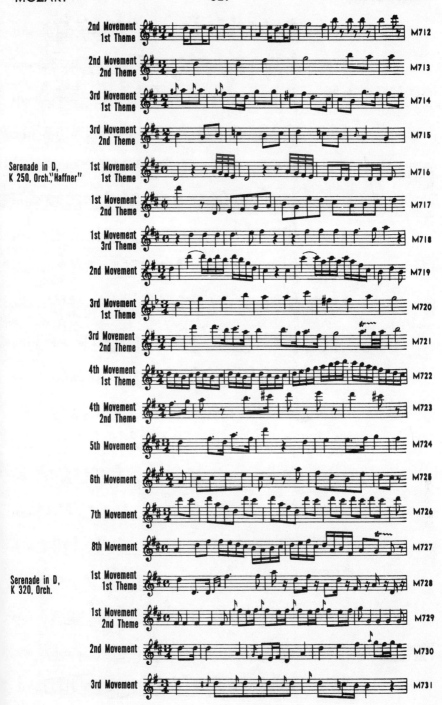

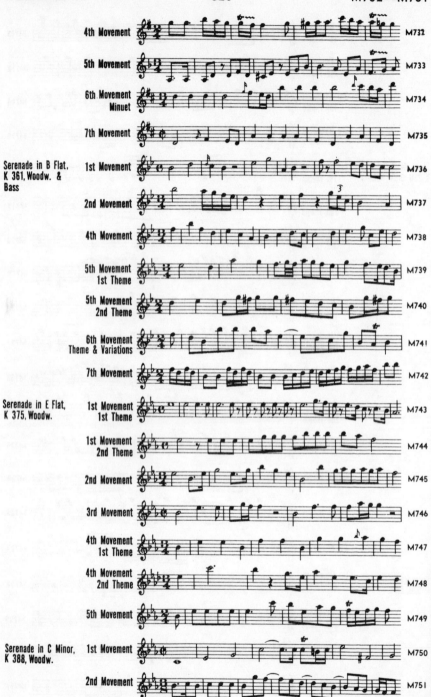

Serenade in B Flat,
K 361, Woodw. &
Bass

Serenade in E Flat,
K 375, Woodw.

Serenade in C Minor,
K 388, Woodw.

4th Movement — M732

5th Movement — M733

6th Movement
Minuet — M734

7th Movement — M735

1st Movement — M736

2nd Movement — M737

4th Movement — M738

5th Movement
1st Theme — M739

5th Movement
2nd Theme — M740

6th Movement
Theme & Variations — M741

7th Movement — M742

1st Movement
1st Theme — M743

1st Movement
2nd Theme — M744

2nd Movement — M745

3rd Movement — M746

4th Movement
1st Theme — M747

4th Movement
2nd Theme — M748

5th Movement — M749

1st Movement — M750

2nd Movement — M751

3rd Movement — M752

4th Movement — M753

Serenade in G, K 525, Str. Orch. Eine Kleine Nachtmusik — 1st Movement — M754

2nd Movement — M755

3rd Movement 1st Theme Minuet — M756

3rd Movement 2nd Theme Trio — M757

4th Movement — M758

Sextet in F, K 522, 2 Vns., Viola, Bass & 2 Horns Ein Musikalischer Spass — 1st Movement — M759

2nd Movement — M760

3rd Movement — M761

4th Movement — M762

Sonata in E Flat K 282, Pft. — 1st Movement — M763

2nd Movement 1st Theme — M764

2nd Movement 2nd Theme — M765

3rd Movement — M766

Sonata in G K 283, Pft. — 1st Movement — M767

2nd Movement — M768

3rd Movement 1st Theme — M769

3rd Movement 2nd Theme — M770

Sonata in C K 309, Pft. — 1st Movement — M771

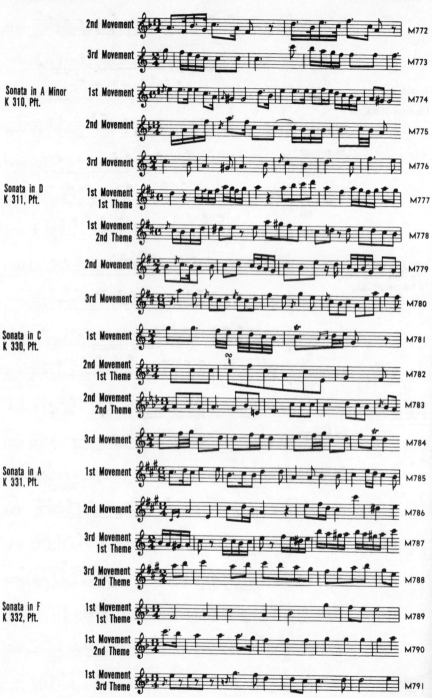

2nd Movement   M772

3rd Movement   M773

Sonata in A Minor
K 310, Pft.

1st Movement   M774

2nd Movement   M775

3rd Movement   M776

Sonata in D
K 311, Pft.

1st Movement
1st Theme   M777

1st Movement
2nd Theme   M778

2nd Movement   M779

3rd Movement   M780

Sonata in C
K 330, Pft.

1st Movement   M781

2nd Movement
1st Theme   M782

2nd Movement
2nd Theme   M783

3rd Movement   M784

Sonata in A
K 331, Pft.

1st Movement   M785

2nd Movement   M786

3rd Movement
1st Theme   M787

3rd Movement
2nd Theme   M788

Sonata in F
K 332, Pft.

1st Movement
1st Theme   M789

1st Movement
2nd Theme   M790

1st Movement
3rd Theme   M791

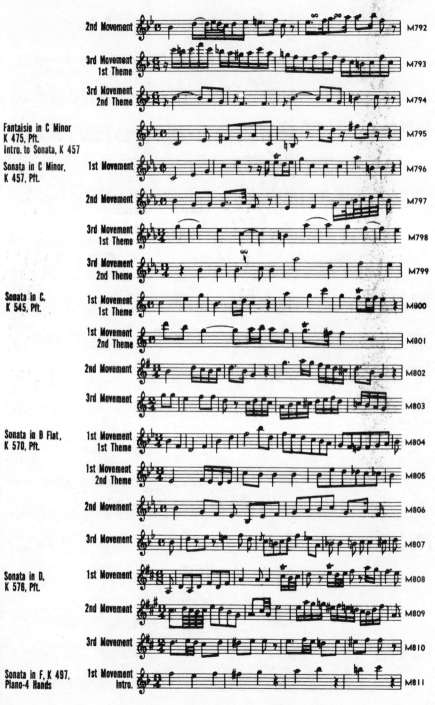

	2nd Movement	M792
	3rd Movement 1st Theme	M793
	3rd Movement 2nd Theme	M794
Fantaisie in C Minor K 475, Pft. Intro. to Sonata, K 457		M795
Sonata in C Minor, K 457, Pft.	1st Movement	M796
	2nd Movement	M797
	3rd Movement 1st Theme	M798
	3rd Movement 2nd Theme	M799
Sonata in C, K 545, Pft.	1st Movement 1st Theme	M800
	1st Movement 2nd Theme	M801
	2nd Movement	M802
	3rd Movement	M803
Sonata in B Flat, K 570, Pft.	1st Movement 1st Theme	M804
	1st Movement 2nd Theme	M805
	2nd Movement	M806
	3rd Movement	M807
Sonata in D, K 576, Pft.	1st Movement	M808
	2nd Movement	M809
	3rd Movement	M810
Sonata in F, K 497, Piano-4 Hands	1st Movement Intro.	M811

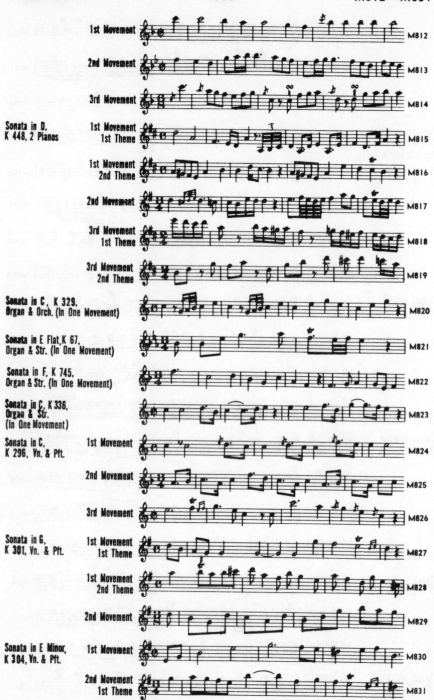

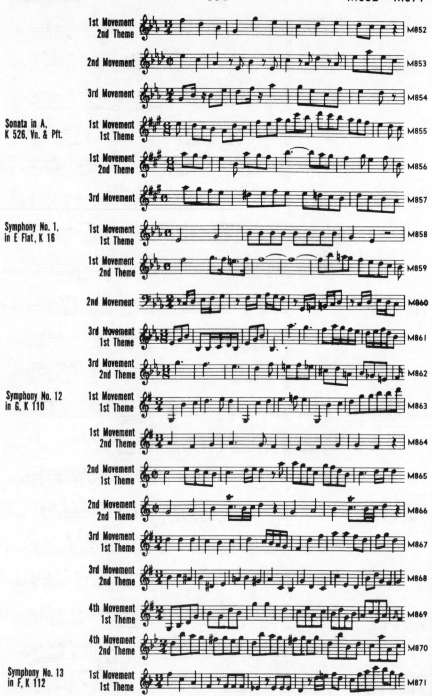

1st Movement 2nd Theme — M852
2nd Movement — M853
3rd Movement — M854
Sonata in A, K 526, Vn. & Pft. — 1st Movement 1st Theme — M855
1st Movement 2nd Theme — M856
3rd Movement — M857
Symphony No. 1, in E Flat, K 16 — 1st Movement 1st Theme — M858
1st Movement 2nd Theme — M859
2nd Movement — M860
3rd Movement 1st Theme — M861
3rd Movement 2nd Theme — M862
Symphony No. 12 in G, K 110 — 1st Movement 1st Theme — M863
1st Movement 2nd Theme — M864
2nd Movement 1st Theme — M865
2nd Movement 2nd Theme — M866
3rd Movement 1st Theme — M867
3rd Movement 2nd Theme — M868
4th Movement 1st Theme — M869
4th Movement 2nd Theme — M870
Symphony No. 13 in F, K 112 — 1st Movement 1st Theme — M871

1st Movement / 2nd Theme — M872
2nd Movement — M873
3rd Movement / 1st Theme — M874
3rd Movement / 2nd Theme — M875
4th Movement / 1st Theme — M876
4th Movement / 2nd Theme — M877
Symphony No. 25 in G Minor, K 183
1st Movement / 1st Theme — M878
1st Movement / 2nd Theme — M879
1st Movement / 3rd Theme — M880
2nd Movement — M881
3rd Movement / 1st Theme — M882
3rd Movement / 2nd Theme — M883
4th Movement / 1st Theme — M884
4th Movement / 2nd Theme — M885
Symphony No. 28 in C, K 200
1st Movement / 1st Theme — M886
1st Movement / 2nd Theme — M887
2nd Movement / 1st Theme — M888
2nd Movement / 2nd Theme — M889
3rd Movement / 1st Theme — M890
3rd Movement / 2nd Theme — M891

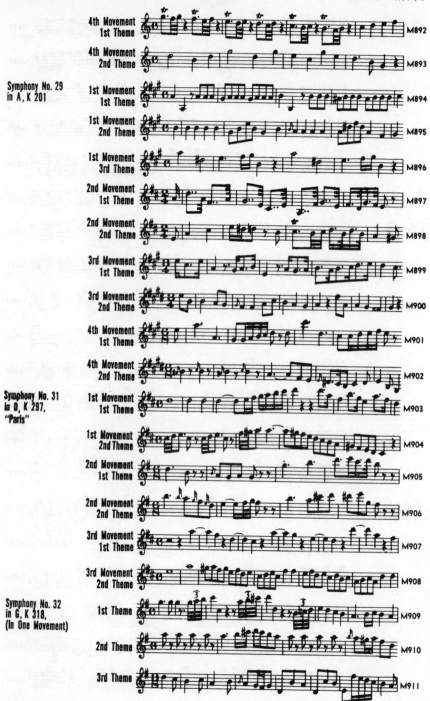

Symphony No. 33
in B Flat, K 319

1st Movement
1st Theme   M912

1st Movement
2nd Theme,
A   M913

1st Movement
2nd Theme.
B   M914

2nd Movement
1st Theme   M915

2nd Movement
2nd Theme   M916

3rd Movement
1st Theme   M917

3rd Movement
2nd Theme   M918

4th Movement
1st Theme   M919

4th Movement
2nd Theme   M920

4th Movement
3rd Theme   M921

Symphony No. 34,
in C, K 338

1st Movement
1st Theme   M922

1st Movement
2nd Theme   M923

2nd Movement
1st Theme   M924

2nd Movement
2nd Theme   M925

3rd Movement
1st Theme   M926

3rd Movement
2nd Theme   M927

Symphony No. 35,
in D, K 385,
"Haffner"

1st Movement
1st Theme   M928

1st Movement
2nd Theme   M929

2nd Movement
1st Theme   M930

2nd Movement
2nd Theme   M931

3rd Movement / 1st Theme — M932
3rd Movement / 2nd Theme — M933
4th Movement / 1st Theme — M934
4th Movement / 2nd Theme — M935

Symphony No. 36, in C, K 425 "Linz"

1st Movement / Intro. — M936
1st Movement / 1st Theme — M937
1st Movement / 2nd Theme — M938
1st Movement / 3rd Theme — M939
2nd Movement / 1st Theme — M940
2nd Movement / 2nd Theme — M941
3rd Movement / 1st Theme — M942
3rd Movement / 2nd Theme — M943
4th Movement / 1st Theme — M944
4th Movement / 2nd Theme — M945
4th Movement / 3rd Theme — M946

Symphony No. 37 in G, K 444

1st Movement / Intro. — M947
1st Movement / 1st Theme — M948
1st Movement / 2nd Theme — M949
2nd Movement / 1st Theme — M950
2nd Movement / 2nd Theme — M951

Symphony No. 40 in G Minor, K 550

1st Movement 1st Theme   M972

1st Movement 2nd Theme   M973

2nd Movement 1st Theme   M974

2nd Movement 2nd Theme   M975

2nd Movement 3rd Theme   M976

3rd Movement 1st Theme   M977

3rd Movement 2nd Theme   M978

4th Movement 1st Theme   M979

4th Movement 2nd Theme   M980

Symphony No. 41, in C K 551, "Jupiter"

1st Movement 1st Theme   M981

1st Movement 2nd Theme   M982

1st Movement 3rd Theme   M983

2nd Movement 1st Theme   M984

2nd Movement 2nd Theme   M985

3rd Movement 1st Theme   M986

3rd Movement 2nd Theme   M987

4th Movement 1st Theme   M988

4th Movement 2nd Theme   M989

4th Movement 3rd Theme   M990

Symphonie Concertante in E Flat, K 364, Vn., Viola & Orch.

1st Movement 1st Theme   M991

1st Movement 2nd Theme   M992

2nd Movement   M993

3rd Movement 1st Theme   M994

3rd Movement 2nd Theme   M995

Trio in B Flat, K 502, Pft., Vn. & Cello   1st Movement   M996

2nd Movement   M997

3rd Movement   M998

Trio in E, K 542, Pft., Vn. & Cello   1st Movement   M999

2nd Movement   M1000

3rd Movement   M1001

Trio in C, K 548, Pft., Vn. & Cello   1st Movement   M1002

2nd Movement   M1003

3rd Movement   M1004

Trio in G, K 564, Pft., Vn. & Cello   1st Movement   M1005

2nd Movement   M1006

3rd Movement   M1007

Variations in C, K 265, Pft. Theme: "Ah, Vous Dirai-Je, Maman"   M1008

Variations, K 455, Pft., (Theme of Gluck)   M1009

Variations on an Allegretto, in B Flat, K 500, Pft.   M1010

Variations, K 573, Pft., (Theme of Duport)   M1011

MUSSORGSKY, Modest Petrovich (1839-1881)

Boris Godunov Opera	Prelude	M1012
	Coronation Scene 1st Theme	M1013
	2nd Theme	M1014
The Fair at Sorochinsk Opera	Hopak	M1015
Khovantstchina Opera	I Prelude 1st Theme	M1016
	2nd Theme	M1017
	II Persian Dance 1st Theme	M1018
	2nd Theme	M1019
A Night on Bald Mountain, Orch.	1st Theme	M1020
	2nd Theme	M1021
	3rd Theme	M1022
	4th Theme	M1023
	5th Theme	M1024
Pictures From an Exposition, Pft. or Orch.	Intro. Promenade	M1025
	I The Gnome 1st Theme	M1026
	2nd Theme	M1027
	3rd Theme	M1028
	II The Old Castle	M1029
	III Tuileries, (Children Quarreling at Play)	M1030

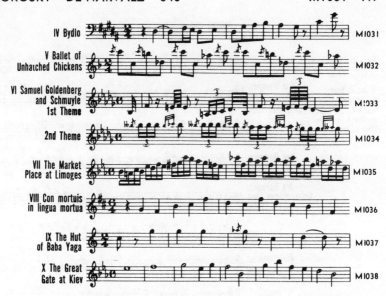

IV Bydlo   M1031

V Ballet of Unhatched Chickens   M1032

VI Samuel Goldenberg and Schmuyle 1st Theme   M1033

2nd Theme   M1034

VII The Market Place at Limoges   M1035

VIII Con mortuis in lingua mortua   M1036

IX The Hut of Baba Yaga   M1037

X The Great Gate at Kiev   M1038

NARDINI, Pietro (1722-1793)

Sonata No. 2 in D, Vn. & Pft.

1st Movement   N1

2nd Movement 1st Theme   N2

2nd Movement 2nd Theme   N3

3rd Movement (Larghetto from another Sonata)   N4

4th Movement   N5

Sonata No. 7 in B Flat, Vn. & Pft.

1st Movement   N6

2nd Movement   N7

3rd Movement   N8

NARVAEZ, Luis de (16th Century)

Tema y Variaciones, Guitar   N9

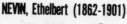

NEVIN, Ethelbert (1862-1901)

Barchetta, Op. 21, No. 3, Pft.
By permisssion of The Boston Music Co.,
copyright owner.

A Day in Venice,
Op. 25, Pft.
Published and copyrighted (1898)
by The John Church Co.
Used by permission.

1st Movement
Dawn
Intro.

Theme

2nd Movement
Gondolieri

3rd Movement
Venetian Love Song
1st Theme

2nd Theme

4th Movement
Good Night

Lullaby, Op. 16, No. 3, Pft.
By permisssion of The Boston Music Co.,
copyright owner.

Narcissus, Op. 13, No. 4, Pft. 1st Theme
By permisssion of The Boston Music Co.,
copyright owner.

2nd Theme

A Shepherd's Tale, Op. 16, No. 1, Pft.
By permisssion of The Boston Music Co.,
copyright owner.

NICOLAI, Otto (1810-1849)

The Merry Wives of Windsor,
Overture

Intro.

1st Theme

2nd Theme

3rd Theme,
A

3rd Theme,
B

4th Theme

NIN, Joaquin (1879-   )

Vals-Serenata from
Chaine de Valses, Pft.
By permission of Associated
Music Publishers, Inc.

Danse Ibérienne, Pft. 1st Theme
By permission of Associated
Music Publishers, Inc.

2nd Theme

3rd Theme

**"1830" Variations sur un
Theme Frivole**
By permission of Associated
Music Publishers, Inc.

**Suite Espagnole,
Vcl. & Pft.**
By permission of
Associated Music
Publishers, Inc.

1st Movement
Old Castile

2nd Movement
1st Theme
Murciana A

2nd Movement
1st Theme,
B

3rd Movement
Asturiana

4th Movement
Andaluza

NIN-KOCHANSKI

Granadina, Vn. & Pft.
By permission of Associated
Music Publishers, Inc.

Saeta, Vn. & Pft.
By permission of Associated
Music Publishers, Inc.

OFFENBACH, Jacques (1819-1880)

**La Belle Hélène,
Opera**
Overture
1st Theme

2nd Theme

Act II Entr'acte

Act III Entr'acte

**La Grande Duchesse de
Gerolstein, Opera**
Overture
1st Theme

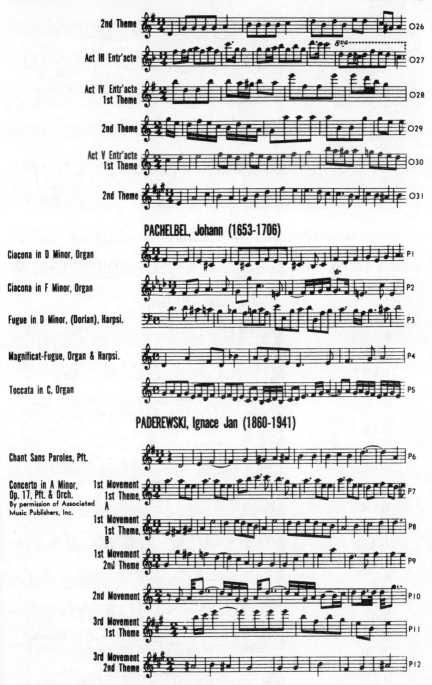

2nd Theme — O26

Act III Entr'acte — O27

Act IV Entr'acte 1st Theme — O28

2nd Theme — O29

Act V Entr'acte 1st Theme — O30

2nd Theme — O31

PACHELBEL, Johann (1653-1706)

Ciacona in D Minor, Organ — P1

Ciacona in F Minor, Organ — P2

Fugue in D Minor, (Dorian), Harpsi. — P3

Magnificat-Fugue, Organ & Harpsi. — P4

Toccata in C, Organ — P5

PADEREWSKI, Ignace Jan (1860-1941)

Chant Sans Paroles, Pft. — P6

Concerto in A Minor, Op. 17, Pft. & Orch. By permission of Associated Music Publishers, Inc. — 1st Movement 1st Theme, A — P7

1st Movement 1st Theme, B — P8

1st Movement 2nd Theme — P9

2nd Movement — P10

3rd Movement 1st Theme — P11

3rd Movement 2nd Theme — P12

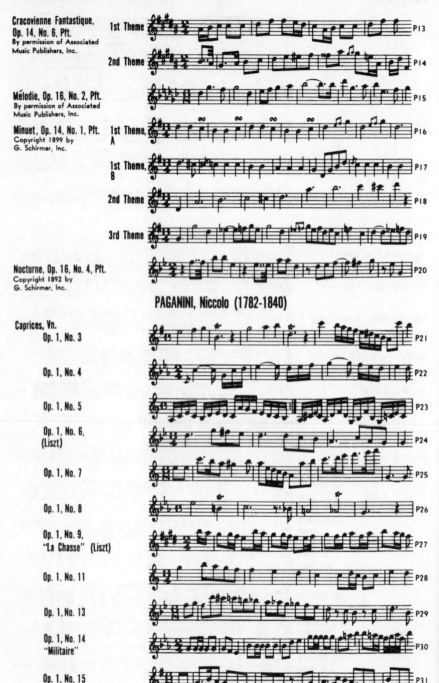

Cracovienne Fantastique,
Op. 14, No. 6, Pft.
By permission of Associated
Music Publishers, Inc.

1st Theme   P13

2nd Theme   P14

Mélodie, Op. 16, No. 2, Pft.
By permission of Associated
Music Publishers, Inc.

P15

Minuet, Op. 14, No. 1, Pft.
Copyright 1899 by
G. Schirmer, Inc.

1st Theme, A   P16

1st Theme, B   P17

2nd Theme   P18

3rd Theme   P19

Nocturne, Op. 16, No. 4, Pft.
Copyright 1892 by
G. Schirmer, Inc.

P20

PAGANINI, Niccolo (1782-1840)

Caprices, Vn.
Op. 1, No. 3   P21

Op. 1, No. 4   P22

Op. 1, No. 5   P23

Op. 1, No. 6,
(Liszt)   P24

Op. 1, No. 7   P25

Op. 1, No. 8   P26

Op. 1, No. 9,
"La Chasse" (Liszt)   P27

Op. 1, No. 11   P28

Op. 1, No. 13   P29

Op. 1, No. 14
"Militaire"   P30

Op. 1, No. 15   P31

Op. 1, No. 17, (Liszt) — P32

Op. 1, No. 18 — P33

Op. 1, No. 20 — P34

Op. 1, No. 21 — P35

Op. 1, No. 22 — P36

Op. 1, No. 24, (Liszt, Brahms, Rachmaninoff) — P37

Concerto No. 1, in D Op. 6, Vn. & Orch. — 1st Movement 1st Theme, A — P38

1st Movement 1st Theme B — P39

1st Movement 2nd Theme — P40

2nd Movement — P41

3rd Movement 1st Theme — P42

3rd Movement 2nd Theme — P43

Concerto No. 2, in B Minor, Op. 7, Vn. & Orch. — 1st Movement 1st Theme — P44

1st Movement 2nd Theme — P45

2nd Movement — P46

Rondo (La Campanella) — 3rd Movement 1st Theme, A — P47

3rd Movement 1st Theme, B — P48

3rd Movement 2nd Theme — P49

Moto Perpetuo, Op. 11, Vn. — P50

I Palpiti, Op. 13, Vn. & Orch. — Intro. — P51

Theme — P52

Le Streghe, Op. 8, Vn. & Pft.   Intro. — P53

Theme — P54

Sonata No. 11, Op. 3, No. 5, Vn. & Guitar   1st Movement — P55

2nd Movement — P56

Sonata No. 12, Op. 3, No. 6, Vn. & Guitar   1st Movement — P57

2nd Movement — P58

PAISIELLO, Giovanni (1740-1816)

Il Barbiere Di Siviglia, Overture   1st Theme — P59

2nd Theme — P60

PALMGREN, Selim (1878-   )

Finnish Romance, Op. 78, No. 5, Vn. & Pft. — P61

May Night, Pft.
By permisssion of The Boston Music Co., copyright owner. — P61a

PARADIES, Pietro Domenico (1707-1791)

Sonata in A, Pft. or Harpsi.   1st Movement — P62

2nd Movement Toccata — P63

Sonata in D, Pft. or Harpsi.   1st Movement Napolitano — P64

2nd Movement — P65

PARADIS, Marie Therese von (1759-1824)

Sicilienne, Vn. & Pft. — P66

PASQUINI, Bernardo (1637-1710)

Aria, Harpsi.   P67

Aria, Harpsi.   P68

Aria, Harpsi.   P69

Toccata Con Lo Scherzo Del Cuccó
Harpsi.   P70

PERGOLESI, Giovanni (1710-1736)

Concertino in F Minor,   1st Movement   P71
Str. Orch.

                           2nd Movement   P72

                           3rd Movement   P73

                           4th Movement   P74

PESCETTI, Giovanni (1704-1766)

Sonata in C Minor,   1st Movement   P75
Harpsi.

                           2nd Movement   P76

                           3rd Movement   P77

PFITZNER, Hans Eric (1869-   )

Palestrina, Musical Legend   1st Theme   P78
  Prelude to Act I
By permission of Associated
Music Publishers, Inc.   2nd Theme   P79

                             3rd Theme   P80

Prelude to Act II   1st Theme   P81

                             2nd Theme   P82

Prelude to Act III — 1st Theme — P83

2nd Theme — P84

PHILIPS, Peter (1560-1633)

Galliardo, Harpsi. — P85

PICK-MANGIAGALLI, Riccardo (1882-   )

Il Carillon Magico, (Ballet) — Intermezzo delle Rose — P86
Copyright 1920 by G. Ricordi & Co., Inc.

La Danse d'Olaf, Op. 33, No. 2 Orch. or Pft. — 1st Theme — P87
Copyright 1916 by G. Ricordi & Co., Inc.

2nd Theme — P88

Notturno, Op. 28, No. 1, Orch. — 1st Theme — P89
Copyright 1923 by G. Ricordi & Co., Inc.

2nd Theme — P90

I Piccoli Soldati, Orch. — 1st Theme — P91
Copyright by G. Ricordi & Co., Inc.

2nd Theme — P92

Rondo Fantastico, Op. 28, No. 2, Orch. — 1st Theme — P93
Copyright by G. Ricordi & Co., Inc.

2nd Theme — P94

3rd Theme — P95

PIERNÉ, Gabriel (1863-1937)

Cydalise et le Chèvre-pied, Ballet Suite, Orch. — March of the Little Fauns 1st Theme, A — P96
By permission of the copyright owner, Heugel Ltd., London.

1st Theme, B — P97

Dance Lesson in the Hypo-Lydian Mode — P98

Finale — P99

Impressions de Music
Hall, Ballet, Op. 47

Chorus Girls
1st Theme — P100

2nd Theme — P101

L'excentrique
1st Theme — P102

2nd Theme — P103

Spanish Routine
1st Theme — P104

2nd Theme — P105

Musical Clowns
(The Fratellinis)
1st Theme — P106

2nd Theme — P107

Sonata da Camera,
Op. 48, Fl., Vcl. & Pft.
Permission for reprint granted
by Durand & Cie, Paris.
Elkan-Vogel Co., Philadelphia,
Copyright Owners, Inc.

Prelude
1st Theme — P108

2nd Theme — P109

Sarabande
1st Theme — P110

2nd Theme — P111

Finale
1st Theme — P112

2nd Theme — P113

PISTON, Walter (1894-   )

Concertino
Pft. & Orch.
Copyright 1938.
by Arrow Music Press, Inc., N.Y.

1st Theme — P113a

2nd Theme — P113b

3rd Theme — P113c

The Incredible Flutist,
Suite from Ballet
Copyright by Arrow
Music Press, Inc., N.Y.

Intro. — P114

1st Theme — P115

2nd Theme — P116
3rd Theme — P117
4th Theme — P118
5th Theme — P119
6th Theme — P120
7th Theme — P121
8th Theme — P122
9th Theme — P123
10th Theme — P124

Quartet No. 1, Str.
Copyright Cos Cob Press, Inc.

1st Movement 1st Theme, A — P125
1st Movement 1st Theme, B — P126
1st Movement 2nd Theme, A — P127
1st Movement 2nd Theme, B — P128
2nd Movement 1st Theme, A — P129
2nd Movement 1st Theme, B — P130
3rd Movement 1st Theme — P131
3rd Movement 2nd Theme — P132

Suite for Oboe and Pft.
Copyright 1934 by E. C. Schirmer, Boston.

1st Movement Prelude — P133
2nd Movement Sarabande — P134
3rd Movement Minuet — P135

4th Movement
Nocturne   P136

5th Movement
Gigue   P137

PIZZETTI, Ildebrando (1880-   )

Sonata in A, Vn. & Pft.
By permission of the
copyright holders,
J. & W. Chester, Ltd., 11
Great Marlborough Street,
London, W. 1.

1st Movement
1st Theme.
A   P138

1st Movement
1st Theme,
B   P139

1st Movement
2nd Theme   P140

2nd Movement
Prayer for the Innocent   P141

3rd Movement
1st Theme   P142

3rd Movement
2nd Theme   P143

Tre Canti (Three Songs),
Vn. & Pft.
Copyright 1925
by G. Ricordi & Co., Inc.

No. 1   P144

No. 2   P145

No. 3   P146

PLATTI, Giovanni (1690-1762)

Sonata No. 1 in E Minor,
Fl. or Vn. & Pft.

1st Movement   P147

2nd Movement   P148

3rd Movement
Minuet
1st Theme   P149

3rd Movement
2nd Theme   P150

4th Movement
Gigue   P151

POLDINI, Eduard (1869-   )

Poupée Valsante
(Dancing Doll), Pft.

1st Theme   P152

2nd Theme — P153

PONCHIELLI, Amilcare (1834-1886)

La Gioconda
Opera
Dance of the Hours
1st Theme — P154

2nd Theme — P155

3rd Theme — P156

4th Theme — P157

I Promessi Sposi, Overture   1st Theme — P158

2nd Theme — P159

3rd Theme — P160

POPPER, David (1843-1913)

Gavotte No. 2, Op. 23,
Vcl. & Pft.
1st Theme — P161

2nd Theme — P162

Mazurka, Op. 11, No. 3,
Vcl. & Pft.
1st Theme — P163

2nd Theme — P164

PORPORA, Niccolo (1686-1766 or '67)

Sonata in G,
Vn. & Pft.
1st Movement — P165

2nd Movement
Fugue — P166

3rd Movement
Aria — P167

4th Movement — P168

POULENC, Francis (1899-   )

Mouvements Perpétuels, Pft.
By permission of the copyright holders,
J. & W. Chester, Ltd., 11
Great Marlborough Street,
London, W. 1.

No. 1  P169

No. 2 P170

No. 3
1st Theme P171

2nd Theme P172

Novelette No. 1, Pft.
By permission of the copyright holders,
J. & W. Chester, Ltd., 11
Great Marlborough Street,
London, W. 1.

1st Theme P173

2nd Theme P174

Novelette No. 2, Pft.
By permission of the copyright holders,
J. & W. Chester, Ltd., 11
Great Marlborough Street,
London, W. 1.

1st Theme P175

2nd Theme P176

Toccato, Pft.
By permission of the copyright owner,
Heugel Ltd., London.

Intro. P177

1st Theme P178

PROKOFIEFF, Serge (1891-   )

Alexander Nevsky, Cantata for Solo, Chorus and Orch., Op. 78
Copyright 1945 by
Leeds Music Corp., N. Y.
Reprinted here by permission of the copyright owner.

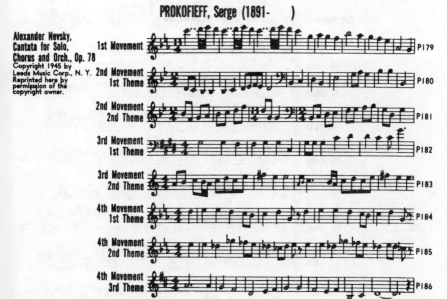

1st Movement P179

2nd Movement
1st Theme P180

2nd Movement
2nd Theme P181

3rd Movement
1st Theme P182

3rd Movement
2nd Theme P183

4th Movement
1st Theme P184

4th Movement
2nd Theme P185

4th Movement
3rd Theme P186

4th Movement / 4th Theme — P187

5th Movement / 1st Theme — P188

5th Movement / 2nd Theme — P189

5th Movement / 3rd Theme — P190

5th Movement / 4th Theme — P191

5th Movement / 5th Theme — P192

5th Movement / 6th Theme — P193

6th Movement — P194

7th Movement — P195

Classical Symphony, Op. 25
By permission of the copyright owner, Boosey and Hawkes, Inc.

1st Movement / 1st Theme — P196

1st Movement / 2nd Theme — P197

2nd Movement — P198

3rd Movement / Gavotte / 1st Theme — P199

3rd Movement / 2nd Theme — P200

4th Movement / 1st Theme — P201

4th Movement / 2nd Theme — P202

Concerto No. 3, Op. 26, Pft. & Orch.
Copyright 1945 by Leeds Music Corp., N. Y. Reprinted here by permission of the copyright owner.

1st Movement / 1st Theme, A — P203

1st Movement / 1st Theme, B — P204

1st Movement / 2nd Theme — P205

2nd Movement — P206

1st Movement
3rd Theme — P227

2nd Movement
Romance
1st Theme — P228

2nd Movement
2nd Theme — P229

2nd Movement
3rd Theme — P230

3rd Movement
Kije's Wedding
1st Theme — P231

3rd Movement
2nd Theme — P232

4th Movement
Troika — P233

Love of Three Oranges, Op. 33
Opera
By permission of the
copyright owner,
Boosey and Hawkes, Inc.   March — P234

Scherzo — P235

March, Op. 12, No. 1, Pft. — P236

Music for Children, Op. 65, Pft.   March
Copyright 1946 by Leeds
Music Corp., N. Y.
Reprinted here by permisssion
of the copyright owner. — P237

Waltz — P238

Overture on Hebrew Themes,
Op. 34, Cl., Pft. &
Str. Quartet   1st Theme — P239
By permission of the
copyright owner,
Boosey and Hawkes, Inc.   2nd Theme — P240

Peter and the Wolf,
Op. 67, Orch.   1st Theme
Peter — P241
Copyright 1946 by
Leeds Music Corp., N. Y.
Reprinted here by
permission of the
copyright owner.   2nd Theme
The Bird — P242

3rd Theme
The Duck — P243

4th Theme
The Cat — P244

5th Theme
The Grandfather — P245

6th Theme
The Wolf — P246

7th Theme
March of the Hunters

Quartet, Op. 50
Str.
By permission of
International Music Co.

1st Movement 1st Theme

1st Movement 2nd Theme

2nd Movement 1st Theme

2nd Movement 2nd Theme

2nd Movement 3rd Theme

2nd Movement 4th Theme

3rd Movement

Romeo and Juliet,
Op. 64, Suite No. 1,
Orch.
Copyright 1946 by
Leeds Music Corp., N. Y.
Reprinted here by
permission of the
copyright owner.

1st Movement Folk Dance 1st Theme

1st Movement 2nd Theme

2nd Movement A Scene 1st Theme, A

2nd Movement 1st Theme, B

3rd Movement Madrigal 1st Theme

3rd Movement 2nd Theme

4th Movement Minuet 1st Theme

4th Movement 2nd Theme

5th Movement Masks

6th Movement Romeo and Juliet

7th Movement Death of Tybalt 1st Theme

7th Movement 2nd Theme

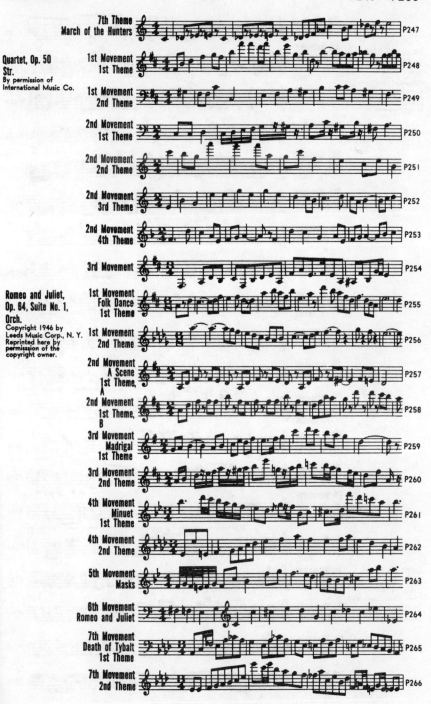

7th Movement
3rd Theme — P267

Romeo and Juliet, The Montagues and
Op. 64, Suite No. 2, the Capulets
Orch.
1st Movement
1st Theme — P268

1st Movement
2nd Theme — P269

1st Movement
3rd Theme — P270

2nd Movement
Juliet—The Little Girl
1st Theme — P271

2nd Movement
2nd Theme — P272

2nd Movement
3rd Theme,
A — P273

2nd Movement
3rd Theme,
B — P274

3rd Movement
Friar Lawrence
1st Theme — P275

3rd Movement
2nd Theme — P276

4th Movement
Dance — P277

5th Movement
Romeo and Juliet Before Parting
1st Theme — P278

5th Movement
2nd Theme — P279

5th Movement
3rd Theme — P280

6th Movement
Dance of the Maids
From the Antilles — P281

7th Movement
Romeo at Juliet's
Grave — P282

Sonata No. 6,
Op. 82, Pft.
1st Movement
1st Theme — P283

1st Movement
2nd Theme — P284

2nd Movement
1st Theme — P285

2nd Movement
2nd Theme — P286

Sonata No. 7, Op. 83
Pft.
Copyright 1945 by
Leeds Music Corp., N. Y.
Reprinted here by
permission of the
copyright owner.

Sonata in D, Op. 94,
Vn. & Pft.
Copyright 1946 by
Leeds Music Corp., N. Y.
Reprinted here by
permission of the
copyright owner.

3rd Movement 1st Theme — P287
3rd Movement 2nd Theme — P288
4th Movement 1st Theme — P289
4th Movement 2nd Theme — P290
4th Movement 3rd Theme — P291
1st Movement 1st Theme — P292
1st Movement 2nd Theme — P293
2nd Movement — P294
3rd Movement — P295
1st Movement 1st Theme — P296
1st Movement 2nd Theme — P297
2nd Movement 1st Theme — P298
2nd Movement 2nd Theme — P299
2nd Movement 3rd Theme — P300
3rd Movement — P301
4th Movement 1st Theme — P302
4th Movement 2nd Theme — P303
4th Movement 3rd Theme — P304
4th Movement 4th Theme — P305

Suggestion Diabolique, Op. 4, No. 4,
Pft. — P306

Symphony No. 5
in B Flat, Op. 100

1st Movement 1st Theme — P307
1st Movement 2nd Theme — P308
1st Movement 3rd Theme — P309
1st Movement 4th Theme — P310
2nd Movement 1st Theme — P311
2nd Movement 2nd Theme — P312
2nd Movement 3rd Theme — P313
3rd Movement 1st Theme — P314
3rd Movement 2nd Theme A — P315
3rd Movement 2nd Theme B — P316
3rd Movement — P317
4th Movement 1st Theme — P318
4th Movement 2nd Theme — P319
4th Movement 3rd Theme — P320

PUGNANI, Gaetano (1731-1798)

Sonata in E, No. 1, Vn. & Pft.

1st Movement — P321
2nd Movement — P322
3rd Movement — P323

PURCELL, Henry (c. 1659-1695)

Bonduca, or
The British Heroine
Opera

Air No. 1 — P324

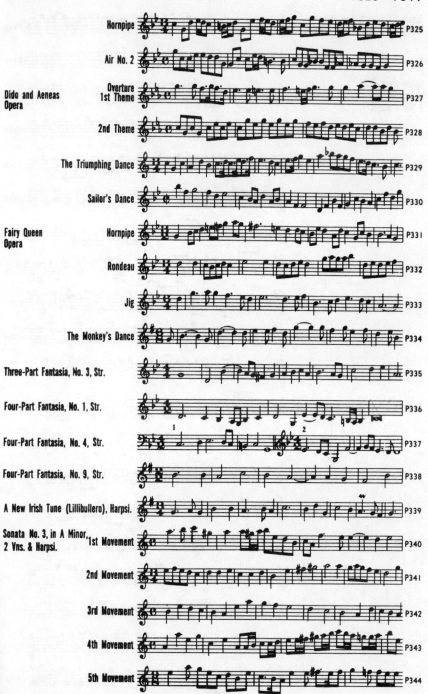

PURCELL 366 P345—P364

Jig  P365

QUANTZ, Johann (1697-1773)

Concerto in G, Fl. & Str.

1st Movement
1st Theme, A

1st Movement
1st Theme, B

2nd Movement
Arioso

3rd Movement

Q1

Q2

Q3

Q4

QUILTER, Roger (1877-   )

A Children's Overture, Orch.

1st Theme
Girls & Boys, Come Out to Play

2nd Theme
Upon Paul's Steeple Stands a Tree

3rd Theme
Dance, Get Up and Bake Your Pies

4th Theme
I Saw Three Ships Go Sailing By

5th Theme
Sing a Song of Sixpence

6th Theme
There Was a Lady Loved a Swine

7th Theme
Over the Hills and Far Away

8th Theme
The Frog and the Crow

9th Theme
A Frog He Would A-Wooing Go

10th Theme
Baa, Baa, Black Sheep

11th Theme
Here We Go Round the Mulberry Bush

12th Theme
Oranges and Lemons

Q5

Q6

Q7

Q8

Q9

Q10

Q11

Q12

Q13

Q14

Q15

Q16

RACHMANINOFF, Sergei (1873-1943)

Concerto No. 1, in F Sharp Minor, Op. 1, Pft. & Orch.
By permission of the copyright owner, Boosey and Hawkes, Inc.

1st Movement 1st Theme 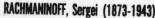 R1

1st Movement 2nd Theme — R2

2nd Movement — R3

3rd Movement 1st Theme — R4

3rd Movement 2nd Theme — R5

3rd Movement 3rd Theme — R6

Concerto No. 2, in C Minor, Op. 18, Pft. & Orch.

1st Movement 1st Theme — R7

1st Movement 2nd Theme — R8

2nd Movement 1st Theme, A — R9

2nd Movement 1st Theme, B — R10

3rd Movement 1st Theme — R11

3rd Movement 2nd Theme — R12

Concerto No. 3, Op. 30, Pft. & Orch.
By permission of the copyright owner, Boosey and Hawkes, Inc.

1st Movement 1st Theme — R13

1st Movement 2nd Theme — R14

2nd Movement 1st Theme — R15

2nd Movement 2nd Theme — R16

3rd Movement 1st Theme — R17

3rd Movement 2nd Theme — R18

3rd Movement 3rd Theme — R19

No. 3 — R40
No. 4 — R41
No. 5 — 1st Theme — R42
2nd Theme — R43
No. 6 — R44
No. 7 — R45
No. 8 — R46
No. 9 — R47
No. 10 — R48
Op. 32, No. 5
By permission of the
copyright owner,
Boosey and Hawkes, Inc.
No. 10 — R49
No. 10 — R50
No. 12 — R51
Serenade, Op. 3, No. 5
Copyright by
Charles Foley,
New York — R52
Sonata in G Minor,
Op. 19, Vcl. & Pft.
By permission of
International Music Co.
1st Movement
1st Theme — R53
1st Movement
2nd Theme — R54
2nd Movement
1st Theme — R55
2nd Movement
2nd Theme — R56
2nd Movement
3rd Theme — R57
3rd Movement — R58
4th Movement
1st Theme — R59

4th Movement
2nd Theme — R60

Suite No. 2, Op. 17,
2 Pfts., 4 Hands
By permission of
International Music Co.

1st Movement
Intro. — R61

2nd Movement
Valse
1st Theme — R62

2nd Movement
2nd Theme — R63

2nd Movement
3rd Theme — R64

3rd Movement
Romance — R65

4th Movement
Tarantelle (Italian Folksong) — R66

Symphony No. 2 in
E Minor, Op. 27
By permission of the
copyright owner,
Boosey and Hawkes, Inc.

1st Movement
1st Theme — R67

1st Movement
2nd Theme — R68

2nd Movement
1st Theme — R69

2nd Movement
2nd Theme — R70

3rd Movement
Intro. — R71

3rd Movement
1st Theme — R72

3rd Movement
2nd Theme — R73

4th Movement
1st Theme — R74

4th Movement
2nd Theme — R75

Waltz, Op. 10, No. 2, Pft.
By permission of the
copyright owner,
Boosey and Hawkes, Inc. — R76

RAFF, Joseph Joachim (1822-1882)

Cavatina, Op. 85, No. 3, Vn. & Pft. — R77

La Fileuse, Op. 157, No. 2, Pft. — R78

RAMEAU, Jean Philippe (1683-1764)

Castor et Pollux, Opera	Gavotte No. 1	R79
	Gavotte No. 2	R80
	Minuet No. 1	R81
	Minuet No. 2	R82
	Passepied No. 1	R83
	Passepied No. 2	R84
Dardanus, Opera	Rigaudon No. 1	R85
	Air en Rondeau	R86
	Rigaudon No. 2	R87
Les Fêtes de Hebe Opera	Tambourin	R88
	Musette	R89
La Follette, Harpsi.		R90
Gavotte Variée, Harpsi.		R91
L'Indifferente, Harpsi.		R92
La Joyeuse, Harpsi.	1st Theme	R93
	1st Theme	R94
Minuet No. 1, Harpsi.		R95
Minuet No. 2, Harpsi.		R96
Pièces de Clavecin en Concert, No. 3, Fl., Vn. & Harpsi.	La Timide	R97

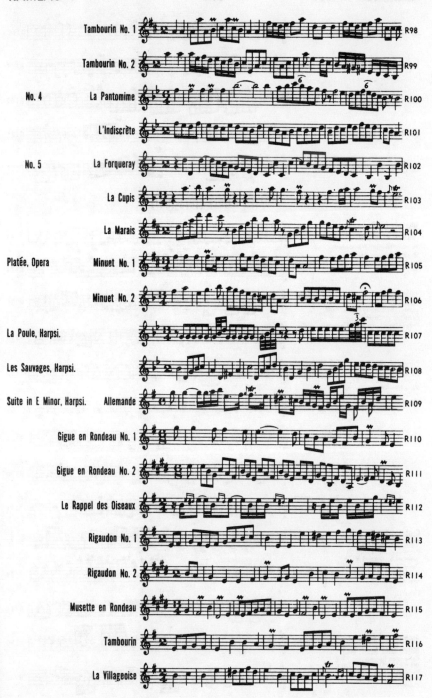

Tambourin No. 1 — R98
Tambourin No. 2 — R99
No. 4 — La Pantomime — R100
L'Indiscrète — R101
No. 5 — La Forqueray — R102
La Cupis — R103
La Marais — R104
Platée, Opera — Minuet No. 1 — R105
Minuet No. 2 — R106
La Poule, Harpsi. — R107
Les Sauvages, Harpsi. — R108
Suite in E Minor, Harpsi. — Allemande — R109
Gigue en Rondeau No. 1 — R110
Gigue en Rondeau No. 2 — R111
Le Rappel des Oiseaux — R112
Rigaudon No. 1 — R113
Rigaudon No. 2 — R114
Musette en Rondeau — R115
Tambourin — R116
La Villageoise — R117

Les Tendres Plaintes, Harpsi.

Les Tourbillons, Harpsi.

Les Tricotets, Harpsi.

Les Triolets, Harpsi.

La Triompante, Harpsi.

RAVEL, Maurice (1875-1937)

Alborada Del Graciosa (Miroirs No. 4), Pft.
By permission of Associated Music Publishers, Inc.

Theme, A

Theme, B

Bolero, Orch.
Permission for reprint grante ' by Durand & Cie, Paris. Elkan-'o el Co. Inc. Philadelphia, Copyright Owners.

Theme, A

Theme, B

Concerto, Pft. & Orch.
Permission for reprint granted by Durand & Cie, Paris. Elkan-Vogel Co., Inc. Philadelphia, Copyright Owners.

1st Movement 1st Theme

1st Movement 2nd Theme

2nd Movement

3rd Movement 1st Theme

3rd Movement 2nd Theme

Concerto for the Left Hand, Pft. & Orch.
Permission for reprint granted by Durand & Cie, Paris. Elkan-Vogel Co., Inc. Philadelphia, Copyright Owners.

1st Theme, A

1st Theme, B

2nd Theme

Daphnis et Chloe, Ballet Suite No. 1, Orch.
Permission for reprint granted by Durand & Cie, Paris. Elkan-Vogel Co., Inc. Philadelphia, Copyright Owners.

1st Theme

2nd Theme

R118
R119
R120
R121
R122
R123
R124
R125
R126
R127
R128
R129
R130
R131
R132
R133
R134
R135
R136

3rd Theme — R137

4th Theme — R138

5th Theme — R139

Daphnis et Chloe, Ballet Suite No. 2, Orch.
Permission for reprint granted by Durand & Cie, Paris. Elkan-Vogel Co., Inc. Philadelphia, Copyright Owners,

1st Theme, A — R140

1st Theme, B — R141

2nd Theme — R142

3rd Theme — R143

4th Theme — R144

5th Theme — R145

6th Theme — R146

Gaspard de la Nuit, Pft.
Permission for reprint granted by Durand & Cie, Paris. Elkan-Vogel Co., Inc. Philadelphia, Copyright Owners,

No. 1 Ondine — R147

No. 2 La Gibet — R148

No. 3 Scarbo — R149

Introduction and Allegro, Harp, Str. Quart., Fl. & Cl.
Permission for reprint granted by Durand & Cie, Paris. Elkan-Vogel Co., Inc., Philadelphia, Copyright Owners.

Intro. 1st Theme, A — R150

1st Theme, B — R151

2nd Theme — R152

Allegro 1st Theme — R153

2nd Theme — R154

Jeux D'Eau, Pft.
Copyright 1930 by Edward B. Marks Music Co. Copyright Assigned 1932 to Edward B. Marks Music Corp. Used by Permission

1st Theme — R155

2nd Theme — R156

RAVEL 376 R157—R176

Ma Mère L'Oye, (Mother Goose Suite) **Orch.**
Permission for reprint granted by Durand & Cie, Paris. Elkan-Vogel Co., Inc., Philadelphia, Copyright Owners.

Pavane of the Sleeping Beauty (Pavane de la Belle au Bois Dormant) — R157

Hop O' My Thumb (Petit Poucet) — R158

Empress of the Pagodas (Laideronnette, Impératrice des Pagodes) — R159

Beauty and the Beast (Les Entretiens de la Belle et de la Bête) — R160

The Enchanted Garden (La Jardin Féerique) — R161

Pavane for a Dead Infanta, Small Orch. or Pft.
By permission of Associated Music Publishers, Inc. — R162

Quartet in F, Str.
By permission of International Music Co.

1st Movement 1st Theme — R163

1st Movement 2nd Theme — R164

2nd Movement Intro. — R165

2nd Movement 1st Theme — R166

2nd Movement 2nd Theme — R167

3rd Movement 1st Theme — R168

3rd Movement 2nd Theme — R169

4th Movement — R170

Rapsodie Espagnole, Orch.
Permission for reprint granted by Durand & Cie, Paris. Elkan-Vogel Co., Inc. Philadelphia, Copyright Owners.

1st Movement Prélude à la Nuit — R171

2nd Movement Malagueña Intro. — R172

2nd Movement 1st Theme — R173

2nd Movement 2nd Theme — R174

3rd Movement Habañera 1st Theme — R175

3rd Movement 2nd Theme — R176

Tzigane, Vn. & Orch.
Permission for reprint granted by Durand & Cie, Paris.
Elkan-Vogel Co., Inc. Philadelphia, Copyright Owners.

Intro. Cadenza

R197

1st Theme

R198

1st Theme

R199

2nd Theme

R200

3rd Theme

R201

La Valse, Orch.
Permission for reprint granted by Durand & Cie, Paris.
Elkan-Vogel Co., Inc. Philadelphia, Copyright Owners.

1st Theme

R202

2nd Theme

R203

3rd Theme
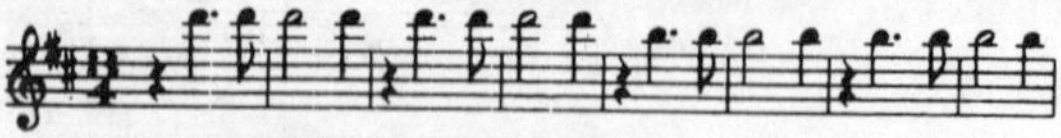
R204

4th Theme

R205

5th Theme

R206

6th Theme

R207

7th Theme

R208

8th Theme

R209

Valses Nobles et Sentimentales Pft. or Orch.
Permission for reprint granted by Durand & Cie, Paris.
Elkan-Vogel Co., Inc. Philadelphia, Copyright Owners.

No. 1

R210

No. 2

R211

No. 3

R212

No. 4

R213

No. 5

R214

No. 6

R215

No. 7

R216

No. 8  R217

REBIKOFF, Vladimir (1866-1920)

The Christmas Tree, Opera — Dance of the Dolls 1st Theme — R218

2nd Theme — R219

March of the Gnomes 1st Theme — R220

2nd Theme — R221

Dance of the Chinese Dolls — R222

REGER, Max (1873-1916)

Balletmusik, Op. 130
By Permission of C. F. Peters, Clayton F. Summy Co., Chicago, — Waltz — R223

Finale — R224

Gavotte, Op. 82, No 5, Pft.
By permission of Associated Music Publishers, Inc. — R225

Konzert im Alten Stil, Op. 123, Orch.
By permission of Associated Music Publishers, Inc. — 1st Movement — R226

2nd Movement — R227

3rd Movement — R228

Quintet, in A, Op. 146, Cl. & Str. Quart.
By permission of Associated Music Publishers, Inc. — 1st Movement 1st Theme — R229

1st Movement 2nd Theme — R230

2nd Movement 1st Theme — R231

2nd Movement 2nd Theme — R232

3rd Movement — R233

4th Movement — R234

Romance, Op. 87, No. 2, Vn. & Pft. — R235

Serenade, Op. 77a, Fl., Vn. & Vla.
1st Movement — R236
2nd Movement — R237
3rd Movement 1st Theme — R238
3rd Movement 2nd Theme — R239

Suite in A Minor, Op. 103a, Vn. & Pft.
By permission of Associated Music Publishers, Inc.
1st Movement Präludium — R240
2nd Movement Gavotte 1st Theme — R241
2nd Movement 2nd Theme — R242
3rd Movement Aria — R243
4th Movement Burleske — R244
5th Movement Minuet 1st Theme — R245
5th Movement 2nd Theme — R246
6th Movement Gigue — R247

RESPIGHI, Ottorino (1879-1936)

Adagio con Variazioni, Vcl. & Pft. — R248

Antiche Danze Ed Arie Per Liuto
Copyright 1920 by G. Ricordi & Co., Inc.
Suite No 1, Orch.
1st Movement Balletto "Il Conte Orlando" (After Simone Molinaro) — R249
2nd Movement Gagliarda (After Vincenzo Galilei) 1st Theme — R250
2nd Movement 2nd Theme — R251
3rd Movement Villanella (After Ignoto) 1st Theme — R252
3rd Movement 2nd Theme — R253

The Villa Medici Fountain at Sunset
1st Theme — R274

2nd Theme — R275

Notturno, Pft. — R276

Pines of Rome, Orch.
Copyright 1925 by G. Ricordi & Co., Inc.
The Pines of the Villa Borghese
1st Theme — R277

2nd Theme — R278

3rd Theme — R279

Pines Near a Catacomb — R280

Pines of the Gianicolo
1st Theme — R281

2nd Theme — R282

Pines of the Appian Way
1st Theme — R283

2nd Theme — R284

Rossiniana,
Suite for Orch.
1st Movement
Capri and Taormina
(Barcarola & Siciliana) — R285

1st Theme
1st Movement
2nd Theme — R286

2nd Movement
Lament
1st Theme — R287

2nd Movement
2nd Theme — R288

3rd Movement
Intermezzo
1st Theme — R289

3rd Movement
2nd Theme — R290

4th Movement
Tarantella & Procession
1st Theme — R291

4th Movement
2nd Theme — R292

Trittico Botticelliano,
Chamber Orch.
Copyright 1928 by G.
Ricordi & Co., Inc.
1st Movement
La Primavera
1st Theme — R293

1st Movement
2nd Theme   R294

2nd Movement
Adoration of the Magi
1st Theme   R295

2nd Movement
2nd Theme   R296

3rd Movement
The Birth of Venus
1st Theme   R297

3rd Movement
2nd Theme   R298

REYER, Ernest (1823-1909)

Sigurd, Overture
By permission of
the copyright owner,
Heugel & Cie, Paris.

1st Theme   R299

2nd Theme   R300

3rd Theme   R301

REZNIČEK, Emil Nikolaus von (1860-1945)

Donna Diana, Overture
By permission of Associated
Music Publishers, Inc.

1st Theme   R302

2nd Theme   R303

RIEGGER, Wallingford (1885-   )

New Dance, 2 Pfts.
Copyright 1940 by Arrow
Music Press, Inc., N. Y.

R303a

Accompanying Figure
A   R303b

Accompanying Figure
B   R303c

RIMSKY-KORSAKOFF, Nicolas (1844-1908)

Antar Symphony, Op. 9

1st Movement
Intro.
1st Theme   R304

1st Movement
Intro.
2nd Theme   R305

1st Movement
1st Theme   R306

1st Movement 2nd Theme ... R307
1st Movement 3rd Theme ... R308
2nd Movement 1st Theme ... R309
2nd Movement 2nd Theme ... R310
3rd Movement 1st Theme ... R311
3rd Movement 2nd Theme ... R312
4th Movement ... R313

Capriccio Espagnol, Op. 34, Orch. By permission of Associated Music Publishers, Inc.

Intro. and Alborada ... R314
Variations ... R315
Scene and Gypsy Song 1st Theme ... R316
2nd Theme ... R317
Fandango Asturiano ... R318

Le Coq D'Or, Suite Orch. By permission of Associated Music Publishers, Inc.

1st Movement 1st Theme ... R319
1st Movement 2nd Theme ... R320
1st Movement 3rd Theme ... R321
2nd Movement ... R322
3rd Movement 1st Theme ... R323
3rd Movement 2nd Theme ... R324
3rd Movement 3rd Theme ... R325
3rd Movement 4th Theme ... R326

La Grande Paque Russe, Overture, Op. 36
By permission of Associated Music Publishers, Inc.

1st Theme — R327
2nd Theme — R328
3rd Theme — R329
4th Theme — R330
5th Theme — R331

May Night, Overture
By permission of Associated Music Publishers, Inc.

1st Theme — R332
2nd Theme — R333
3rd Theme — R334

Mlada, Ballet
By permission of Associated Music Publishers, Inc.

1st Theme Cortège des Nobles — R335
2nd Theme — R336

Scheherezade, Op. 35, Orch.
By permission of Associated Music Publishers, Inc.

1st Movement, The Sea & Sinbad's Ship Intro. A — R337
1st Movement Intro. B — R338
1st Movement 1st Theme — R339
1st Movement 2nd Theme — R340
1st Movement 3rd Theme — R341

2nd Movement, The Story of the Kalander Prince 1st Theme, A — R342
2nd Movement 1st Theme, B — R343
2nd Movement 2nd Theme — R344

3rd Movement, The Young Prince & the Young Princess 1st Theme — R345
3rd Movement 2nd Theme — R346

4th Movement
Festival at Bagdad — R347

Snow Maiden,
(Snegourotchka), Opera

Dance of the
Buffoons
1st Theme — R348

2nd Theme — R349

3rd Theme — R350

Tale of the
Invisible City
of Kitezh, Opera

Battle of Kershenetz
1st Theme — R351

2nd Theme — R352

Tsar Saltan, Opera

Flight of the
Bumble Bee
1st Theme — R353

2nd Theme — R354

The Tsar's Bride, Overture
By permission of Associated
Music Publishers, Inc.

1st Theme — R355

2nd Theme — R356

3rd Theme — R357

ROSAS, J. (1868-1894)

Over the Waves, Waltzes

1st Theme — R358

2nd Theme — R359

ROSSINI, Gioacchino Antonio (1792-1868)

The Barber of Seville, Overture

Intro. — R360

1st Theme — R361

2nd Theme — R362

3rd Theme — R363

La Boutique Fantasque,
Ballet

1st Movement
Overture
1st Theme — R364

ROUSSEL, Albert (1869-1937)

2nd Theme R404

Sinfonietta, Op. 52, Str. Orch.
Permission for reprint granted by Durand & Cie, Paris. Elkan-Vogel Co., Inc. Philadelphia, Copyright Owners.

1st Movement 1st Theme R405

1st Movement 2nd Theme R406

2nd Movement R407

3rd Movement 1st Theme R408

3rd Movement 2nd Theme R409

Symphony No. 3 in G Minor, Op. 42
Permission for reprint granted by Durand & Cie, Paris. Elkan-Vogel Co., Inc. Philadelphia, Copyright Owners.

1st Movement 1st Theme R410

1st Movement 2nd Theme R411

2nd Movement 1st Theme R412

2nd Movement 2nd Theme R413

3rd Movement 1st Theme R414

3rd Movement 2nd Theme R415

4th Movement 1st Theme R416

4th Movement 2nd Theme R417

Symphony No. 4, Op. 53
Permission for reprint granted by Durand & Cie, Paris. Elkan-Vogel Co., Inc. Philadelphia, Copyright Owners,

1st Movement 1st Theme R418

1st Movement 2nd Theme R419

2nd Movement R420

3rd Movement 1st Theme R421

3rd Movement 2nd Theme R422

4th Movement 1st Theme R423

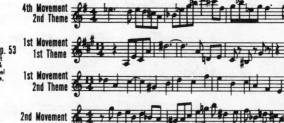

RUBINSTEIN, Anton (1829-1894)

Barcarolle, Op. 30, No. 1, Pft.
By permission of Associated Music Publishers, Inc.
1st Theme   R424
2nd Theme   R425

Concerto No. 4 in D Minor, Op. 70, Pft. & Orch.
By permission of Associated Music Publishers, Inc.
1st Movement 1st Theme, A   R426
1st Movement 1st Theme, B   R427
1st Movement 2nd Theme   R428
2nd Movement   R429
3rd Movement 1st Theme   R430
3rd Movement 2nd Theme   R431

Cracovienne, Op. 5, No. 3, Pft.
1st Theme   R432
2nd Theme   R433

Etude, Op. 23, No. 2, Pft. "Staccato"
1st Theme   R434
2nd Theme   R435

Feramors (Lalla Rookh) Opera
By permission of Associated Music Publishers, Inc.
Bridal March 1st Theme   R436
2nd Theme   R437

Kamennoi-Ostrow, Op. 10, No. 22, Pft.
1st Theme   R438
2nd Theme   R439

Melody in F, Op. 3, No. 1, Pft.
1st Theme   R440
2nd Theme   R441

Romance, Op. 44, No. 1, Pft.   1st Theme   R442

2nd Theme — R443

Toreador et Andalouse, Op. 103, No. 7, from Bal Costumé, Pft., 4 Hands
By permission of Associated Music Publishers, Inc.

1st Theme — R444

2nd Theme — R445

Valse in F, Pft.
By permission of Associated Music Publishers, Inc.

R446

Valse Caprice, Pft.
By permission of Associated Music Publishers, Inc.

1st Theme — R447

2nd Theme — R448

3rd Theme — R449

SACCHINI, Antonio (1730-1786)

Sonata in F Harpsi.

1st Movement — S1

2nd Movement 1st Theme — S2

2nd Movement 2nd Theme — S3

SAINT-SAËNS, Camille (1835-1921)

Caprice Arabe, Op. 96, 2 Pfts.
Permission for reprint granted by Durand & Cie, Paris. Elkan-Vogel Co., Inc. Philadelphia, Copyright Owners.

1st Theme — S4

2nd Theme — S5

3rd Theme — S6

Carnaval des Animaux, Orch. & 2 Pfts.
Permission for reprint granted by Durand & Cie, Paris. Elkan-Vogel Co., Inc. Philadelphia, Copyright Owners.

March Royale du Lion — S7

Poules et Coqs — S8

Tortues (Theme from Orpheus in Hades — Offenbach) — S9

L'Éléphant — S10

Kangorous — S11

Aquarium — S12
Le Coucou au Fond des Bois — S13
Fossiles — S14
The Swan — S15
Finale — S16

Concertos

No. 1 in A Minor, Op. 33, Vcl. & Orch.
Permission for reprint granted by Durand & Cie, Paris, Elkan-Vogel Co., Inc. Philadelphia, Copyright Owners,

1st Movement 1st Theme — S17
1st Movement 2nd Theme — S18
2nd Movement — S19
3rd Movement 1st Theme — S20
3rd Movement 2nd Theme — S21
3rd Movement Coda — S22

No. 2 in G Minor, Op. 22, Pft. & Orch.
Permission for reprint granted by Durand & Cie, Paris, Elkan-Vogel Co., Inc. Philadelphia, Copyright Owners,

1st Movement 1st Theme — S23
1st Movement 2nd Theme — S24
2nd Movement 1st Theme — S25
2nd Movement 2nd Theme — S26
3rd Movement 1st Theme — S27
3rd Movement 2nd Theme — S28

No. 4 in C Minor, Op. 44, Pft. & Orch.
Permission for reprint granted by Durand & Cie, Paris, Elkan-Vogel Co., Inc. Philadelphia, Copyright Owners,

1st Movement 1st Theme — S29
1st Movement 2nd Theme, A — S30
1st Movement 2nd Theme, B — S31

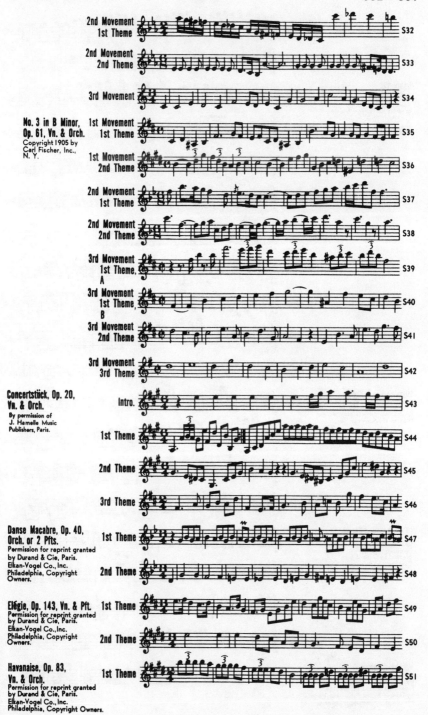

2nd Movement
1st Theme — S32

2nd Movement
2nd Theme — S33

3rd Movement — S34

No. 3 in B Minor,
Op. 61, Vn. & Orch.
Copyright 1905 by
Carl Fischer, Inc.,
N. Y.

1st Movement
1st Theme — S35

1st Movement
2nd Theme — S36

2nd Movement
1st Theme — S37

2nd Movement
2nd Theme — S38

3rd Movement
1st Theme,
A — S39

3rd Movement
1st Theme,
B — S40

3rd Movement
2nd Theme — S41

3rd Movement
3rd Theme — S42

Concertstück, Op. 20,
Vn. & Orch.
By permission of
J. Hamelle Music
Publishers, Paris.

Intro. — S43

1st Theme — S44

2nd Theme — S45

3rd Theme — S46

Danse Macabre, Op. 40,
Orch. or 2 Pfts.
Permission for reprint granted
by Durand & Cie, Paris.
Elkan-Vogel Co., Inc.
Philadelphia, Copyright
Owners.

1st Theme — S47

2nd Theme — S48

Elégie, Op. 143, Vn. & Pft.
Permission for reprint granted
by Durand & Cie, Paris.
Elkan-Vogel Co., Inc.
Philadelphia, Copyright
Owners.

1st Theme — S49

2nd Theme — S50

Havanaise, Op. 83,
Vn. & Orch.
Permission for reprint granted
by Durand & Cie, Paris.
Elkan-Vogel Co., Inc.
Philadelphia, Copyright Owners.

1st Theme — S51

Henry VIII Ballet Music
Permission for reprint granted by Durand & Cie, Paris. Elkan-Vogel Co., Inc., Philadelphia, Copyright Owners.

Introduction & Rondo Capriccioso, Op. 28, Vn. & Orch.
Copyright renewal assigned 1928 to G. Schirmer, Inc.

La Jeunesse d'Hercule, Op. 50, Orch.
Permission for reprint granted by Durand & Cie, Paris. Elkan-Vogel Co., Inc. Philadelphia, Copyright Owners.

Marche Héroique, Op. 34, Orch.
Permission for reprint granted by Durand & Cie, Paris. Elkan-Vogel Co., Inc. Philadelphia, Copyright Owners.

2nd Theme — S52
3rd Theme — S53
Entry of the Clans 1st Theme — S54
2nd Theme — S55
Scotch Idyll — S56
Dance of the Gypsy 1st Theme — S57
2nd Theme — S58
Scherzetto — S59
Gigue & Finale 1st Theme — S60
2nd Theme — S61
3rd Theme — S62
Intro. — S63
1st Theme — S64
2nd Theme — S65
3rd Theme — S66
1st Theme — S67
2nd Theme — S68
3rd Theme — S69
4th Theme — S70
1st Theme — S71

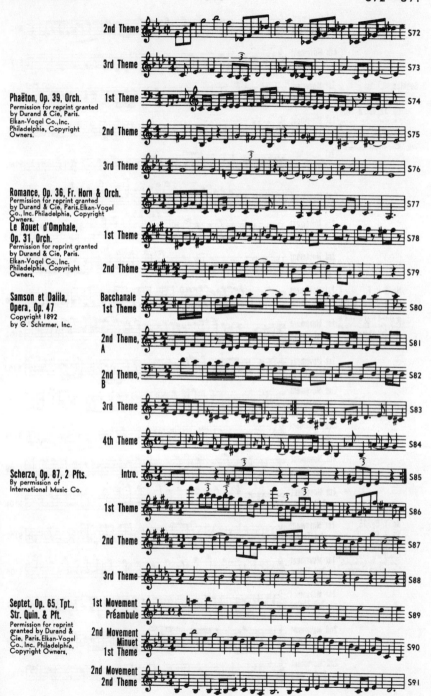

Phaëton, Op. 39, Orch.
Permission for reprint granted by Durand & Cie, Paris. Elkan-Vogel Co.,Inc. Philadelphia, Copyright Owners.

Romance, Op. 36, Fr. Horn & Orch.
Permission for reprint granted by Durand & Cie, Paris.Elkan-Vogel Co., Inc. Philadelphia, Copyright Owners.

Le Rouet d'Omphale, Op. 31, Orch.
Permission for reprint granted by Durand & Cie, Paris. Elkan-Vogel Co.,Inc. Philadelphia, Copyright Owners.

Samson et Dalila, Opera, Op. 47
Copyright 1892 by G. Schirmer, Inc.

Scherzo, Op. 87, 2 Pfts.
By permission of International Music Co.

Septet, Op. 65, Tpt., Str. Quin. & Pft.
Permission for reprint granted by Durand & Cie, Paris.Elkan-Vogel Co., Inc. Philadelphia, Copyright Owners,

2nd Theme — S72
3rd Theme — S73
1st Theme — S74
2nd Theme — S75
3rd Theme — S76
S77
1st Theme — S78
2nd Thème — S79
Bacchanale 1st Theme — S80
2nd Theme, A — S81
2nd Theme, B — S82
3rd Theme — S83
4th Theme — S84
Intro. — S85
1st Theme — S86
2nd Theme — S87
3rd Theme — S88
1st Movement Préambule — S89
2nd Movement Minuet 1st Theme — S90
2nd Movement 2nd Theme — S91

3rd Movement Intermède — S92

4th Movement Gavotte & Finale — S93

Sonatas
No. 1 in C Minor, Op. 32, Vcl. & Pft.
Permission for reprint granted by Durand & Cie, Paris. Elkan-Vogel Co., Inc. Philadelphia, Copyright Owners.

1st Movement Intro. — S94

1st Movement 1st Theme — S95

1st Movement 2nd Theme — S96

2nd Movement — S97

3rd Movement 1st Theme — S98

3rd Movement 2nd Theme — S99

No. 2 in F, Op. 123, Vcl. & Pft.
Permission for reprint granted by Durand & Cie, Paris. Elkan-Vogel Co., Inc. Philadelphia, Copyright Owners.

1st Movement Intro. — S100

1st Movement 1st Theme — S101

1st Movement 2nd Theme — S102

2nd Movement Scherzo con Variazione — S103

3rd Movement Romance — S104

4th Movement 1st Theme — S105

4th Movement 2nd Theme — S106

No. 1, Op. 75, Vn. & Pft.
Permission for reprint granted by Durand & Cie, Paris. Elkan-Vogel Co., Inc. Philadelphia, Copyright Owners.

1st Movement 1st Theme — S107

1st Movement 2nd Theme — S108

1st Movement 3rd Theme — S109

2nd Movement 1st Theme — S110

2nd Movement 2nd Theme — S111

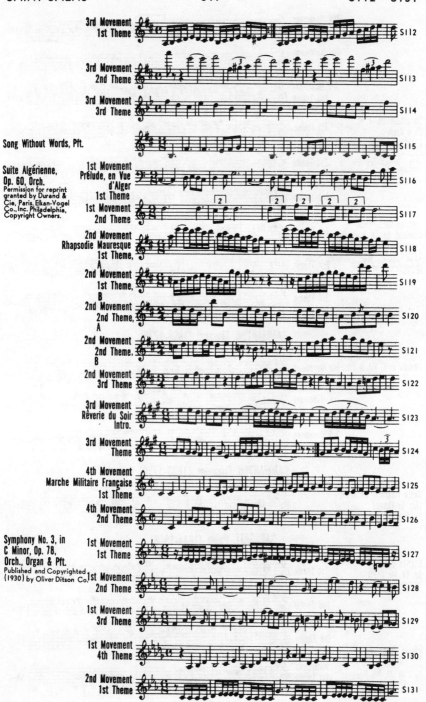

3rd Movement 1st Theme — S112
3rd Movement 2nd Theme — S113
3rd Movement 3rd Theme — S114

Song Without Words, Pft. — S115

Suite Algérienne, Op. 60, Orch.
Permission for reprint granted by Durand & Cie, Paris. Elkan-Vogel Co., Inc. Philadelphia, Copyright Owners.

1st Movement Prélude, en Vue d'Alger 1st Theme — S116
1st Movement 2nd Theme — S117
2nd Movement Rhapsodie Mauresque 1st Theme, A — S118
2nd Movement 1st Theme, B — S119
2nd Movement 2nd Theme, A — S120
2nd Movement 2nd Theme, B — S121
2nd Movement 3rd Theme — S122
3rd Movement Rêverie du Soir Intro. — S123
3rd Movement Theme — S124
4th Movement Marche Militaire Française 1st Theme — S125
4th Movement 2nd Theme — S126

Symphony No. 3, in C Minor, Op. 78, Orch., Organ & Pft.
Published and Copyrighted (1930) by Oliver Ditson Co.

1st Movement 1st Theme — S127
1st Movement 2nd Theme — S128
1st Movement 3rd Theme — S129
1st Movement 4th Theme — S130
2nd Movement 1st Theme — S131

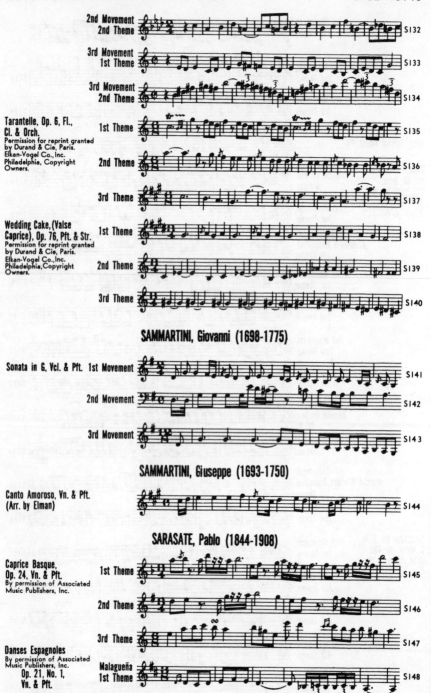

2nd Movement
2nd Theme — S132

3rd Movement
1st Theme — S133

3rd Movement
2nd Theme — S134

Tarantelle, Op. 6, Fl.,
Cl. & Orch.
Permission for reprint granted
by Durand & Cie, Paris.
Elkan-Vogel Co., Inc.
Philadelphia, Copyright
Owners.

1st Theme — S135

2nd Theme — S136

3rd Theme — S137

Wedding Cake, (Valse
Caprice), Op. 76, Pft. & Str.
Permission for reprint granted
by Durand & Cie, Paris.
Elkan-Vogel Co., Inc.
Philadelphia, Copyright
Owners.

1st Theme — S138

2nd Theme — S139

3rd Theme — S140

SAMMARTINI, Giovanni (1698-1775)

Sonata in G, Vcl. & Pft. 1st Movement — S141

2nd Movement — S142

3rd Movement — S143

SAMMARTINI, Giuseppe (1693-1750)

Canto Amoroso, Vn. & Pft.
(Arr. by Elman) — S144

SARASATE, Pablo (1844-1908)

Caprice Basque,
Op. 24, Vn. & Pft.
By permission of Associated
Music Publishers, Inc.

1st Theme — S145

2nd Theme — S146

3rd Theme — S147

Danses Espagnoles
By permission of Associated
Music Publishers, Inc.
Op. 21, No. 1,
Vn. & Pft.

Malagueña
1st Theme — S148

4th Theme 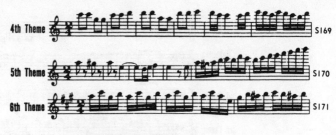 S169

5th Theme S170

6th Theme S171

SATIE, Erik (1866-1925)

Gnossiennes, Pft.
No. 1   S172

No. 2   S173

No. 3   S174

Gymnopédies, Pft.
No. 1   S175

No. 2   S176

No. 3   S177

Parade Ballet Rag-Time S178

Trois Petites Pièces Montées, (after Rabelais), Orch. De L'Enfance de Pantagruel S179

Marche de Cocagne S180

Jeux de Gargantua S181

SAUVEPLANE, Henri (1892-)

Habañera, Vn. & Pft. S182

SCARLATTI, Alessandro (1660-1725)

Fuga, Pft. S183

SCARLATTI, Domenico (1685-1757)

Sonatas, Harpsi.
Longo 22 in E Minor S184

Longo 23 in E — S185

Longo 33 in B Minor — S186

Longo 58 in D Minor "Gavotte" — S187

Longo 104 in C — S188

Longo 107 in D — S189

Longo 108 in D Minor — S190

Longo 129 in G — S191

Longo 142 in E Flat — S192

Longo 152 in A — S193

Longo 205 in C — S194

Longo 208 in D — S195

Longo 232 in G — S196

Longo 239 in A Minor — S197

Longo 243 in A Minor, "Pastorale" — S198

Longo 256 in C Sharp Minor — S199

Longo 257 in E — S200

Longo 261 in D — S201

Longo 263 in B Minor — S202

Longo 294 in F Sharp Minor, — S203

Longo 338 in G Minor "Burlesca" — S204

Longo 345 in A   S205

Longo 352 in C Minor   S206

Longo 375 in E,   S207

Longo 382 in F Minor   S208

Longo 384 in F   S209

Longo 387 in G   S210

Longo 395 in A   S211

Longo 407 in C Minor   S212

Longo 411 in D   S213

Longo 413 in D Minor
"Pastorale"   S214

Longo 422 in D Minor
"Toccata"   S215

Longo 429 in A Minor   S216

Longo 434 in B Flat   S217

Longo 438 in F Minor   S218

Longo 449 in B Minor   S219

Longo 463 in D
"Tempo di Ballo"   S220

Longo 465 in D   S221

Longo 474 in F   S222

Longo 475 in F Minor   S223

Longo 479 in F   S224

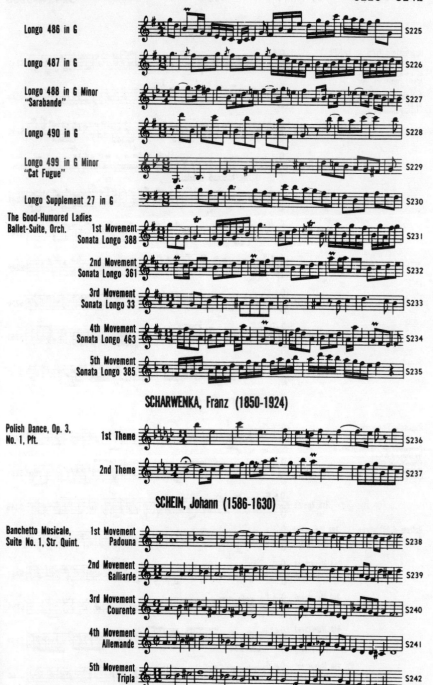

Longo 486 in G — S225

Longo 487 in G — S226

Longo 488 in G Minor "Sarabande" — S227

Longo 490 in G — S228

Longo 499 in G Minor "Cat Fugue" — S229

Longo Supplement 27 in G — S230

The Good-Humored Ladies Ballet-Suite, Orch. — 1st Movement Sonata Longo 388 — S231

2nd Movement Sonata Longo 361 — S232

3rd Movement Sonata Longo 33 — S233

4th Movement Sonata Longo 463 — S234

5th Movement Sonata Longo 385 — S235

SCHARWENKA, Franz (1850-1924)

Polish Dance, Op. 3, No. 1, Pft. — 1st Theme — S236

2nd Theme — S237

SCHEIN, Johann (1586-1630)

Banchetto Musicale, Suite No. 1, Str. Quint. — 1st Movement Padouna — S238

2nd Movement Galliarde — S239

3rd Movement Courente — S240

4th Movement Allemande — S241

5th Movement Tripla — S242

SCHELLING, Ernest (1876-1939)

Impressions from an Artist's
Life (Variations), Orch. & Pft.
By permission of Associated
Music Publishers, Inc.

A Victory Ball, Orch.
By permission of Associated
Music Publishers, Inc.

SCHMITT, Florent (1870-   )

Rapsodie Viennoise,
Op. 53, No. 3, Orch.
Permission for reprint granted
by Durand & Cie, Paris.
Elkan-Vogel Co., Inc.
Philadelphia, Copyright
Owners.

Reflets d'Allemagne,
Orch.

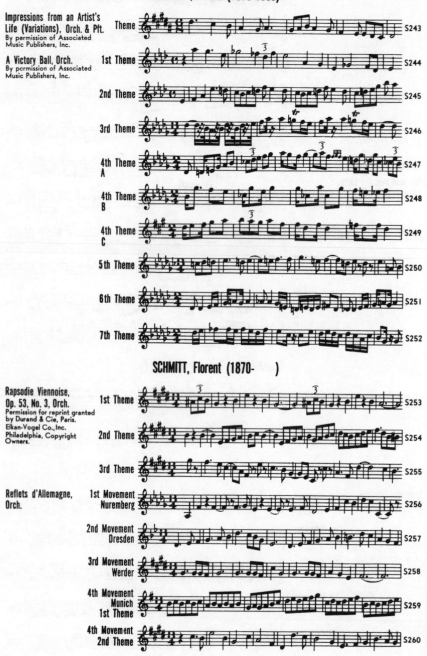

SCHOBERT, Johann (c. 1720-1767)

Sonata in F, Op. 8, Pft.

1st Movement — S261

2nd Movement — S262

3rd Movement
Polonaise — S263

4th Movement
1st Theme — S264

4th Movement
2nd Theme — S265

SCHÖNBERG, Arnold (1874-   )

Six Little Piano Pieces, Op. 19
By permission of Associated Music Publishers, Inc.

No. 1 — S266

No. 2 — S267

No. 3 — S268

No. 4 — S269

No. 5 — S270

Verklärte Nacht, Op. 4, Str. Sextet

1st Theme — S271

2nd Theme — S272

3rd Theme — S273

4th Theme — S274

5th Theme — S275

SCHREKER, Franz (1878-1934)

Birthday of the Infanta, Orch.
By permission of Associated Music Publishers, Inc.

1st Movement
"Reigen" (Rounds)
1st Theme — S276

1st Movement
2nd Theme — S277

2nd Movement
Marionetten   S278

3rd Movement
Minuet der Tanzknaben (Dancing Boys)   S279
1st Theme

3rd Movement
2nd Theme   S280

4th Movement
Tänze des Zwerges   S281
(Dances of the Dwarf)

4th Movement
2nd Theme   S282

4th Movement
3rd Theme   S283

Kleine Suite,
Chamber Orch.   1st Movement
By permission of   Präludium   S284
Associated Music
Publishers, Inc.

2nd Movement
Marcia   S285

3rd Movement
Canon   S286

4th Movement
Fughette   S287

5th Movement
Intermezzo   S288

6th Movement
Capriccio   S289

SCHUBERT, Franz (1797-1828)

Allegretto in C Minor, Pft.   S290

Deutsche Tänze, Pft.
Op. 33, No. 2   S291

Op. 33, No. 6   S292

Op. 33, No. 7   S293

Fantaisie in C, "Wanderer"   1st Theme   S294
Op. 15, Pft.

2nd Theme   S295

3rd Theme   S296

4th Theme — S297

Impromptus, Pft.
Op. 90, No. 1 in C Minor — S298

Op. 90, No. 2, in E Flat   1st Theme — S299

2nd Theme — S300

Op. 90, No. 3, in G Flat — S301

Op. 90, No. 4, in A Flat   1st Theme — S302

2nd Theme — S303

Op. 142, No. 1, in F Minor — S304

Op. 142, No. 2, in A Flat — S305

Op. 142, No. 3 in B Flat, (Theme & Variations) — S306

Op. 142, No. 4, in F Minor — S307

March, Op. 40, No. 2, Pft.,   1st Theme — S308

2nd Theme — S309

Military Marches, Pft. 4 Hands   Op. 51, No. 1   1st Theme — S310

2nd Theme — S311

3rd Theme — S312

Op. 51, No. 2 — S313

Op. 51, No. 3   1st Theme — S314

2nd Theme — S315

Moments Musicals Op. 94, Pft.   No. 1, in C — S316

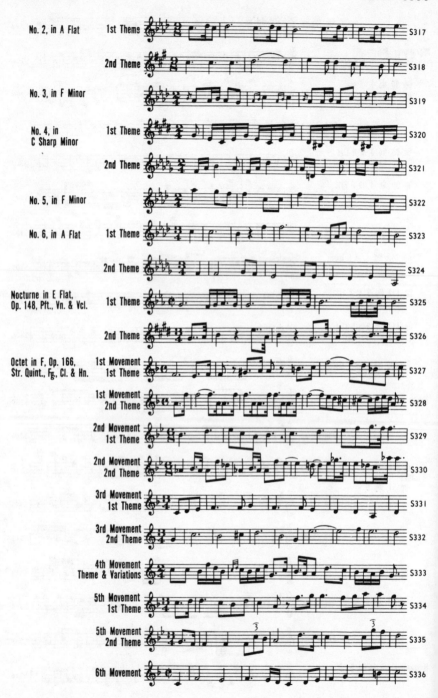

SCHUBERT

410

S357—S376

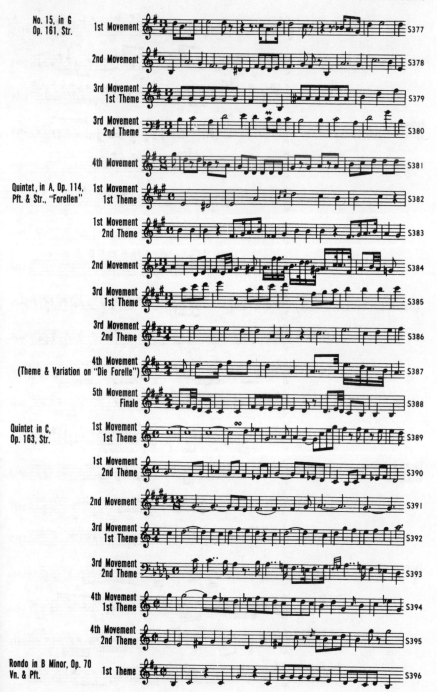

No. 15, in G
Op. 161, Str.   1st Movement   S377

2nd Movement   S378

3rd Movement
1st Theme   S379

3rd Movement
2nd Theme   S380

4th Movement   S381

Quintet, in A, Op. 114,
Pft. & Str., "Forellen"   1st Movement
1st Theme   S382

1st Movement
2nd Theme   S383

2nd Movement   S384

3rd Movement
1st Theme   S385

3rd Movement
2nd Theme   S386

4th Movement
(Theme & Variation on "Die Forelle")   S387

5th Movement
Finale   S388

Quintet in C,
Op. 163, Str.   1st Movement
1st Theme   S389

1st Movement
2nd Theme   S390

2nd Movement   S391

3rd Movement
1st Theme   S392

3rd Movement
2nd Theme   S393

4th Movement
1st Theme   S394

4th Movement
2nd Theme   S395

Rondo in B Minor, Op. 70
Vn. & Pft.   1st Theme   S396

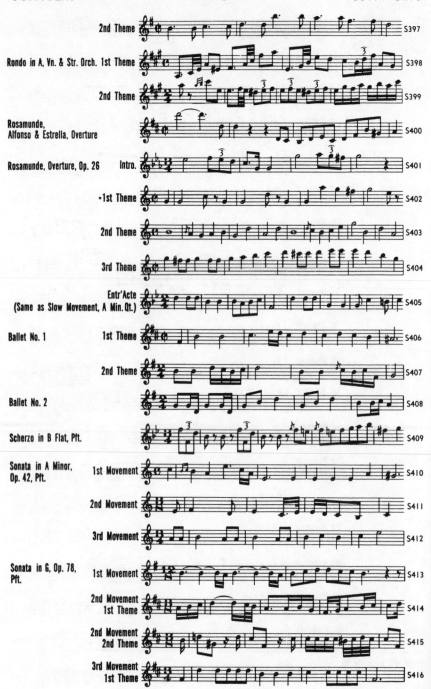

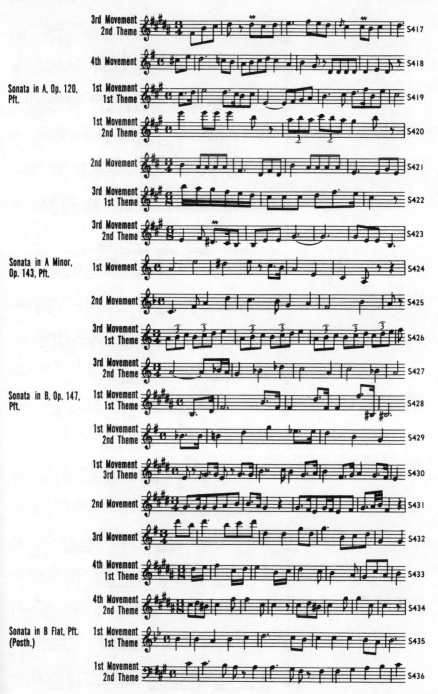

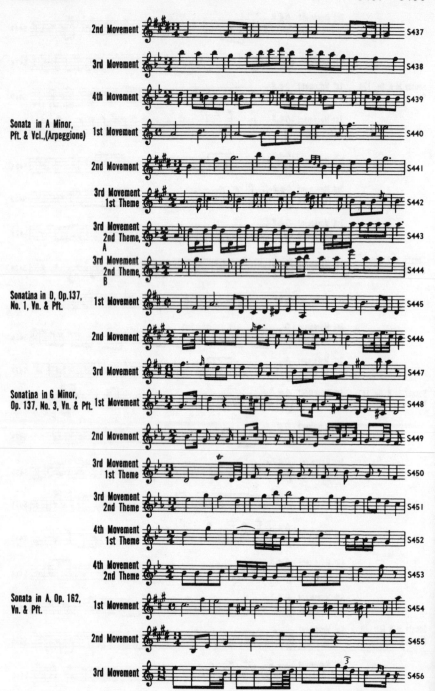

2nd Movement — S437

3rd Movement — S438

4th Movement — S439

Sonata in A Minor, Pft. & Vcl..(Arpeggione) 1st Movement — S440

2nd Movement — S441

3rd Movement 1st Theme — S442

3rd Movement 2nd Theme, A — S443

3rd Movement 2nd Theme, B — S444

Sonatina in D, Op.137, No. 1, Vn. & Pft. 1st Movement — S445

2nd Movement — S446

3rd Movement — S447

Sonatina in G Minor, Op. 137, No. 3, Vn. & Pft. 1st Movement — S448

2nd Movement — S449

3rd Movement 1st Theme — S450

3rd Movement 2nd Theme — S451

4th Movement 1st Theme — S452

4th Movement 2nd Theme — S453

Sonata in A, Op. 162, Vn. & Pft. 1st Movement — S454

2nd Movement — S455

3rd Movement — S456

4th Movement 1st Theme — S457
4th Movement 2nd Theme — S458
4th Movement 3rd Theme — S459

Symphony No. 1 in D

1st Movement Intro. — S460
1st Movement 1st Theme, A — S461
1st Movement 1st Theme, B — S462
1st Movement 2nd Theme — S463
2nd Movement 1st Theme — S464
2nd Movement 2nd Theme — S465
3rd Movement 1st Theme — S466
3rd Movement 2nd Theme — S467
4th Movement 1st Theme — S468
4th Movement 2nd Theme — S469
4th Movement 3rd Theme — S470

Symphony No. 2 in B Flat

1st Movement 1st Theme — S471
1st Movement 2nd Theme — S472
2nd Movement — S473
3rd Movement 1st Theme — S474
3rd Movement 2nd Theme — S475
4th Movement 1st Theme — S476

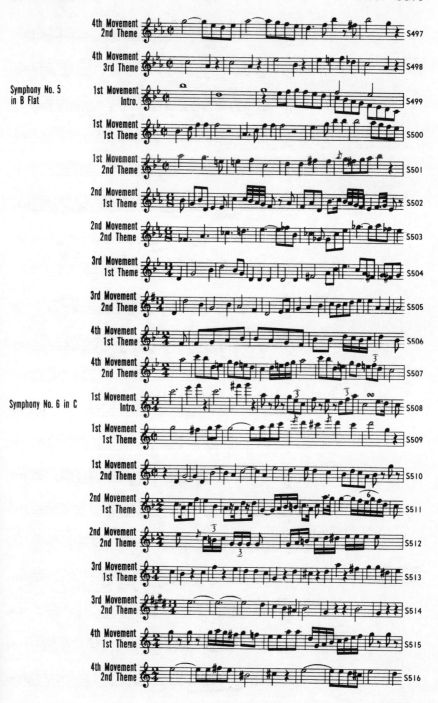

4th Movement / 3rd Theme — S517

Symphony No. 7 in C, "Great"

1st Movement / Intro. — S518

1st Movement / 1st Theme — S519

1st Movement / 2nd Theme — S520

1st Movement / 3rd Theme — S521

2nd Movement / 1st Theme — S522

2nd Movement / 2nd Theme — S523

2nd Movement / 3rd Theme — S524

2nd Movement / 4th Theme — S525

3rd Movement / 1st Theme — S526

3rd Movement / 2nd Theme — S527

3rd Movement / 3rd Theme — S528

3rd Movement / 4th Theme — S529

4th Movement / Intro. — S530

4th Movement / 1st Theme — S531

4th Movement / 2nd Theme — S532

Symphony No. 8 in B Minor, "Unfinished"

1st Movement / Intro. — S533

1st Movement / 1st Theme — S534

1st Movement / 2nd Theme — S535

2nd Movement / (Intro-motive) — S536

2nd Movement 1st Theme S537
2nd Movement 2nd Theme S538
Trio in B Flat, Op. 99, Vn., Pft. & Vcl. 1st Movement 1st Theme S539
1st Movement 2nd Theme S540
2nd Movement S541
3rd Movement 1st Theme S542
3rd Movement 2nd Theme S543
4th Movement 1st Theme S544
4th Movement 2nd Theme S545
Trio in E Flat, Op. 100, Vn., Pft. & Vcl. 1st Movement 1st Theme S546
1st Movement 2nd Theme S547
1st Movement 3rd Theme S548
2nd Movement S549
3rd Movement S550
4th Movement 1st Theme S551
4th Movement 2nd Theme S552
Trio in B Flat, (1817), Vn., Vla. & Vcl. 1st Movement S553
2nd Movement S554
3rd Movement S555
4th Movement S556

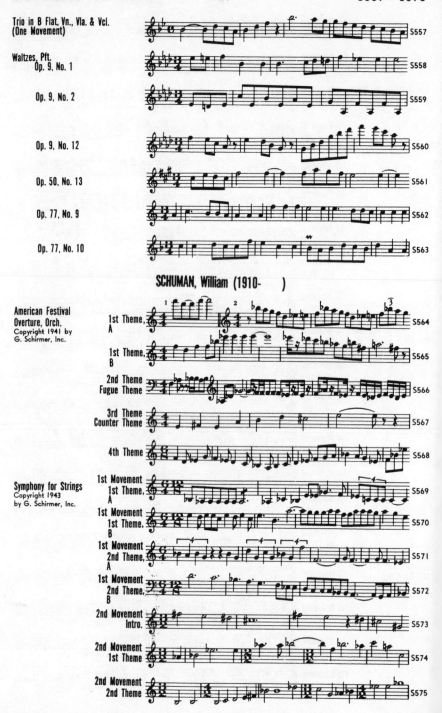

Trio in B Flat, Vn., Vla. & Vcl.
(One Movement)   S557

Waltzes, Pft.
     Op. 9, No. 1   S558

     Op. 9, No. 2   S559

     Op. 9, No. 12   S560

     Op. 50, No. 13   S561

     Op. 77, No. 9   S562

     Op. 77, No. 10   S563

SCHUMAN, William (1910-   )

American Festival
Overture, Orch.
Copyright 1941 by
G. Schirmer, Inc.   1st Theme, A   S564

                         1st Theme, B   S565

                         2nd Theme
                         Fugue Theme   S566

                         3rd Theme
                         Counter Theme   S567

                         4th Theme   S568

Symphony for Strings
Copyright 1943
by G. Schirmer, Inc.   1st Movement
                              1st Theme, A   S569

                              1st Movement
                              1st Theme, B   S570

                              1st Movement
                              2nd Theme, A   S571

                              1st Movement
                              2nd Theme, B   S572

                              2nd Movement
                              Intro.   S573

                              2nd Movement
                              1st Theme   S574

                              2nd Movement
                              2nd Theme   S575

	3rd Movement / 1st Theme — S576
	3rd Movement / 2nd Theme — S577
Symphony No. 3 / Part I / Passacaglia & Fugue / Copyright 1942 by / G. Schirmer, Inc.	1st Theme / Passacaglia — S578
	2nd Theme / Fugue — S579
Part II / Chorale & Toccata	1st Theme / Chorale — S580
	2nd Theme / Toccata — S581

SCHUMANN, Robert (1810-1856)

Abegg Variations, Op. 1, Pft.		S582
Abendlied (Evening Song), Op. 85, No. 12, Pft., 4 Hands		S583
Des Abends, Op. 12, No. 1, Pft.		S584
Album for the Young, Op. 68, Pft.	Soldiers' March	S584a
	The Wild Horseman	S584b
	Folk Song	S584c
	The Happy Farmer	S584d
	Sicilienne	S584e
	Little Romance	S584f
	The Strange Man	S584g
	Italian Sailors' Song	S584h
Arabeske, Op. 18, Pft.	1st Theme	S585
	2nd Theme	S586

3rd Theme S587

Aufschwung (Soaring), Op. 12, No. 2, Pft. 1st Theme S588

2nd Theme S589

Carnaval, Op. 9, Pft. Préambule S590

Pierrot S591

Arlequin S592

Valse Noble S593

Eusebius S594

Florestan S595

Lettres Dansantes S596

Chopin S597

Estrella S598

Reconnaissance S599

March of the Davidsbündler S600

Concerto in A Minor, Op. 129, Vcl. & Orch. 1st Movement 1st Theme S601

1st Movement 2nd Theme S602

1st Movement 3rd Theme S603

2nd Movement S604

3rd Movement 1st Theme S605

3rd Movement 2nd Theme S606

SCHUMANN

3rd Movement
3rd Theme — S607

Concerto in A Minor,
Op. 54, Pft. & Orch.

1st Movement
1st Theme — S608

1st Movement
2nd Theme,
A — S609

1st Movement
2nd Theme,
B — S610

1st Movement
3rd Theme — S611

1st Movement
Coda — S612

2nd Movement
Intermezzo
1st Theme — S613

2nd Movement
2nd Theme — S614

3rd Movement
1st Theme — S615

3rd Movement
2nd Theme — S616

3rd Movement
3rd Theme — S617

Concerto in D Minor,
Vn. & Orch.

1st Movement
1st Theme — S618

1st Movement
2nd Theme — S619

2nd Movement — S620

3rd Movement
1st Theme — S621

3rd Movement
2nd Theme — S622

Davidsbündler, Op. 6, Pft.

No. 1 — S623

No. 2 — S624

No. 5 — S625

No. 9 — S626

2nd Movement 1st Theme Scherzo   S667

2nd Movement 2nd Theme Intermezzo   S668

3rd Movement   S669

4th Movement   S670

Quartet in F, Op. 41, No. 2, Str.

1st Movement 1st Theme   S671

1st Movement 2nd Theme   S672

2nd Movement   S673

3rd Movement 1st Theme   S674

3rd Movement 2nd Theme   S675

4th Movement 1st Theme   S676

4th Movement 2nd Theme, A   S677

4th Movement 2nd Theme, B   S678

Quartet in A, Op. 41, No. 3, Str.

1st Movement 1st Theme   S679

1st Movement 2nd Theme   S680

2nd Movement 1st Theme   S681

2nd Movement 2nd Theme   S682

2nd Movement 3rd Theme   S683

3rd Movement 1st Theme   S684

3rd Movement 2nd Theme   S685

4th Movement 1st Theme   S686

Quartet in E Flat,
Op. 47, Pft. & Str.

Quintet in E Flat,
Op. 44, Pft. & Str.

4th Movement 2nd Theme S687
4th Movement 3rd Theme S688
1st Movement Intro. S689
1st Movement 1st Theme S690
1st Movement 2nd Theme S691
2nd Movement 1st Theme S692
2nd Movement 2nd Theme S693
3rd Movement Intro. S694
3rd Movement 1st Theme S695
3rd Movement 2nd Theme S696
4th Movement 1st Theme S697
4th Movement 2nd Theme S698
1st Movement 1st Theme S699
1st Movement 2nd Theme S700
2nd Movement 1st Theme S701
2nd Movement 2nd Theme S702
2nd Movement 3rd Theme S703
3rd Movement 1st Theme S704
3rd Movement 2nd Theme S705
3rd Movement 3rd Theme S706

4th Movement / 1st Theme — S707

4th Movement / 2nd Theme — S708

4th Movement / 3rd Theme — S709

Romanze, Op. 28, No. 2, Pft. — S710

Scenes from Childhood, Op. 15, Pft.   From Foreign Lands — S711

Curious Story — S712

Träumerei — S713

At the Hearth — S714

Hobby Horse — S715

Slumbersong, Op. 124, No. 16, Pft. — S716

Sonatas
No. 2 in G Minor, Op. 22, Pft.   1st Movement / 1st Theme — S717

1st Movement / 2nd Theme — S718

2nd Movement — S719

3rd Movement — S720

4th Movement / 1st Theme — S721

4th Movement / 2nd Theme — S722

A Minor, Op. 105, Vn. & Pft.   1st Movement / 1st Theme — S723

1st Movement / 2nd Theme — S724

2nd Movement / 1st Theme, A — S725

2nd Movement / 1st Theme, B — S726

2nd Movement 2nd Theme — S727

3rd Movement 1st Theme — S728

3rd Movement 2nd Theme — S729

3rd Movement 3rd Theme — S730

D Minor, Op. 121, Vn. & Pft. — 1st Movement Intro. — S731

1st Movement 1st Theme — S732

1st Movement 2nd Theme — S733

2nd Movement 1st Theme — S734

2nd Movement 2nd Theme — S735

2nd Movement 3rd Theme — S736

3rd Movement 1st Theme — S737

3rd Movement 2nd Theme — S738

4th Movement 1st Theme — S739

4th Movement 2nd Theme — S740

Symphonic Etudes, in C Sharp Minor, Op. 13, Pft. — Theme — S741

Etude I — S742

Etude II — S743

Etude III — S744

Etude VI — S745

Finale 1st Theme — S746

2nd Theme — S747

Symphony No. 1 in B Flat, Op. 38, "Spring"

1st Movement Intro. — S748

1st Movement 1st Theme — S749

1st Movement 2nd Theme — S750

1st Movement 3rd Theme — S751

1st Movement 4th Theme — S752

1st Movement 5th Theme — S753

2nd Movement — S754

2nd Movement 2nd Theme — S755

3rd Movement 1st Theme — S756

3rd Movement 2nd Theme — S757

3rd Movement 3rd Theme — S758

3rd Movement 4th Theme — S759

4th Movement Intro. — S760

4th Movement 1st Theme — S761

4th Movement 2nd Theme — S762

4th Movement 3rd Theme — S763

Symphony No. 2 in C, Op. 61

1st Movement Intro. A 1 — S764

1st Movement Intro. A 2 — S765

1st Movement Intro. B — S766

1st Movement 1st Theme — S767
1st Movement 2nd Theme — S768
1st Movement 3rd Theme — S769
2nd Movement 1st Theme — S770
2nd Movement 2nd Theme — S771
2nd Movement 3rd Theme — S772
2nd Movement 4th Theme — S773
3rd Movement 1st Theme — S774
3rd Movement 2nd Theme — S775
4th Movement Intro. — S776
4th Movement 1st Theme — S777
4th Movement 2nd Theme — S778
4th Movement 3rd Theme — S779

Symphony No. 3 in E Flat, Op. 97, "Rhenish"

1st Movement 1st Theme — S780
1st Movement 2nd Theme — S781
2nd Movement 1st Theme — S782
2nd Movement 2nd Theme — S783
3rd Movement 1st Theme — S784
3rd Movement 2nd Theme — S785
4th Movement — S786

1st Theme — S807

2nd Theme — S808

Vogel Als Prophet,
(Bird as Prophet),
Op. 82, No. 7, Pft.
1st Theme — S809

2nd Theme — S810

Warum? (Why?), Op. 12, No. 3, Pft. — S811

SCOTT, Cyril (1879-   )

Danse Nègre, Op. 58, No. 5, Pft.
Copyright 1911 by
Elkin & Co., Ltd.
By permission of Galaxy
Music Corporation, N. Y. — S812

Lotus Land, Op. 47,
No. 1, Pft.
Copyright 1905 by
Elkin & Co., Ltd.
By permission of Galaxy
Music Corporation, N. Y.
1st Theme — S813

2nd Theme — S814

A Song from the East,
Op. 54, No. 2, Pft.
Copyright 1907
by Elkin & Co., Ltd.
By permission of Galaxy
Music Corporation, N. Y. — S815

SCRIABIN, Alexander (1872-1915)

Etudes
By permisssion of The Boston Music Co.,
Op. 2, No. 1, Pft. copyright owner. — S816

Op. 8, No. 10, Pft.
By permission of Associated
Music Publishers, Inc. — S817

Op. 8, No. 12, Pft.
By permission of Associated
Music Publishers, Inc. — S818

Fantaisie, Op. 28, Pft.   1st Theme
By permission of Associated
Music Publishers, Inc. — S819

2nd Theme — S820

Mazurka, Op. 25, No. 3, Pft.
By permission of Associated
Music Publishers, Inc. — S821

Nocturne, Pft. (For Left Hand Alone)
By permission of Associated
Music Publishers, Inc. — S822

Poème, Op. 32, No. 1, Pft.
By permission of Associated
Music Publishers, Inc. — S823

Poème, Op. 32, No. 2, Pft.
By permission of Associated
Music Publishers, Inc. — S824

Poème D'Extase, Op. 34, Orch.
By permission of Associated Music Publishers, Inc.
1st Theme — S825

2nd Theme — S826

3rd Theme — S827

Preludes
Op. 9, No. 1, Pft.
(For Left Hand Alone)
By permission of Associated Music Publishers, Inc. — S828

Op. 11, No. 2, Pft.
By permission of Associated Music Publishers, Inc. — S829

No. 9, Pft. — S830

No. 10, Pft. — S831

Sonata, No. 4, Op. 30, Pft.
By permission of International Music Co.
1st Movement — S932

2nd Movement — S833

Symphony No. 3, Op. 43
"Le Divin Poème"
By permission of Associated Music Publishers, Inc.
Intro. — S834

1st Movement Luttes 1st Theme — S835

1st Movement 2nd Theme — S836

2nd Movement Voluptés — S837

3rd Movement Jeu Divin 1st Theme — S838

3rd Movement 2nd Theme — S839

Waltz, Op. 38, Pft.
By permission of Associated Music Publishers, Inc. — S840

SGAMBATI, Giovanni (1841-1914)

Serenata Napoletana, Op. 24, No. 2, Vn. & Pft.
1st Theme, A — S841

1st Theme, B — S842

2nd Theme — S843

Vecchio Minuetto, Op. 18, Pft.   S844

SHOSTAKOVICH, Dmitri (1906-   )

Concerto, Op. 35,   1st Movement   S845
Pft. & Orch.   1st Theme
By permission of
Broude Brothers

                        1st Movement   S846
                        2nd Theme

                        2nd Movement   S847

                        3rd Movement   S848
                        Finale
                        1st Theme

                        3rd Movement   S849
                        2nd Theme

                        3rd Movement   S850
                        3rd Theme

The Golden Age, Op. 22,   1st Theme   S851
Ballet   Polka
Copyright 1941 by Leeds
Music Corp., N. Y.
Reprinted here by permisssion
of the copyright owner.

                        2nd Theme   S852

                        3rd Theme   S853

Quartet, Op. 49, Str.   1st Movement   S854
By permission of   1st Theme
International Music Co.

                        1st Movement   S855
                        2nd Theme

                        2nd Movement   S856

                        3rd Movement   S857
                        1st Theme

                        3rd Movement   S858
                        2nd Theme

                        4th Movement   S859
                        1st Theme

                        4th Movement   S860
                        2nd Theme

Quintet, Op. 57,   1st Movement   S861
Pft. & Str.   Prelude
                       1st Theme

                       1st Movement   S862
                       2nd Theme

2nd Movement
Fugue   S863

3rd Movement
Scherzo
1st Theme   S864

3rd Movement
2nd Theme   S865

4th Movement
Intermezzo   S866

5th Movement
Finale
1st Theme, A   S867

5th Movement
1st Theme,
B   S868

5th Movement
2nd Theme   S869

5th Movement
3rd Theme   S870

Sonata, Op. 40
Cello & Pft.
Copyright 1947 by Leeds
Music Corp., N. Y.
Reprinted here by
permisssion of the
copyright owner.

1st Movement
1st Theme   S870a

1st Movement
2nd Theme   S870b

2nd Movement
1st Theme   S870c

2nd Movement
2nd Theme   S870d

3rd Movement
1st Theme   S870e

3rd Movement
2nd Theme   S870f

4th Movement   S870g

Symphony No. 1 in F,
Op. 10
Copyright 1946 by
Leeds Music Corp., N. Y.
Reprinted here by
permisssion of the
copyright owner.

1st Movement
Intro.   S871

1st Movement
1st Theme   S872

1st Movement
2nd Theme   S873

2nd Movement
1st Theme   S874

2nd Movement
2nd Theme   S875

3rd Movement 1st Theme — S876
3rd Movement 2nd Theme — S877
4th Movement 1st Theme — S878
4th Movement 2nd Theme — S879

Symphony No. 5, Op. 47
Copyright 1945 by Leeds
Music Corp., N. Y.
Reprinted here by
permisssion of the
copyright owner.

1st Movement 1st Theme A — S880
1st Movement 1st Theme B — S881
1st Movement 1st Theme C — S882
1st Movement 1st Theme D — S883
1st Movement 2nd Theme A — S884
1st Movement 2nd Theme B — S885
2nd Movement 1st Theme, A — S886
2nd Movement 1st Theme, B — S887
2nd Movement 2nd Theme — S888
2nd Movement 3rd Theme — S889
2nd Movement 4th Theme — S890
3rd Movement 1st Theme — S891
3rd Movement 2nd Theme — S892
3rd Movement 3rd Theme — S893
3rd Movement 4th Theme — S894
4th Movement — S895

Symphony No. 6, Op. 53
Copyright 1946 by Leeds
Music Corp., N. Y.
Reprinted here by
permisssion of the
copyright owner.

1st Movement
1st Theme   S896

1st Movement
2nd Theme   S897

2nd Movement
1st Theme   S898

2nd Movement
2nd Theme   S899

3rd Movement
1st Theme   S900

3rd Movement
2nd Theme   S901

3rd Movement
3rd Theme   S902

Symphony No. 7, Op. 60
Copyright 1945 by Leeds
Music Corp., N. Y.
Reprinted here by
permisssion of the
copyright owner.

1st Movement
1st Theme   S903

1st Movement
2nd Theme   S904

1st Movement
3rd Theme   S905

2nd Movement
1st Theme   S906

2nd Movement
2nd Theme   S907

2nd Movement
3rd Theme   S908

3rd Movement
1st Theme   S909

3rd Movement
2nd Theme   S910

3rd Movement
3rd Theme   S911

4th Movement
1st Theme   S912

4th Movement
2nd Theme   S913

Symphony No. 9, Op. 70

1st Movement
1st Theme   S914

1st Movement
2nd Theme   S915

2nd Movement 1st Theme — S916
2nd Movement 2nd Theme — S917
3rd Movement 1st Theme — S918
3rd Movement 2nd Theme — S919
4th Movement — S920
5th Movement 1st Theme — S921
5th Movement 2nd Theme — S922

Three Fantastic Dances, Op. 1, Pft.
Copyright 1944 and 1945 by Leeds Music Corp., N. Y. Reprinted here by permisssion of the copyright owner.

No. 1 — S923
No. 2 — S924
No. 3 — S925

Two Pieces for String Octet, Op. 11
Copyright 1946 by Leeds Music Corp., N. Y. Reprinted here by permisssion of the copyright owner.

No. 1 Prelude 1st Theme — S925a
2nd Theme — S925b
No. 2 Scherzo 1st Theme — S925c
2nd Theme — S925d

SIBELIUS, Jean (1865-   )

The Bard, Op. 64, Orch.
By permission of Associated Music Publishers, Inc.

1st Theme — S926
2nd Theme — S927

Concerto, Op. 47, Vn. & Orch.
By permission of International Music Co.

1st Movement 1st Theme — S928
1st Movement 2nd Theme, A — S929
1st Movement 2nd Theme, B — S930

2nd Movement Intro. S931

2nd Movement S932

3rd Movement 1st Theme S933

3rd Movement 2nd Theme S934

En Saga, Op. 9, Orch.
By permission of Associated Music Publishers, Inc.
1st Theme S935

2nd Theme S936

3rd Theme S937

4th Theme S938

5th Theme S939

6th Theme S940

Finlandia, Op. 26, No. 7, Orch.
By permission of Associated Music Publishers, Inc.
1st Theme S941

2nd Theme S942

3rd Theme S943

In Memoriam, Op. 59 (Funeral March), Orch.
By permission of Associated Music Publishers, Inc.
S944

Karelia, Op. 11, Suite for Orch.
By permission of Associated Music Publishers, Inc.
1st Movement Intermezzo S945

2nd Movement Ballade S946

3rd Movement Alla Marcia 1st Theme S947

3rd Movement 2nd Theme S948

King Christian II, Op. 27, Suite for Orch.
By permission of Associated Music Publishers, Inc.
Nocturne 1st Theme S949

2nd Theme S950

Elégie and Musette
1st Theme Elégie — S951

2nd Theme Musette — S952

Serenade 1st Theme — S953

2nd Theme — S954

Ballade 1st Theme — S955

2nd Theme — S956

Lemminkäinen's Homeward Journey, Op. 22, No. 4 Orch.
By permission of Associated Music Publishers, Inc.
1st Theme — S957

2nd Theme — S958

3rd Theme — S959

Nightride and Sunrise, Op. 55, Orch.
1st Theme — S960

2nd Theme — S961

3rd Theme — S962

The Oceanides, Op. 73, Orch.
By permission of Associated Music Publishers, Inc.
1st Theme — S963

2nd Theme — S964

Pelléas et Mélisande, (Incidental Music) Op. 46, Orch.
Mélisande — S965

A Spring in the Park — S966

Pastorale — S967

Entr'acte — S968

Death of Mélisande — S969

Pohjola's Daughter, Op. 49, Orch.
Copyright by Lienau, Licensed by SESAC, Inc., N. Y.
1st Theme A — S970

1st Theme, B — S971

2nd Theme — S972

3rd Theme — S973

4th Theme — S974

4th Theme — S975

5th Theme — S976

Quartet, Op. 56, Str. "Voces Intimae" By permission of Associated Music Publishers, Inc.

1st Movement 1st Theme, A — S977

1st Movement 1st Theme, B — S978

1st Movement 2nd Theme — S979

2nd Movement 1st Theme — S980

2nd Movement 2nd Theme — S981

3rd Movement 1st Theme, A — S982

3rd Movement 1st Theme, B — S983

4th Movement 1st Theme — S984

4th Movement 2nd Theme — S985

4th Movement 3rd Theme — S986

5th Movement 1st Theme — S987

5th Movement 2nd Theme — S988

5th Movement 3rd Theme — S989

Rakastava, (The Lover), Op. 14, Suite for Orch. By permission of Associated Music Publishers, Inc.

1st Movement — S990

SIBELIUS

2nd Movement — S991

3rd Movement — S992

Romance, Op. 24, No. 9, Pft. 1st Theme — S993

2nd Theme — S994

The Swan of Tuonela,
(from Kalevala)
Op. 22, No. 3
Orch.
By permission of Associated
Music Publishers, Inc.

1st Theme, A — S995

1st Theme, B — S996

1st Theme, C — S997

2nd Theme — S998

Symphony No. 1
in E Minor, Op. 39
By permission of Associated
Music Publishers, Inc.

1st Movement Intro. — S999

1st Movement 1st Theme — S1000

1st Movement 2nd Theme — S1001

1st Movement 3rd Theme — S1002

2nd Movement 1st Theme, A — S1003

2nd Movement 1st Theme, B — S1004

2nd Movement 2nd Theme — S1005

3rd Movement 1st Theme — S1006

3rd Movement 2nd Theme — S1007

4th Movement 1st Theme — S1008

4th Movement 2nd Theme — S1009

4th Movement 3rd Theme — S1010

Symphony No. 2
in D, Op. 43
By permission of Associated
Music Publishers, Inc.

1st Movement / 1st Theme — S1011

1st Movement / 2nd Theme — S1012

1st Movement / 3rd Theme — S1013

2nd Movement / Intro. — S1014

2nd Movement / 1st Theme — S1015

2nd Movement / 2nd Theme — S1016

3rd Movement / 1st Theme — S1017

3rd Movement / 2nd Theme — S1018

3rd Movement / 3rd Theme — S1019

4th Movement / 1st Theme — S1020

4th Movement / 2nd Theme — S1021

4th Movement / 3rd Theme — S1022

4th Movement / 4th Theme — S1023

Symphony No. 3
in C, Op. 52
Copyright by Lienau,
Licensed by SESAC
Inc., N. Y.

1st Movement / 1st Theme — S1024

1st Movement / 2nd Theme — S1025

1st Movement / 3rd Theme — S1026

2nd Movement — S1027

3rd Movement / 1st Theme — S1028

3rd Movement / 2nd Theme — S1029

3rd Movement / 3rd Theme — S1030

Symphony No. 4
in A Minor, Op. 63
By permission of Associated
Music Publishers, Inc.

1st Movement / 1st Theme — S1031

1st Movement / 2nd Theme — S1032

1st Movement / 3rd Theme — S1033

2nd Movement / 1st Theme — S1034

2nd Movement / 2nd Theme — S1035

2nd Movement / 3rd Theme — S1036

2nd Movement / 4th Theme — S1037

2nd Movement / 5th Theme — S1038

3rd Movement / 1st Theme — S1039

3rd Movement / 2nd Theme — S1040

4th Movement / 1st Theme — S1041

4th Movement / 2nd Theme — S1042

4th Movement / 3rd Theme — S1043

4th Movement / 4th Theme — S1044

4th Movement / 5th Theme — S1045

Symphony No. 5
in E Flat, Op. 82
By permission of Associated
Music Publishers, Inc.

1st Movement / 1st Theme — S1046

1st Movement / 2nd Theme — S1047

1st Movement / 3rd Theme — S1048

1st Movement / 4th Theme — S1049

1st Movement / 5th Theme — S1050

Symphony No. 6
in D Minor, Op. 104
By permission of Associated
Music Publishers, Inc.

SIBELIUS

4th Movement
2nd Theme — S1071

4th Movement
3rd Theme — S1072

4th Movement
4th Theme — S1073

Symphony No. 7
in C, Op. 105
By permission of Associated
Music Publishers, Inc.

1st Theme — S1074

2nd Theme — S1075

3rd Theme
A — S1076

3rd Theme
B — S1077

4th Theme — S1078

5th Theme — S1079

6th Theme — S1080

7th Theme — S1081

8th Theme — S1082

9th Theme — S1083

10th Theme — S1084

11th Theme — S1085

Tapiola, Op. 112, Orch.
By permission of Associated
Music Publishers, Inc.

1st Theme — S1086

2nd Theme — S1087

3rd Theme — S1088

Valse Triste (from
Kuolema), Op. 44
Orch.
Copyright 1926
by G. Schirmer, Inc.

1st Theme — S1089

2nd Theme — S1090

3rd Theme  S1091

4th Theme S1092

SINDING, Christian (1856-1941)

Marche Grotesque, Op. 32, No. 1, Pft.  S1093

Rustle of Spring
(Frühlingsrauschen),
Op. 32, No. 3, Pft.
Copyright renewal assigned
1931 to G. Schirmer, Inc.

1st Theme, A S1094

1st Theme, B S1095

SMETANA, Bedřich (1824-1884)

Aus Meinem Leben,
Quartet No. 1
in E Minor, Str.

1st Movement 1st Theme 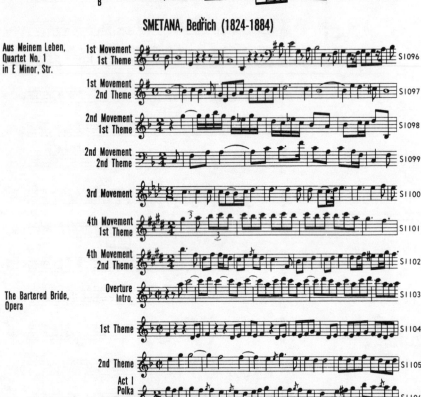 S1096

1st Movement 2nd Theme S1097

2nd Movement 1st Theme S1098

2nd Movement 2nd Theme S1099

3rd Movement S1100

4th Movement 1st Theme S1101

4th Movement 2nd Theme S1102

The Bartered Bride,
Opera

Overture Intro. S1103

1st Theme S1104

2nd Theme S1105

Act I
Polka
1st Theme S1106

2nd Theme, A S1107

2nd Theme, B S1108

Act III
Dance of the Comedians
1st Theme — S1109

2nd Theme — S1110

3rd Theme — S1111

4th Theme — S1112

5th Theme — S1113

My Country (Symphonic Cycle)
No. 2, The Moldau
Orch.
1st Theme — S1114

2nd Theme — S1115

3rd Theme — S1116

4th Theme — S1117

No. 4 From Bohemia's
Meadows and Forests
Intro. — S1118

1st Theme — S1119

2nd Theme — S1120

3rd Theme — S1121

4th Theme — S1122

5th Theme — S1123

Slepicka (The Little Hen), Pft. — S1124

Trio in G Minor, Op. 15, 1st Movement
Vn., Vcl. & Pft.
1st Theme — S1125

1st Movement
2nd Theme — S1126

2nd Movement
1st Theme,
A — S1127

2nd Movement
1st Theme,
B — S1128

2nd Movement 2nd Theme — S1129

2nd Movement 3rd Theme — S1130

3rd Movement 1st Theme — S1131

3rd Movement 2nd Theme — S1132

SOLER, Padre Antonio (1729-1783)

Sonatas
F, Harpsi. — S1133

A Minor, Harpsi. — S1134

D, Harpsi. — S1135

SOUSA, John Philip (1854-1932)

El Capitan, March
1st Theme — S1136

2nd Theme — S1137

3rd Theme — S1138

4th Theme — S1139

Hail to the Spirit of Liberty, March
1st Theme — S1140

2nd Theme — S1141

3rd Theme — S1142

The High School Cadets, March
1st Theme — S1143

2nd Theme — S1144

3rd Theme — S1145

4th Theme — S1146

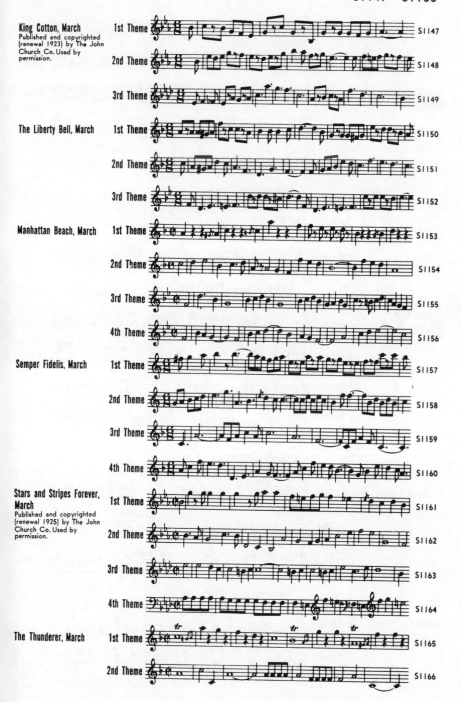

King Cotton, March
Published and copyrighted
(renewal 1923) by The John
Church Co. Used by
permission.

1st Theme   S1147

2nd Theme   S1148

3rd Theme   S1149

The Liberty Bell, March

1st Theme   S1150

2nd Theme   S1151

3rd Theme   S1152

Manhattan Beach, March

1st Theme   S1153

2nd Theme   S1154

3rd Theme   S1155

4th Theme   S1156

Semper Fidelis, March

1st Theme   S1157

2nd Theme   S1158

3rd Theme   S1159

4th Theme   S1160

**Stars and Stripes Forever,
March**
Published and copyrighted
(renewal 1925) by The John
Church Co. Used by
permission.

1st Theme   S1161

2nd Theme   S1162

3rd Theme   S1163

4th Theme   S1164

The Thunderer, March

1st Theme   S1165

2nd Theme   S1166

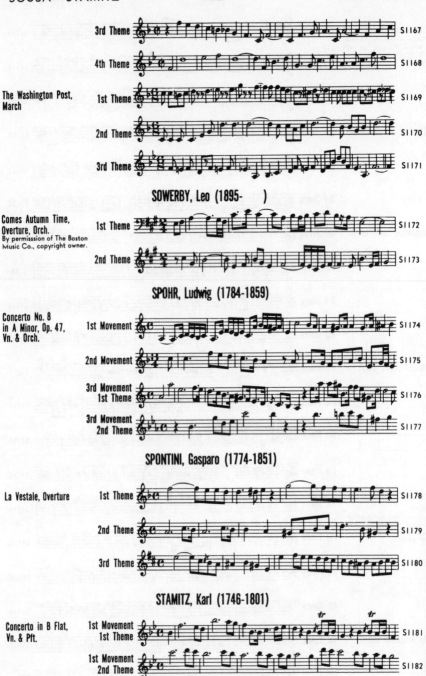

3rd Theme — S1167

4th Theme — S1168

The Washington Post, March

1st Theme — S1169

2nd Theme — S1170

3rd Theme — S1171

SOWERBY, Leo (1895-   )

Comes Autumn Time, Overture, Orch.
By permisssion of The Boston Music Co., copyright owner.

1st Theme — S1172

2nd Theme — S1173

SPOHR, Ludwig (1784-1859)

Concerto No. 8 in A Minor, Op. 47, Vn. & Orch.

1st Movement — S1174

2nd Movement — S1175

3rd Movement 1st Theme — S1176

3rd Movement 2nd Theme — S1177

SPONTINI, Gasparo (1774-1851)

La Vestale, Overture

1st Theme — S1178

2nd Theme — S1179

3rd Theme — S1180

STAMITZ, Karl (1746-1801)

Concerto in B Flat, Vn. & Pft.

1st Movement 1st Theme — S1181

1st Movement 2nd Theme — S1182

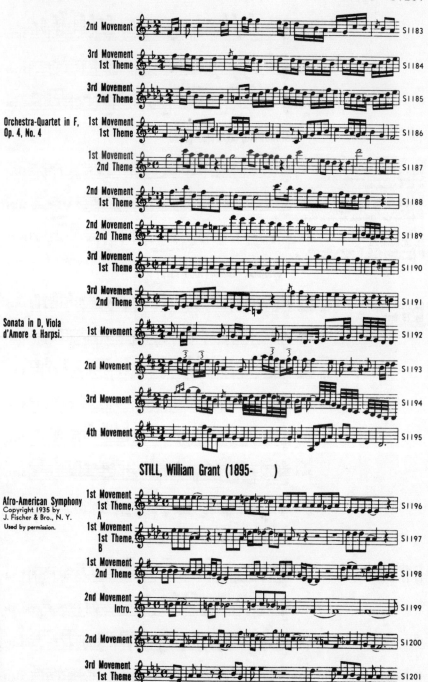

2nd Movement — S1183

3rd Movement
1st Theme — S1184

3rd Movement
2nd Theme — S1185

Orchestra-Quartet in F,
Op. 4, No. 4   1st Movement
1st Theme — S1186

1st Movement
2nd Theme — S1187

2nd Movement
1st Theme — S1188

2nd Movement
2nd Theme — S1189

3rd Movement
1st Theme — S1190

3rd Movement
2nd Theme — S1191

Sonata in D, Viola
d'Amore & Harpsi.   1st Movement — S1192

2nd Movement — S1193

3rd Movement — S1194

4th Movement — S1195

STILL, William Grant (1895-   )

Afro-American Symphony
Copyright 1935 by
J. Fischer & Bro., N. Y.
Used by permission.

1st Movement
1st Theme, A — S1196

1st Movement
1st Theme, B — S1197

1st Movement
2nd Theme — S1198

2nd Movement
Intro. — S1199

2nd Movement — S1200

3rd Movement
1st Theme — S1201

3rd Movement
2nd Theme — S1202

4th Movement
1st Theme — S1203

4th Movement
2nd Theme — S1204

STOJOWSKI, Sigismond (1870-   )

Chant d'Amour, Op. 26, No. 3, Pft.
Copyright renewal assigned 1939
to G. Schirmer, Inc. — S1205

Melodie, Op. 26, No. 1, Pft.
By Permission of C. F. Peters, Clayton
F. Summy Co., Chicago, Agents in the U. S. — S1206

Thème Cracovien Varié,
Op. 26, No. 4, Pft.
By Permission of C. F. Peters, Clayton
F. Summy Co., Chicago, Agents in the U. S. — S1207

STRAUSS, Eduard (1835-1916)

Doctrinen Waltzes,
Op. 79, Orch.

No. 1
1st Theme — S1208

2nd Theme — S1209

No. 2
1st Theme — S1210

2nd Theme — S1211

No. 3 — S1212

No. 4 — S1213

No. 5 — S1214

STRAUSS, Johann, Jr. (1825-1899)

Perpetuum Mobile,
Op. 257, Orch.

Theme — S1215

Variation — S1216

Variation — S1217

Die Fledermaus, Overture   1st Theme — S1218

2nd Theme — S1219

3rd Theme — S1220

4th Theme — S1221

5th Theme — S1222

Eine Nacht in Venedig, Overture   1st Theme — S1223

2nd Theme — S1224

3rd Theme — S1225

4th Theme — S1226

5th Theme — S1227

Der Zigeunerbaron, Overture   1st Theme — S1228

2nd Theme — S1229

3rd Theme — S1230

4th Theme — S1231

An Der Schönen Blauen Donau (On the Beautiful Blue Danube), Op. 317 Waltzes, Orch.   No. 1 1st Theme — S1232

2nd Theme — S1233

No. 2 1st Theme — S1234

2nd Theme — S1235

No. 3 1st Theme — S1236

2nd Theme — S1237

No. 4 1st Theme — S1238

2nd Theme — S1239

No. 5 1st Theme — S1240

2nd Theme — S1241

Du Und Du, Waltzes from Die Fledermaus, Op. 367, Orch.

No. 1 1st Theme — S1242

2nd Theme — S1243

No. 2 1st Theme — S1244

2nd Theme — S1245

No. 3 1st Theme — S1246

2nd Theme — S1247

Frühlingsstimmen (Voices of Spring), Op. 410 Waltz, Orch.

1st Theme — S1248

2nd Theme — S1249

3rd Theme — S1250

4th Theme — S1251

5th Theme — S1252

6th Theme — S1253

G'schichten Aus Dem Wienerwald (Tales of the Vienna Woods), Op. 325 Waltzes, Orch.

No. 1 1st Theme — S1254

2nd Theme — S1255

No. 2 1st Theme — S1256

2nd Theme — S1257

No. 3 — S1258

Kuss (Kiss) Waltz from Der
Lustige Krieg , Op. 400,
Orch.
1st Theme — S1279
2nd Theme — S1280
3rd Theme — S1281
4th Theme — S1282

Lagunen-Waltzes, from
Eine Nacht in Venedig
(Same as Artist's Life), Orch.
1st Theme — S1283
2nd Theme — S1284
3rd Theme — S1285
4th Theme — S1286
5th Theme — S1287

Morgenblätter Waltz,
Op. 279, Orch.
1st Theme — S1288
2nd Theme — S1289
3rd Theme — S1290
4th Theme — S1291
5th Theme — S1292

O Schöner Mai,
Waltzes, Op. 375, Orch.
No. 1 — S1293
No. 2
1st Theme — S1294
2nd Theme — S1295
No. 3 — S1296

Roses From the South
Waltzes, Op. 388, Orch.
No. 1
1st Theme — S1297
2nd Theme — S1298

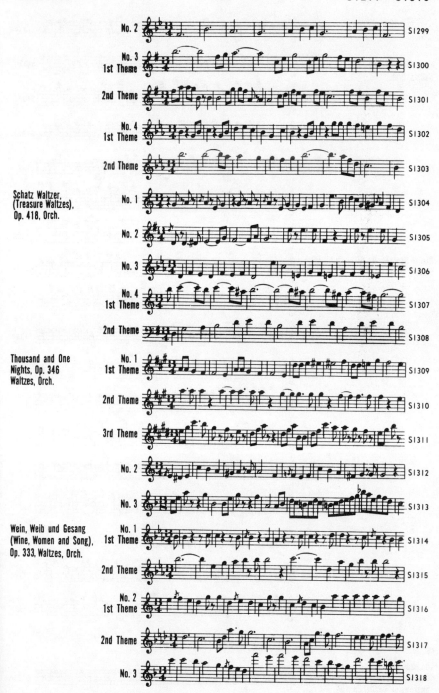

No. 2 — S1299

No. 3 1st Theme — S1300

2nd Theme — S1301

No. 4 1st Theme — S1302

2nd Theme — S1303

Schatz Waltzer, (Treasure Waltzes), Op. 418, Orch.

No. 1 — S1304

No. 2 — S1305

No. 3 — S1306

No. 4 1st Theme — S1307

2nd Theme — S1308

Thousand and One Nights, Op. 346 Waltzes, Orch.

No. 1 1st Theme — S1309

2nd Theme — S1310

3rd Theme — S1311

No. 2 — S1312

No. 3 — S1313

Wein, Weib und Gesang (Wine, Women and Song), Op. 333, Waltzes, Orch.

No. 1 1st Theme — S1314

2nd Theme — S1315

No. 2 1st Theme — S1316

2nd Theme — S1317

No. 3 — S1318

No. 4   S1319

Wiener-Blut, Op. 354
Waltzes, Orch.

No. 1
1st Theme   S1320

2nd Theme   S1321

No. 2   S1322

No. 3
1st Theme   S1323

2nd Theme   S1324

No. 4   S1325

Wiener-Bonbons, Op. 307
Waltzes, Orch.

No. 1
1st Theme   S1326

2nd Theme   S1327

No. 2   S1328

No. 3
1st Theme   S1329

2nd Theme   S1330

No. 4   S1331

No. 5
1st Theme   S1332

2nd Theme   S1333

STRAUSS, Johann, Sr. (1804-1849)

Radetsky March, Orch.

1st Theme   S1334

2nd Theme   S1335

STRAUSS, Joseph (1827-1870)

Dorfschwalben Aus
Oesterreich (Village
Swallows of Austria),Op. 164
Waltzes, Orch.

No. 1
1st Theme   S1336

Sphärenklange, Op. 235
Waltzes, Orch.

Wiener Kinder, Op. 61
Waltzes, Orch.

STRAUSS, Richard (1864-)

Alpensinfonie, Op. 64
Orch.
By permission of Associated
Music Publishers, Inc.

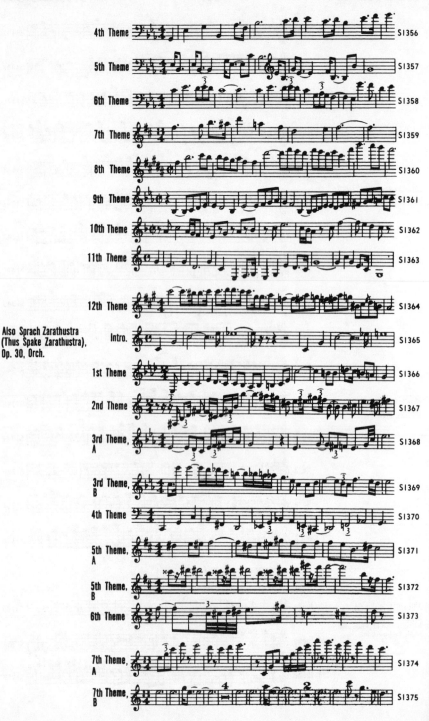

4th Theme S1356

5th Theme S1357

6th Theme S1358

7th Theme S1359

8th Theme S1360

9th Theme S1361

10th Theme S1362

11th Theme S1363

12th Theme S1364

Also Sprach Zarathustra
(Thus Spake Zarathustra),
Op. 30, Orch.

Intro. S1365

1st Theme S1366

2nd Theme S1367

3rd Theme, A S1368

3rd Theme, B S1369

4th Theme S1370

5th Theme, A S1371

5th Theme, B S1372

6th Theme S1373

7th Theme, A S1374

7th Theme, B S1375

Aus Italien,
Symphonic Fantasy,
Op. 16

In the Campagna
(Auf der Campagna)
1st Theme — S1376

2nd Theme — S1377

3rd Theme — S1378

In the Roman Ruins
(In Roms Ruinen)
1st Theme — S1379

2nd Theme — S1380

3rd Theme — S1381

4th Theme — S1382

5th Theme — S1383

The Beach at Sorrento
(Am Strande von Sorrent)
1st Theme — S1384

2nd Theme — S1385

3rd Theme — S1386

4th Theme — S1387

Neapolitan Folk Life
(Neapolitanisches Volksleben)
1st Theme
A — S1388

1st Theme
B — S1389

2nd Theme — S1390

3rd Theme — S1391

4th Theme — S1392

Der Bürger Als
Edelmann, Op. 60,
Orch.
By permission of the
copyright owner,
Boosey and Hawkes, Inc.

Overture
1st Theme — S1393

2nd Theme — S1394

Minuet — S1395

The Fencing Master
1st Theme — S1396

2nd Theme — S1397

Entry & Dance of the Tailors
1st Theme — S1398

2nd Theme — S1399

Minuet of Lully
1st Theme — S1400

2nd Theme — S1401

Courante
1st Theme, A — S1402

1st Theme, B — S1403

2nd Theme — S1404

Entrance of Cleonte
1st Theme — S1405

2nd Theme — S1406

Intermezzo
(Prelude to Act II) — S1407

The Dinner
1st Theme — S1408

2nd Theme — S1409

3rd Theme — S1410

4th Theme — S1411

5th Theme — S1412

6th Theme
Dance of the Kitchen Boys — S1413

Burleske, Pft. & Orch. 1st Theme — S1414

2nd Theme — S1415

STRAUSS

3rd Theme — S1416
4th Theme — S1417
5th Theme — S1418

Don Juan, Op. 20, Orch.
1st Theme — S1419
2nd Theme — S1420
3rd Theme — S1421
4th Theme — S1422
5th Theme — S1423
6th Theme — S1424

Don Quixote, Op. 35, Orch.
1st Theme — S1425
2nd Theme — S1426
3rd Theme — S1427
4th Theme — S1428
5th Theme, A — S1429
5th Theme, B — S1430

Ein Heldenleben, Op. 40, Orch.
By permission of Associated Music Publishers, Inc.
1st Theme — S1431
2nd Theme, A — S1432
2nd Theme, B — S1433
2nd Theme, C — S1434
3rd Theme — S1435

4th Theme — S1436

5th Theme — S1437

6th Theme — S1438

7th Theme — S1439

8th Theme — S1440

9th Theme — S1441

Rêverie, Op. 9, No. 4,
Pft. or Pft. & Vn. — S1442

Der Rosenkavalier, Waltz Themes,
Op. 59.
By permission of the copyright
owner, Boosey and Hawkes, Inc. — S1443

S1444

S1445

S1446

S1447

Salome, Opera,
Op. 54
By permission of the
copyright owner,
Boosey and Hawkes, Inc.
Dance of the
Seven Veils
1st Theme — S1448

2nd Theme — S1449

3rd Theme — S1450

4th Theme — S1451

5th Theme — S1452

Sonata in E Flat,
Op. 18, Vn. & Pft.
1st Movement
1st Theme
A — S1453

1st Movement
1st Theme
B — S1454

1st Movement
2nd Theme — S1455

2nd Theme — S1476

3rd Theme — S1477

4th Theme — S1478

5th Theme — S1479

STRAVINSKY, Igor (1882-   )

Apollon Musagètes, Ballet
By permission of the copyright owner, Boosey and Hawkes, Inc.

Birth of Apollo, Prologue 1st Theme, A — S1480

1st Theme, B — S1481

2nd Theme — S1482

Variation of Apollo — S1483

Pas d'Action 1st Theme — S1484

2nd Theme — S1485

Variation of Calliope — S1486

Variation of Polymnie — S1487

Variation of Terpsichore — S1488

Pas de Deux — S1489

Coda — S1490

Apotheosis — S1491

Le Baiser de la Fée, Ballet on Tschaikovsky Themes
By permission of the copyright owner, Boosey and Hawkes, Inc.

1st Movement Berceuse de la Tempête 1st Theme — S1492

1st Movement 2nd Theme — S1493

2nd Movement Fête au Village 1st Theme — S1494

Capriccio
Pft. & Orch.
By permission of the
copyright owner,
Boosey and Hawkes, Inc.

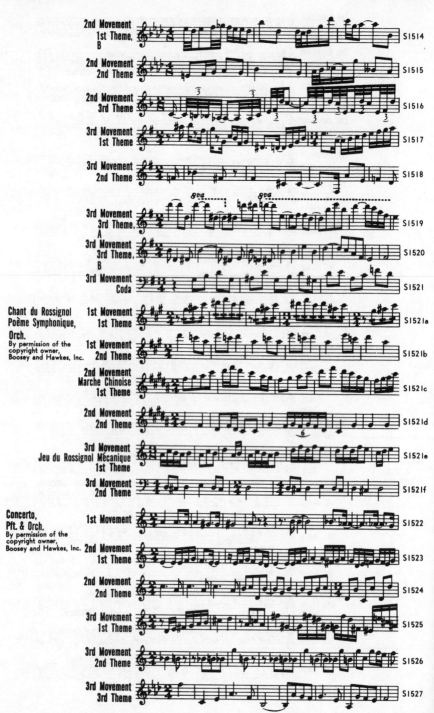

Concerto in D, Vn. & Orch.
By permission of Associated Music Publishers, Inc.

1st Movement 1st Theme — S1528

1st Movement 2nd Theme, A — S1529

1st Movement 2nd Theme, B — S1530

2nd Movement Aria, A — S1531

3rd Movement Aria, B — S1532

4th Movement Intro. — S1533

4th Movement Theme — S1534

Dumbarton Oaks Concerto, Chamber Orch.
By permission of Associated Music Publishers, Inc.

1st Movement 1st Theme — S1534a

1st Movement 2nd Theme — S1534b

1st Movement 3rd Theme — S1534c

2nd Movement — S1534d

3rd Movement 1st Theme — S1534e

3rd Movement 1st Theme — S1534f

3rd Movement 2nd Theme — S1534g

The Fire Bird Ballet Suite, Orch.
By permission of the copyright holders, J. & W. Chester, Ltd., 11 Great Marlborough Street, London, W. 1.

Intro. — S1535

Ronde des Princesses 1st Theme — S1536

2nd Theme — S1537

Dance of Kastchei — S1538

Berceuse — S1539

Finale — S1540

Octet for Fl., Cl.,
2 Fg., 2 Trpts.,
2 Tromb.
By permission of the
copyright owner,
Boosey and Hawkes, Inc.

1st Movement Intro. — S1541
1st Movement 1st Theme — S1542
1st Movement 2nd Theme — S1543
2nd Movement Theme & Variations — S1544
3rd Movement Finale — S1545

Pastorale
Vn. & Pft.
By permission of the copyright
owner, Boosey and Hawkes, Inc.

Intro. — S1546
Theme — S1547

Petrouchka, Suite
Ballet, Orch.
By permission of the
copyright owner,
Boosey and Hawkes, Inc.

Tableau 1 1st Theme — S1548
2nd Theme — S1549
3rd Theme — S1550
4th Theme — S1551
Le Tour de Passe-passe — S1552
Danse Russe 1st Theme — S1553
2nd Theme — S1554
3rd Theme — S1555
Tableau 2 Chez Petrouchka 1st Theme — S1556
2nd Theme, A — S1557
2nd Theme, B — S1558
Tableau 3 Chez le Maure — S1559
Danse de la Ballerina — S1560

Waltz
La Ballerina et le Maure
1st Theme — S1561

2nd Theme, A — S1562

2nd Theme, B — S1563

Tableau 4
Fête De Grand Semaine
Dance of the Nurses
1st Theme — S1564

2nd Theme — S1565

The Peasant and the Bear — S1566

The Merchant — S1567

Dance of the Gypsies — S1568

Dance of the Coachmen — S1569

Dance of the Maskers — S1570

General Dance — S1571

Pulcinella
Ballet after Pergolesi, Orch.
By permission of the
copyright owner,
Boosey and Hawkes, Inc.
Overture — S1572

Larghetto — S1573

Gavotte — S1574

Finale — S1575

Le Sacre du Printemps
(Rites of Spring), Orch.
By permission of the copyright
owner, Boosey and Hawkes, Inc.
Part I,
Adoration of
the Earth
Intro. — S1576

Dance of the Adolescents
1st Theme — S1577

2nd Theme — S1578

3rd Theme — S1579

Rounds of Spring — S1580

1st Movement
3rd Theme  S1601

1st Movement
4th Theme S1602

2nd Movement
1st Theme S1603

2nd Movement
2nd Theme S1604

2nd Movement
3rd Theme S1605

3rd Movement
1st Theme S1606

3rd Movement
2nd Theme S1607

3rd Movement
3rd Theme S1608

SUK, Joseph (1874-1935)

Serenade, Op. 6
Str. Orch.
By permission of
Associated Music
Publishers, Inc.

1st Movement
1st Theme  S1609

1st Movement
2nd Theme S1610

2nd Movement
1st Theme S1611

2nd Movement
2nd Theme S1612

3rd Movement
1st Theme S1613

3rd Movement
2nd Theme S1614

4th Movement S1615

SUPPÉ, Franz von (1819-1895)

Banditenstreiche,
Overture

1st Theme 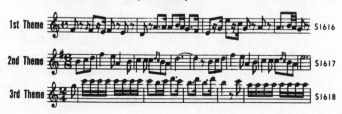 S1616

2nd Theme S1617

3rd Theme S1618

5th Theme — S1634

Pique Dame, Overture — 1st Theme — S1635

2nd Theme — S1636

3rd Theme — S1637

4th Theme — S1638

Poet and Peasant, Overture — Intro. — S1639

1st Theme, A — S1640

1st Theme, B — S1641

2nd Theme, A — S1642

2nd Theme, B — S1643

3rd Theme — S1644

4th Theme — S1645

Die Schöne Galathe, Overture — 1st Theme — S1646

2nd Theme — S1647

2nd Theme — S1648

3rd Theme — S1649

SVENDSEN, Johan Severin (1840-1911)

Carnival in Paris, Op. 9, Orch. — 1st Theme — S1650

2nd Theme — S1651

3rd Theme — S1652

Festival Polonaise, Op. 12, Orch.
By permission of Associated Music Publishers, Inc.
- 1st Theme — S1653
- 2nd Theme — S1654
- 3rd Theme — S1655

Norwegian Artists' Carnival, Op. 14, Orch.
- 1st Theme — S1656
- 2nd Theme — Italian Folk Song — S1657
- 3rd Theme — Norwegian Dance Tune — S1658

Romance, Op. 26, Vn. & Pft.
- 1st Theme — S1659
- 2nd Theme — S1660

SZYMANOWSKI, Karol (1883-1937)

The Fountain of Arethusa, Op. 30, No. 1, Vn. & Pft.
By permission of Associated Music Publishers, Inc.
- 1st Theme — S1661
- 2nd Theme — S1662

Mazurkas, Pft.
By permission of Associated Music Publishers, Inc.
Op. 50, No. 1
- 1st Theme — S1663
- 2nd Theme — S1664

Op. 50, No. 2
- 1st Theme — S1665
- 2nd Theme — S1666

Notturno, Op. 28, No. 1, Vn. & Pft.
By permission of Associated Music Publishers, Inc.
- 1st Theme — S1667
- 2nd Theme — S1668

Romance, Op. 23, Vn. & Pft.
By permission of Associated Music Publishers, Inc.
- 1st Theme — S1669
- 2nd Theme — S1670

Tarantella, Op. 28, No. 2, Vn. & Pft.
By permission of Associated Music Publishers, Inc.
- 1st Theme — S1671

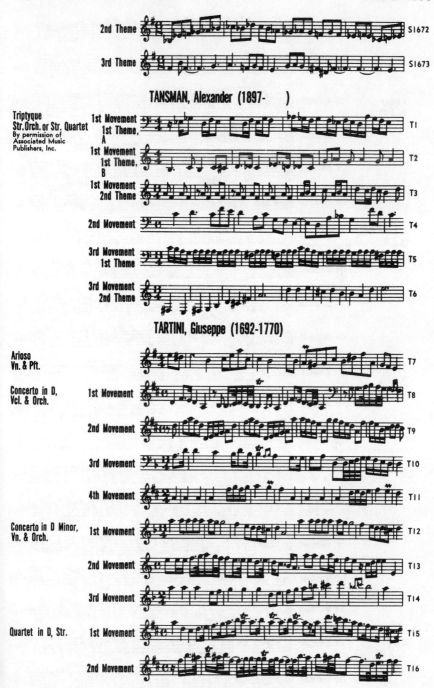

2nd Theme S1672

3rd Theme S1673

TANSMAN, Alexander (1897-   )

Triptyque
Str. Orch. or Str. Quartet
By permission of
Associated Music
Publishers, Inc.

1st Movement
1st Theme, A   T1

1st Movement
1st Theme, B   T2

1st Movement
2nd Theme   T3

2nd Movement   T4

3rd Movement
1st Theme   T5

3rd Movement
2nd Theme   T6

TARTINI, Giuseppe (1692-1770)

Arioso
Vn. & Pft.   T7

Concerto in D,
Vcl. & Orch.
1st Movement   T8

2nd Movement   T9

3rd Movement   T10

4th Movement   T11

Concerto in D Minor,
Vn. & Orch.
1st Movement   T12

2nd Movement   T13

3rd Movement   T14

Quartet in D, Str.
1st Movement   T15

2nd Movement   T16

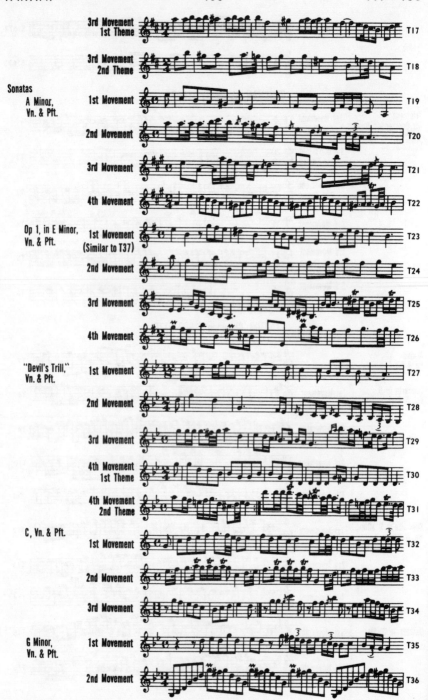

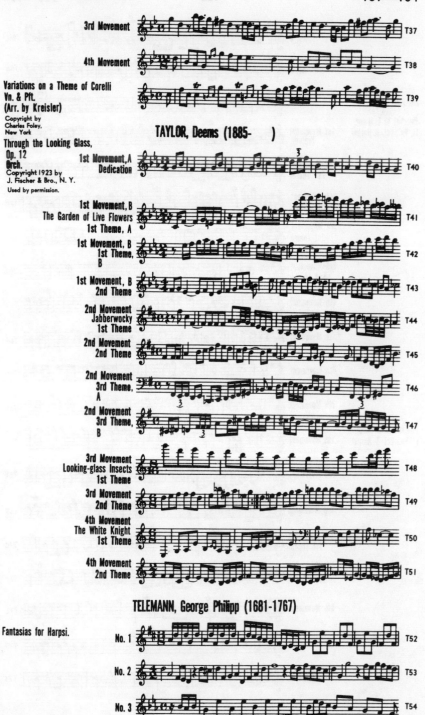

3rd Movement — T37

4th Movement — T38

Variations on a Theme of Corelli
Vn. & Pft.
(Arr. by Kreisler)
Copyright by
Charles Foley,
New York

— T39

Through the Looking Glass,
Op. 12
Orch.
Copyright 1923 by
J. Fischer & Bro., N. Y.
Used by permission.

TAYLOR, Deems (1885-   )

1st Movement, A
Dedication — T40

1st Movement, B
The Garden of Live Flowers
1st Theme, A — T41

1st Movement, B
1st Theme,
B — T42

1st Movement, B
2nd Theme — T43

2nd Movement
Jabberwocky
1st Theme — T44

2nd Movement
2nd Theme — T45

2nd Movement
3rd Theme,
A — T46

2nd Movement
3rd Theme,
B — T47

3rd Movement
Looking-glass Insects
1st Theme — T48

3rd Movement
2nd Theme — T49

4th Movement
The White Knight
1st Theme — T50

4th Movement
2nd Theme — T51

TELEMANN, George Philipp (1681-1767)

Fantasias for Harpsi.

No. 1 — T52

No. 2 — T53

No. 3 — T54

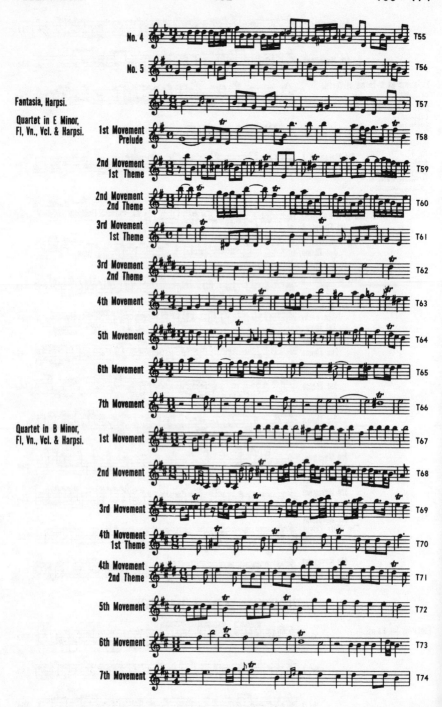

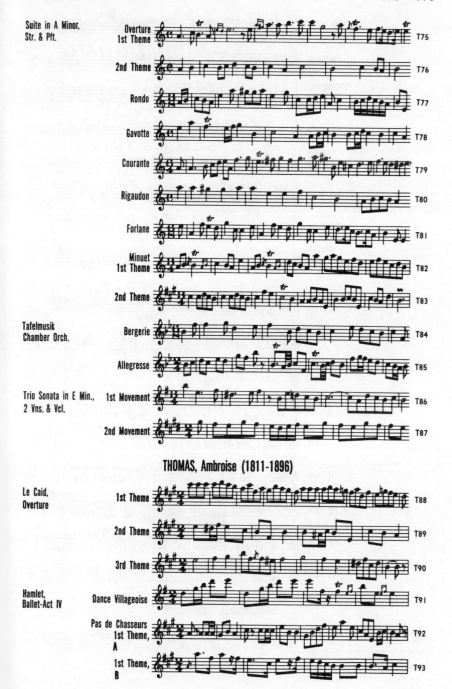

Suite in A Minor, Str. & Pft.

Overture 1st Theme — T75

2nd Theme — T76

Rondo — T77

Gavotte — T78

Courante — T79

Rigaudon — T80

Forlane — T81

Minuet 1st Theme — T82

2nd Theme — T83

Tafelmusik Chamber Orch.

Bergerie — T84

Allegresse — T85

Trio Sonata in E Min., 2 Vns. & Vcl.

1st Movement — T86

2nd Movement — T87

THOMAS, Ambroise (1811-1896)

Le Caid, Overture

1st Theme — T88

2nd Theme — T89

3rd Theme — T90

Hamlet, Ballet-Act IV

Dance Villageoise — T91

Pas de Chasseurs 1st Theme, A — T92

1st Theme, B — T93

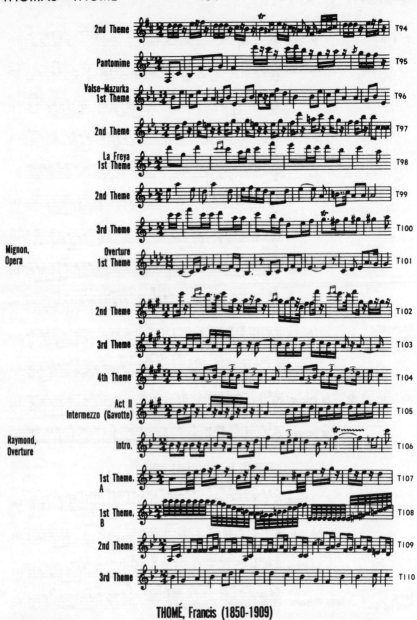

2nd Theme   T94

Pantomime   T95

Valse-Mazurka 1st Theme   T96

2nd Theme   T97

La Freya 1st Theme   T98

2nd Theme   T99

3rd Theme   T100

Mignon, Opera   Overture 1st Theme   T101

2nd Theme   T102

3rd Theme   T103

4th Theme   T104

Act II Intermezzo (Gavotte)   T105

Raymond, Overture   Intro.   T106

1st Theme, A   T107

1st Theme, B   T108

2nd Theme   T109

3rd Theme   T110

THOMÉ, Francis (1850-1909)

Simple Confession (Simple Aveu)

Permission for reprint granted by Durand & Cie, Paris. Elkan-Vogel Co., Inc. Philadelphia, Copyright Owners.

T111

THOMSON, Virgil (1896-)

Filling Station,
Ballet
Copyright by Arrow
Music Press, Inc., N. Y.

No. 1
Intro.
1st Theme   TIIIa

2nd Theme   TIIIb

No. 2
Mac's Dance   TIIIc

No. 3
Motorist and Mac   TIIId

No. 4
Truck Drivers' Dance   TIIIe

2nd Theme   TIIIf

No. 7
Tango   TIIIg

No. 8
Waltz
1st Theme   TIIIh

2nd Theme   TIIIi

No. 9
The Big Apple   TIIIj

No. 11
The Chase   TIIIk

The Plow That
Broke the Plains
(Suite from film score)
Orch.
By permission of
Music Press, Inc.

1st Movement
Prelude
1st Theme   TII2

1st Movement
2nd Theme   TII3

2nd Movement
Pastorale
(Grass)   TII4

3rd Movement
Cattle   TII5

4th Movement
Blues (Speculation)
1st Theme   TII6

4th Movement
2nd Theme   TII7

5th Movement
Drought
(6th Movement repeats
previous Themes)   TII8

Quartet, No. 2
Str.
Copyright by Arrow
Music Press, Inc., N. Y.

1st Movement
1st Theme   TII8a

1st Movement 2nd Theme — T118b

2nd Movement 1st Theme — T118c

2nd Movement 2nd Theme — T118d

3rd Movement — T118e

4th Movement 1st Theme — T118f

4th Movement 2nd Theme — T118g

The River
Film Suite
Small Orch.
By permission of
the Composer

1st Movement
The Old South
1st Theme — T118h

1st Movement 2nd Theme — T118i

1st Movement 3rd Theme — T118j

1st Movement 4th Theme — T118k

Intro.
2nd Movement
Industrial Expansion
in the Mississippi Valley — T118l

2nd Movement
1st Theme
(Hot Time in the Old Town Tonight) — T118m

2nd Movement
2nd Theme
(Oh, My Name is Samuel Hall) — T118n

3rd Movement
Soil Erosion & Floods — T118o

4th Movement
Finale
1st Theme — T118p

4th Movement
2nd Theme — T118q

4th Movement
3rd Theme — T118r

TOCH, Ernst (1887-   )

The Chinese Flute,
Op. 29, Chamber Orch.
(2nd & 4th Movements
are Vocal)
By permission of Associated
Music Publishers, Inc.

1st Movement — T119

3rd Movement
1st Theme — T120

TSCHAIKOVSKY, Peter Ilyich (1840-1893)

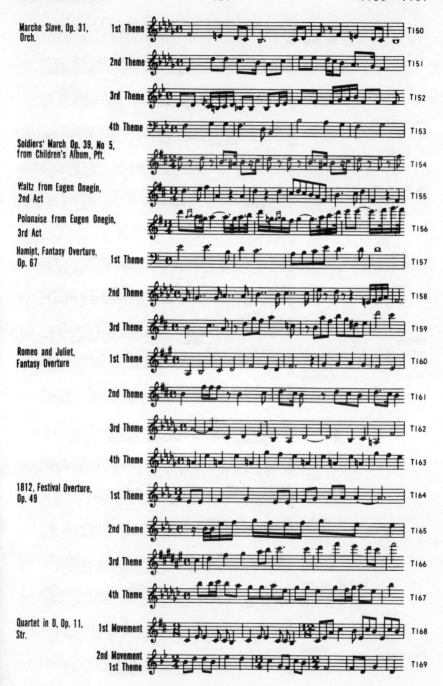

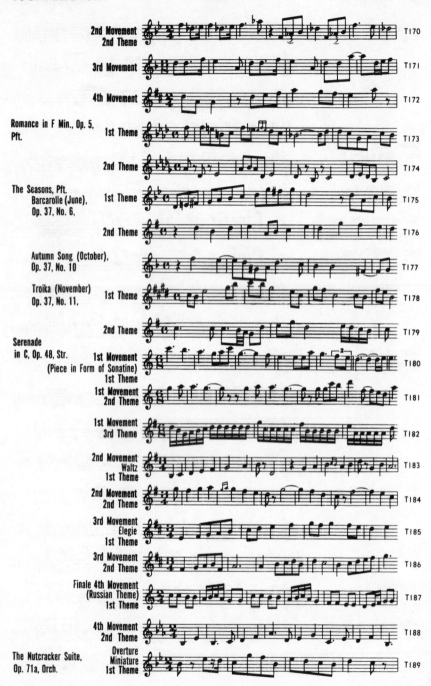

5th Movement Waltz — T210

Swan Lake, Suite from the Ballet, Op. 20a, Orch.
1st Movement Intro. — T211

2nd Movement Waltz — T212

3rd Movement Dance of the Swans — T213

4th Movement Hungarian Dance and Czardas 1st Theme — T214

4th Movement 2nd Theme — T215

Symphony No. 1, Op. 13, "Rêverie d'Hiver"
1st Movement 1st Theme, A — T216

1st Movement 1st Theme, B — T217

1st Movement 2nd Theme — T218

2nd Movement 1st Theme — T219

2nd Movement 2nd Theme, A — T220

2nd Movement 2nd Theme, B — T221

3rd Movement 1st Theme — T222

3rd Movement 2nd Theme — T223

4th Movement 1st Theme — T224

4th Movement 2nd Theme — T225

Symphony No. 2, in C Minor, Op. 17, "Little Russia"
1st Movement 1st Theme — T226

1st Movement 2nd Theme — T227

1st Movement 3rd Theme, A — T228

1st Movement 3rd Theme, B — T229

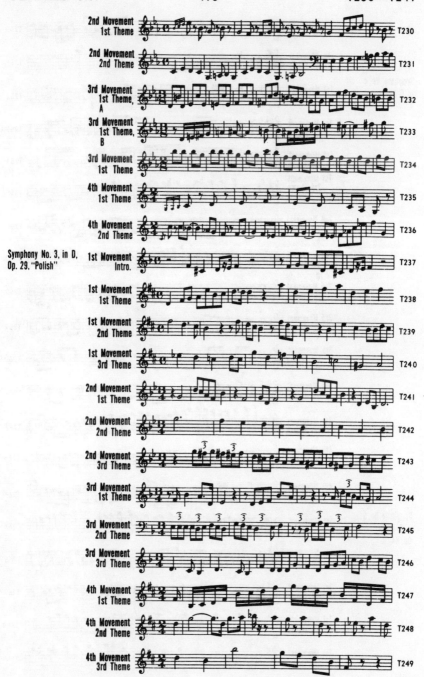

Symphony No. 4,
in F Minor.
Op. 36

Symphony No. 5,
in E Minor,
Op. 64

5th Movement
1st Theme — T250

5th Movement
2nd Theme — T251

1st Movement
Intro. — T252

1st Movement
1st Theme — T253

1st Movement
2nd Theme — T254

1st Movement
3rd Theme
(Variant of T253) — T255

2nd Movement
1st Theme,
A — T256

2nd Movement
1st Theme,
B — T257

2nd Movement
2nd Theme — T258

3rd Movement
1st Theme,
A — T259

3rd Movement
1st Theme,
B — T260

3rd Movement
2nd Theme — T261

4th Movement
1st Theme — T262

4th Movement
2nd Theme — T263

4th Movement
3rd Theme — T264

1st Movement
Intro. — T265

1st Movement
1st Theme — T266

1st Movement
2nd Theme — T267

1st Movement
3rd Theme — T268

1st Movement
4th Theme — T269

2nd Movement 1st Theme — T270

2nd Movement 2nd Theme — T271

2nd Movement 3rd Theme — T272

3rd Movement 1st Theme — T273

3rd Movement 2nd Theme — T274

4th Movement 1st Theme — T275

4th Movement 2nd Theme — T276

4th Movement 3rd Theme — T277

4th Movement 4th Theme — T278

4th Movement 5th Theme — T279

Symphony No. 6,
in B Minor, Op. 74
"Pathétique"
By permission of
Associated Music
Publishers, Inc.

1st Movement Intro. — T280

1st Movement 1st Theme — T281

1st Movement 2nd Theme — T282

1st Movement 3rd Theme — T283

2nd Movement 1st Theme — T284

2nd Movement 2nd Theme — T285

3rd Movement 1st Theme — T286

3rd Movement 2nd Theme — T287

3rd Movement 3rd Theme — T288

4th Movement 1st Theme — T289

4th Movement / 2nd Theme   T290

Theme & Variations, Op. 19, No. 6, Pft.   T291

Trio in A Min., Op. 50, Pft., Vn. & Vcl.   1st Movement / 1st Theme   T292

1st Movement / 2nd Theme   T293

2nd Movement / Theme & Variations   T294

TURINA, Joaquin (1882-   )

Danzas Fantásticas, Orch. or Pft.   Ensueño / 1st Theme, A   T295

1st Theme, B   T296

2nd Theme   T297

3rd Theme   T298

Orgia / 1st Theme   T299

2nd Theme   T300

Fandanguillo, Guitar / By permission of Associated Music Publishers, Inc.   1st Theme   T301

2nd Theme   T302

Femmes d'Espagne (Mujeres Españolas) / Copyright by Editions Salabert / Editions Salabert, 22 Rue Chaucat, Paris Salabert, Inc., 1 East 57 St., N. Y.   L'Andalouse Sentimentale / 1st Theme   T303

2nd Theme   T304

3rd Theme   T305

La Oración del Torero / Quart., Str.   1st Theme   T306

2nd Theme   T307

3rd Theme   T308

4th Theme — T309

La Procésion del Rocío, Pft. or Orch.
Copyright by Editions Salabert
Editions Salabert, 22 Rue
Chaucat, Paris Salabert, Inc.,
I East 57 St., N. Y.

Triana
en Fête
1st Theme — T310

2nd Theme — T311

3rd Theme — T312

La Procésion
1st Theme — T313

2nd Theme — T314

Sevilla
Orch.

1st Movement
Sous les Orangers
1st Theme — T315

1st Movement
2nd Theme — T316

2nd Movement
Le Jeudi Saint et Procession
1st Theme — T317

2nd Movement
2nd Theme — T318

3rd Movement
La Feria
1st Theme — T319

3rd Movement
2nd Theme — T320

VARDELL, Charles (1893-   )

Joe Clark Steps Out, Orch.
Copyright 1937 by Eastman
School of Music,
Rochester, N. Y.

Theme, A — V1

Theme, B — V2

VAUGHAN WILLIAMS, Ralph (1872-   )

Concerto Accademico
in D Min.,
Vn. & Str. Orch.
Copyright by the
Oxford University Press
Reproduced by permission.

1st Movement
1st Theme — V3

1st Movement
2nd Theme — V4

1st Movement
3rd Theme — V5

2nd Movement — V6

3rd Movement
1st Theme — V7

3rd Movement
2nd Theme — V8

Fantasia on
a Theme by Tallis
Copyright 1921 by
Goodwin & Tabb,
Ltd., London.

1st Theme,
A — V9

2nd Theme
B — V10

The Lark Ascending
Vn. & Orch.
Copyright by the Oxford
University Press.
Reproduced by permission.

1st Theme — V11

2nd Theme — V12

3rd Theme — V13

4th Theme — V14

A London Symphony
By permission of Galaxy
Music Corp., N. Y.,
Sole Agents in the U. S. A.
for Stainer and Bell, Ltd.,
London: Copyright 1920
by R. Vaughan Williams.

1st Movement
Intro. — V15

1st Movement
1st Theme — V16

1st Movement
2nd Theme — V17

1st Movement
3rd Theme — V18

1st Movement
4th Theme,
A — V19

1st Movement
4th Theme,
B — V20

1st Movement
5th Theme
(Variant of Intro.) — V21

2nd Movement
1st Theme — V22

2nd Movement
2nd Theme — V23

2nd Movement
3rd Theme — V24

2nd Movement
4th Theme — V25

3rd Movement
1st Theme — V26

Symphony No. 4,
in F Minor
Copyright by the
Oxford University Press.
Reproduced by permission.

The Wasps
(Aristophanes)
Orch.

3rd Movement 2nd Theme — V27
3rd Movement 3rd Theme — V28
4th Movement 1st Theme — V29
4th Movement 2nd Theme — V30
1st Movement 1st Theme — V31
1st Movement 2nd Theme — V32
1st Movement 3rd Theme — V33
1st Movement 4th Theme — V34
2nd Movement — V35
3rd Movement 1st Theme — V36
3rd Movement 2nd Theme — V37
3rd Movement 3rd Theme — V38
4th Movement 1st Theme, A — V39
4th Movement 1st Theme, B — V40
4th Movement 2nd Theme — V41
1st Movement Overture 1st Theme — V42
1st Movement 2nd Theme — V43
1st Movement 3rd Theme — V44
2nd Movement Entr'acte — V45
3rd Movement March Past of the Kitchen Utensils 1st Theme — V46

3rd Movement 2nd Theme — V47
4th Movement Entr'acte, 1st Theme A — V48
4th Movement 1st Theme B — V49
5th Movement Ballet & Final Tableau 1st Theme — V50
5th Movement 2nd Theme — V51
5th Movement 3rd Theme — V52
5th Movement 4th Theme — V53
5th Movement 5th Theme — V54
5th Movement 6th Theme — V55
5th Movement 7th Theme — V56

VERACINI, Francesco (1690-1750)

Largo, Vn. & Pft. — V57
Sonata in E Minor Vn. & Pft. — 1st Movement Intro. — V58
1st Movement Theme — V59
2nd Movement — V60
3rd Movement Minuet — V61
4th Movement Gavotte — V62
5th Movement Gigue — V63

VERDI, Giuseppe (1813-1901)

Aïda, Opera — Act I, Dance of the Priestesses 1st Theme — V64

2nd Theme   V65

Act II
Dance of the Moorish Slaves   V66

March   V67

Ballet
1st Theme   V68

2nd Theme   V69

3rd Theme   V70

Un Ballo in Maschera,
Overture   1st Theme   V71

2nd Theme   V72

3rd Theme   V73

La Forza del Destino,
Overture   1st Theme   V74

2nd Theme   V75

3rd Theme   V76

4th Theme   V77

5th Theme   V78

Nabucodonosor
Overture   Intro.   V79

1st Theme   V80

2nd Theme   V81

3rd Theme   V82

Quartet in E Minor,
Str.   1st Movement
1st Theme   V83

1st Movement
2nd Theme   V84

2nd Movement — V85

3rd Movement 1st Theme — V86

3rd Movement 2nd Theme — V87

4th Movement — V88

La Traviata, Opera

Act I, Prelude 1st Theme — V89

2nd Theme — V90

I Vespri Siciliani, Overture

1st Theme — V91

2nd Theme — V92

VIEUXTEMPS, Henri (1820-1881)

Ballade et Polonaise Op. 38 Vn. & Pft.

1st Theme — V93

2nd Theme — V94

3rd Theme — V95

4th Theme — V96

5th Theme — V97

Concerto No. 4 in D Minor, Vn. & Orch.

1st Movement 1st Theme, A — V98

1st Movement 1st Theme, B — V99

1st Movement 2nd Theme — V100

2nd Movement 1st Theme — V101

2nd Movement 2nd Theme — V102

3rd Movement 1st Theme — V103

3rd Movement 2nd Theme — V104

4th Movement 1st Theme — V105

4th Movement 2nd Theme — V106

VILLA-LOBOS, Heitor (1881-)

Bachianas-Brasileiras, No. 4, Pft. 1st Theme — V107

2nd Theme — V108

3rd Theme — V109

Saudades das Selvas Brasileiras, Pft.
By permission of Associated Music Publishers, Inc.
No. 1 — V110

No. 2 — V111

VINCI, Leonardo (1690-1730)

Sonata in D, Fl. & Harpsi. 1st Movement — V112

2nd Movement — V113

3rd Movement — V114

4th Movement — V115

5th Movement — V116

VIOTTI, Giovanni (1753-1824)

Concerto No. 22, in A Minor, Vn. & Orch.
1st Movement 1st Theme — V117

1st Movement 2nd Theme — V118

1st Movement 3rd Theme — V119

2nd Movement 1st Theme — V120

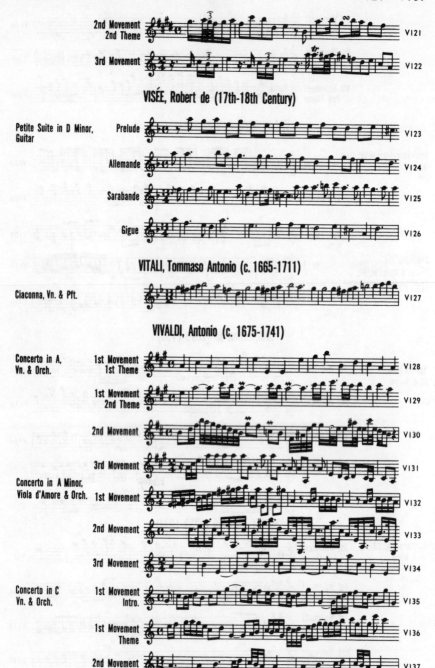

2nd Movement 2nd Theme — V121

3rd Movement — V122

VISÉE, Robert de (17th-18th Century)

Petite Suite in D Minor, Guitar — Prelude — V123

Allemande — V124

Sarabande — V125

Gigue — V126

VITALI, Tommaso Antonio (c. 1665-1711)

Ciaconna, Vn. & Pft. — V127

VIVALDI, Antonio (c. 1675-1741)

Concerto in A, Vn. & Orch. — 1st Movement 1st Theme — V128

1st Movement 2nd Theme — V129

2nd Movement — V130

3rd Movement — V131

Concerto in A Minor, Viola d'Amore & Orch. — 1st Movement — V132

2nd Movement — V133

3rd Movement — V134

Concerto in C Vn. & Orch. — 1st Movement Intro. — V135

1st Movement Theme — V136

2nd Movement — V137

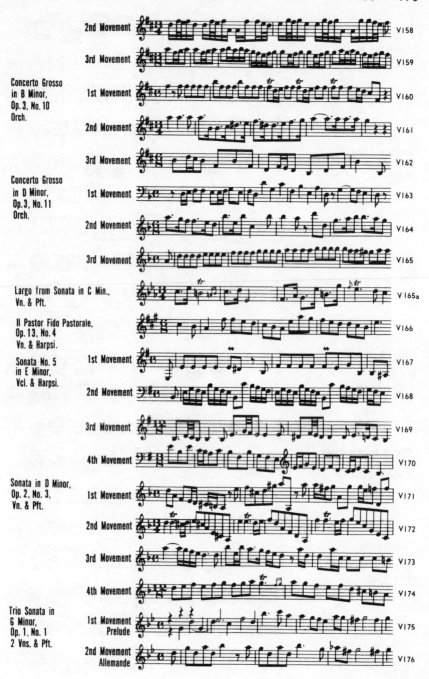

3rd Movement — V177

4th Movement Capriccio — V178

5th Movement Gavotte — V179

WAGENSEIL, Georg Christoph (1715-1777)

Symphony in D

1st Movement 1st Theme — W1

1st Movement 2nd Theme — W2

2nd Movement — W3

3rd Movement — W4

WAGNER, Richard (1813-1883)

Albumblatt, Pft. — W5

A Faust Overture — 1st Theme — W6

2nd Theme — W7

3rd Theme — W8

4th Theme — W9

5th Theme — W10

Die Feen, Opera — Overture 1st Theme — W11

2nd Theme — W12

3rd Theme — W13

4th Theme — W14

The Flying Dutchman, Opera — Overture 1st Theme — W15

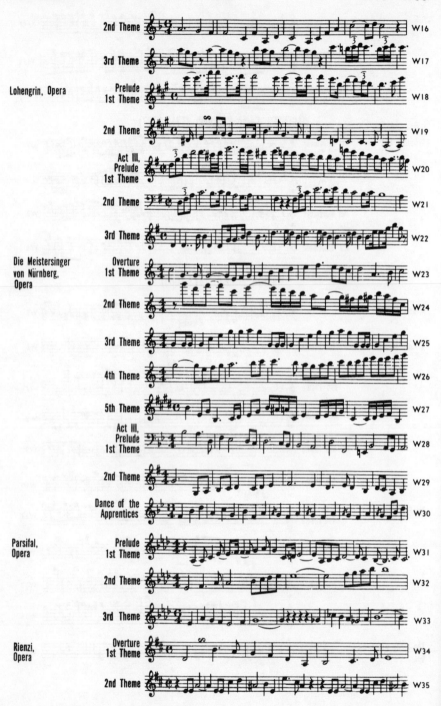

Der Ring Der Nibelungen
(The Ring of the Nibelungs)
Das Rheingold,
Opera   Prelude   W36

Entrance of the
Gods Into Valhalla
1st Theme   W37

2nd Theme   W38

Die Walküre,
Opera   Ride of the Valkyries
1st Theme   W39

2nd Theme   W40

Magic Fire Music
1st Theme   W41

2nd Theme   W42

Waldweben
Siegfried, Opera (Forest Murmurs)
1st Theme   W43

2nd Theme   W44

3rd Theme   W45

4th Theme   W46

5th Theme   W47

6th Theme   W48

Götterdämmerung   Siegfried's
Opera   Rhine Journey
1st Theme   W49

2nd Theme   W50

3rd Theme   W51

4th Theme   W52

5th Theme   W53

6th Theme   W54

Siegfried's
Funeral Music
1st Theme   W55

7th Theme — W75
8th Theme — W76
Act II, March Intro. — W77
1st Theme — W78
2nd Theme — W79
3rd Theme — W80
Bacchanale (Venusberg Music) 1st Theme — W81
2nd Theme — W82
3rd Theme — W83
4th Theme — W84
Tristan und Isolde, Opera — Prelude 1st Theme — W85
2nd Theme — W86
Act III Prelude 1st Theme — W87
2nd Theme — W88
3rd Theme — W89
Love Death 1st Theme — W90
2nd Theme — W91

WALDTEUFEL, Emil (1837-1915)

Dolores Waltzes
Op. 170, Orch.
Courtesy Carl Fischer,
Inc., N.Y.

No. 1 1st Theme — W92
2nd Theme — W93

No. 2   W94

No. 3   W95

No. 4 1st Theme   W96

2nd Theme   W97

España, Waltzes Op. 286, Orch. Courtesy Carl Fischer, Inc., N. Y.

No. 1 1st Theme   W98

2nd Theme   W99

No. 2 1st Theme   W100

2nd Theme   W101

No. 3 1st Theme   W102

2nd Theme   W103

No. 4 1st Theme   W104

2nd Theme   W105

Estudiantina, Waltzes Op. 191, Orch. Courtesy Carl Fischer, Inc., N. Y.

No. 1 1st Theme   W106

2nd Theme   W107

No. 2 1st Theme   W108

2nd Theme   W109

No. 3 1st Theme   W110

2nd Theme   W111

No. 4 1st Theme   W112

2nd Theme   W113

Frühlingskinder Waltz (Violettes), Op. 148 Orch.
1st Theme   W114
2nd Theme   W115
3rd Theme   W116
4th Theme   W117

Ganz Allerliebst (Très Jolie), Waltz Op. 159, Orch.
1st Theme   W118
2nd Theme   W119
3rd Theme   W120
4th Theme   W121

Immer Oder Nimmer (Toujours ou Jamais), Waltzes Op. 156, Orch.
No. 1   W122
No. 2 1st Theme   W123
2nd Theme   W124
No. 3 1st Theme   W125
2nd Theme   W126
No. 4   W127

Mein Traum, Waltzes, Op. 151, Orch.
No. 1   W128
No. 2 1st Theme   W129
2nd Theme   W130
No. 3 1st Theme   W131
2nd Theme   W132
No. 4   W133

Sirenenzauber (Sirens)
Waltzes, Op. 154
Orch.

No. 1 1st Theme — W134

2nd Theme — W135

No. 2 1st Theme — W136

2nd Theme — W137

No. 3 1st Theme — W138

2nd Theme — W139

No. 4 — W140

The Skaters, Waltzes
Op. 183, Orch.
Courtesy Carl Fischer, Inc., N. Y.

No. 1 1st Theme — W141

2nd Theme — W142

No. 2 1st Theme — W143

2nd Theme — W144

No. 3 1st Theme — W145

2nd Theme — W146

No. 4 — W147

WALLACE, William Vincent (1812-1865)

Maritana,
Overture

1st Theme — W148

2nd Theme — W149

3rd Theme — W150

4th Theme — W151

5th Theme — W152

WALTON, William Turner (1902-)

Concerto
Viola & Orch.
Copyright by the Oxford
University Press.
Reproduced by permission.

1st Movement 1st Theme — W153

1st Movement 2nd Theme — W154

2nd Movement 1st Theme — W155

2nd Movement 2nd Theme — W156

2nd Movement 3rd Theme — W157

3rd Movement 1st Theme — W158

3rd Movement 2nd Theme — W159

Concerto
Vn. & Orch.
Copyright by the Oxford
University Press.
Reproduced by permission.

1st Movement 1st Theme — W160

1st Movement 2nd Theme — W161

2nd Movement 1st Theme, A — W162

2nd Movement 1st Theme, B — W163

2nd Movement 2nd Theme — W164

2nd Movement 3rd Theme — W165

3rd Movement 1st Theme — W166

3rd Movement 2nd Theme — W167

Crown Imperial,
Coronation March,
Orch.
Copyright by the Oxford
University Press.
Reproduced by permission.

1st Theme — W168

2nd Theme — W169

3rd Theme — W170

4th Theme — W171

Façade, Suite No. 1, Orch.
Copyright by the Oxford University Press.
Reproduced by permission.

Polka 1st Theme — W172

2nd Theme — W173

3rd Theme — W174

Valse 1st Theme — W175

2nd Theme — W176

A Swiss Yodeling Song 1st Theme — W177

2nd Theme (Parody on William Tell) — W178

3rd Theme — W179

Tango-Pasodoble 1st Theme — W180

2nd Theme — W181

Tarantella-Sevillana 1st Theme — W182

2nd Theme — W183

Façade, Suite No. 2, Orch.
Copyright by the Oxford University Press.
Reproduced by permission.

Fanfare — W184

Scotch Rhapsody 1st Theme — W185

2nd Theme — W186

Country Dance — W187

Noche Española 1st Theme — W188

2nd Theme — W189

Popular Song — W190

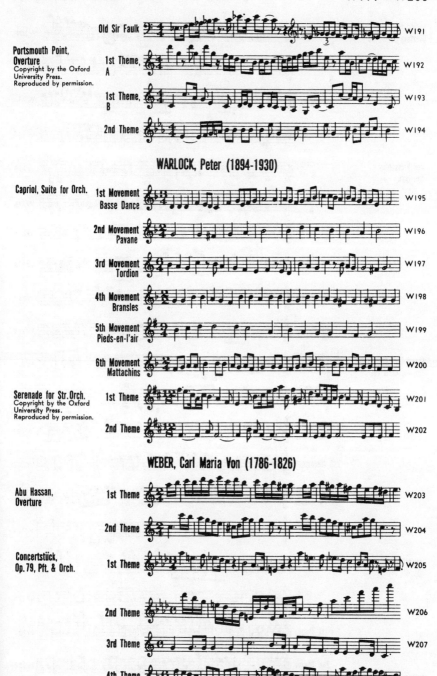

Old Sir Faulk — W191

Portsmouth Point, Overture
Copyright by the Oxford University Press. Reproduced by permission.

1st Theme, A — W192

1st Theme, B — W193

2nd Theme — W194

WARLOCK, Peter (1894-1930)

Capriol, Suite for Orch.

1st Movement Basse Dance — W195

2nd Movement Pavane — W196

3rd Movement Tordion — W197

4th Movement Bransles — W198

5th Movement Pieds-en-l'air — W199

6th Movement Mattachins — W200

Serenade for Str. Orch.
Copyright by the Oxford University Press. Reproduced by permission.

1st Theme — W201

2nd Theme — W202

WEBER, Carl Maria Von (1786-1826)

Abu Hassan, Overture

1st Theme — W203

2nd Theme — W204

Concertstück, Op. 79, Pft. & Orch.

1st Theme — W205

2nd Theme — W206

3rd Theme — W207

4th Theme — W208

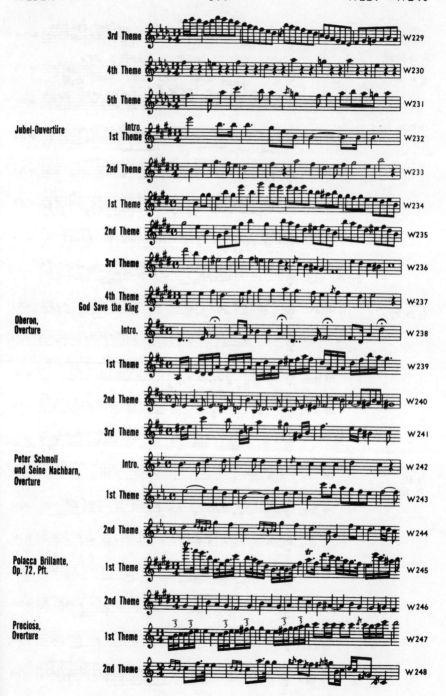

WEBER

3rd Theme — W229
4th Theme — W230
5th Theme — W231

Jubel-Ouvertüre
Intro.
1st Theme — W232
2nd Theme — W233
1st Theme — W234
2nd Theme — W235
3rd Theme — W236
4th Theme
God Save the King — W237

Oberon,
Overture
Intro. — W238
1st Theme — W239
2nd Theme — W240
3rd Theme — W241

Peter Schmoll
und Seine Nachbarn,
Overture
Intro. — W242
1st Theme — W243
2nd Theme — W244

Polacca Brillante,
Op. 72, Pft.
1st Theme — W245
2nd Theme — W246

Preciosa,
Overture
1st Theme — W247
2nd Theme — W248

3rd Theme	W 249
Rondo Brillant "La Gaite" Op. 62, Pft. — 1st Theme	W 250
2nd Theme	W 251
Sonata No. 1 in C, Op. 24, Pft. — 1st Movement	W 252
2nd Movement	W 253
3rd Movement	W 254
3rd Movement 2nd Theme	W 255
4th Movement (Perpetual Motion)	W 256
Sonata No. 2 in A Flat Op. 39. Pft. — 1st Movement	W 257
2nd Movement	W 258
3rd Movement 1st Theme	W 259
3rd Movement 2nd Theme	W 260
4th Movement	W 261
Trio in G Minor, Op. 63, Vn., Vcl. & Pft. — 1st Movement 1st Theme	W 262
1st Movement 2nd Theme	W 263
2nd Movement Intro.	W 264
2nd Movement Theme	W 265
3rd Movement	W 266
4th Movement 1st Theme	W 267
4th Movement 2nd Theme	W 268

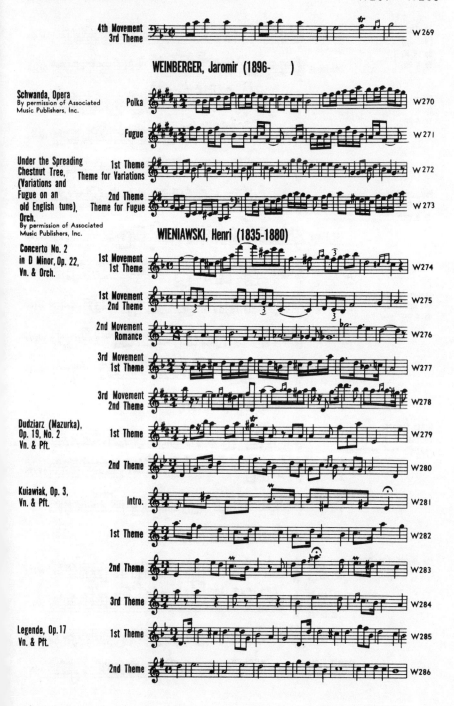

4th Movement
3rd Theme   W 269

WEINBERGER, Jaromir (1896-   )

Schwanda, Opera
By permission of Associated
Music Publishers, Inc.
   Polka   W270

   Fugue   W271

Under the Spreading
Chestnut Tree,
(Variations and
Fugue on an
old English tune),
Orch.
By permission of Associated
Music Publishers, Inc.
   1st Theme
Theme for Variations   W272

   2nd Theme
Theme for Fugue   W273

WIENIAWSKI, Henri (1835-1880)

Concerto No. 2
in D Minor, Op. 22,
Vn. & Orch.
   1st Movement
1st Theme   W274

   1st Movement
2nd Theme   W275

   2nd Movement
Romance   W276

   3rd Movement
1st Theme   W277

   3rd Movement
2nd Theme   W278

Dudziarz (Mazurka),
Op. 19, No. 2
Vn. & Pft.
   1st Theme   W279

   2nd Theme   W280

Kuiawiak, Op. 3,
Vn. & Pft.
   Intro.   W281

   1st Theme   W282

   2nd Theme   W283

   3rd Theme   W284

Legende, Op. 17
Vn. & Pft.
   1st Theme   W285

   2nd Theme   W286

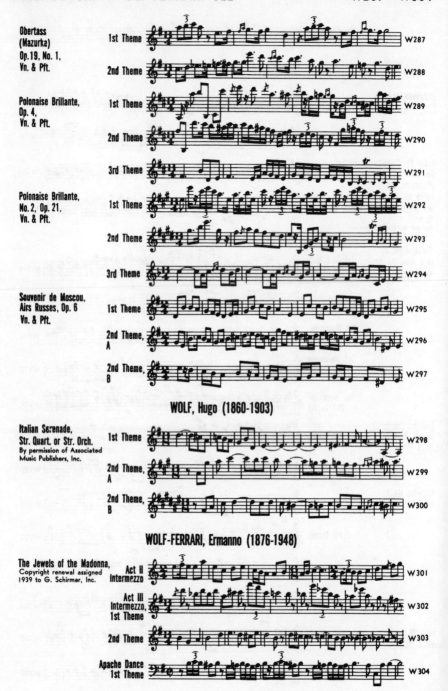

Obertass
(Mazurka)
Op.19, No. 1,
Vn. & Pft.   1st Theme   W287

        2nd Theme   W288

Polonaise Brillante,
Op. 4,
Vn. & Pft.   1st Theme   W289

        2nd Theme   W290

        3rd Theme   W291

Polonaise Brillante,
No.2, Op. 21,
Vn. & Pft.   1st Theme   W292

        2nd Theme   W293

        3rd Theme   W294

Souvenir de Moscou,
Airs Russes, Op. 6
Vn. & Pft.   1st Theme   W295

        2nd Theme,
        A   W296

        2nd Theme,
        B   W297

WOLF, Hugo (1860-1903)

Italian Serenade,
Str. Quart. or Str. Orch.
By permission of Associated
Music Publishers, Inc.   1st Theme   W298

        2nd Theme,
        A   W299

        2nd Theme,
        B   W300

WOLF-FERRARI, Ermanno (1876-1948)

The Jewels of the Madonna,
Copyright renewal assigned
1939 to G. Schirmer, Inc.   Act II
        Intermezzo   W301

        Act III
        Intermezzo,
        1st Theme   W302

        2nd Theme   W303

        Apache Dance
        1st Theme   W304

2nd Theme — W305

The Secret of Suzanne, Overture
Copyright 1910 by Josef Weinberger, Leipzig.

1st Theme — W306

2nd Theme — W307

3rd Theme — W308

YSAŸE, Théo (1865-1918)

Variations, Op. 10, 2 Pfts.
By permission of Associated Music Publishers, Inc.

Theme — Y1

ZANDONAI, Riccardo (1883-1944)

Giulietta E Romeo Symphonic Episode, Orch.
Copyright 1928 by G. Ricordi & Co., Inc.

1st Theme — Z1

2nd Theme — Z2

3rd Theme — Z3

ZARZYCKI, Alexander (1834-1895)

Mazurka, Op. 26, Vn. & Pft.
Copyright 1899 by Carl Fischer, Inc., N. Y.

1st Theme — Z4

2nd Theme — Z5

3rd Theme — Z6

ZIMBALIST, Efrem (1889-   )

Quartet in E Minor, Str.
Copyright 1938 by G. Schirmer, Inc.

1st Movement — Z7

2nd Movement 1st Theme — Z8

2nd Movement 2nd Theme — Z9

3rd Movement 1st Theme — Z10

3rd Movement 2nd Theme — Z11

4th Theme — Z12

TRANSPOSITION KEY

C	D	E	F	G	A	B	C	
C♯	D♯	E♯	F♯	G♯	A♯	B♯	C♯	} enharmonic[x]
D♭	E♭	F	G♭	A♭	B♭	C	D♭	
D	E	F♯	G	A	B	C♯	D	
E♭	F	G	A♭	B♭	C	D	E♭	
E	F♯	G♯	A	B	C♯	D♯	E	
F	G	A	B♭	C	D	E	F	
F♯	G♯	A♯	B	C♯	D♯	E♯	F♯	} enharmonic[x]
G♭	A♭	B♭	C♭	D♭	E♭	F	G♭	
G	A	B	C	D	E	F♯	G	
A♭	B♭	C	D♭	E♭	F	G	A♭	
A	B	C♯	D	E	F♯	G♯	A	
B♭	C	D	E♭	F	G	A	B♭	
B	C♯	D♯	E	F♯	G♯	A♯	B	} enharmonic[x]
C♭	D♭	E♭	F♭	G♭	A♭	B♭	C♭	

x Sounding the same but written differently.

This chart, though not necessary to the use of the notation key, should be helpful to the reader in explaining key relationships. For example, the fifth note in the key of C is G, its equivalent in the key of A is E.

HOW TO USE
THE NOTATION INDEX*

To identify a given theme, play it in the key of C and look it up under its note sequence using the following alphabet as a guide:

A A♭ A♯ **B** B♭ B♯ **C** C♭ C♯ **D** D♭ D♯
E E♭ E♯ **F** F♭ F♯ **G** G♭ G♯

Double flats follow flats; double sharps follow sharps.

The letter and number to the right of the definition indicate the place in the alphabetic section of the book where the theme may be found in its original key with the name of the composition and the composer.

Trills, turns, grace notes, and other embellishments are not taken into consideration here. However, it must be remembered that the appoggiatura is a regular note. In rare cases the grace note may be of such nature as to give the aural impression of being a regular note, in which case it is included in this section.

Keys are, in the main, determined by the harmonic structure of the opening bars, not by the cadence. The phrase that begins in C and goes to G is considered to be in C. Themes that may be analyzed in two keys are listed under both keys. There are themes that defy key definition. However, if the melodic line carries a key implication of its own, if only for the first few notes, that key is used. If the theme carries no such implication, then, for the sake of convenience, the first note is assumed to be C and the rest transposed accordingly.

Memory plays strange tricks and it is possible that the desired theme may be remembered inaccurately. We have occasionally listed a theme incorrectly as well as correctly if there is a popular misconception about it.

Each definition has been carried to six places except in the case of duplication. Duplicates are continued to a point of difference, but in no case to more than eleven places. When a note is repeated many times, for space conservation an exponent is used, *i.e.* G G G G G G $= G^6$.

H. B.

---

* Publisher's note: The Notation Index was conceived by Harold Barlow.

NOTATION INDEX

A A A A A A A A	S1554		A B B C G A	Z11
A A A A A A A G	I 125		A B B E E E	D61
A A A A A Ab	W144		A B C A B C	C587
A A A A A B	D70		A B C A C Bb	F221
A A A A A G	R371		A B C B A C	L195
A A A A B A	P91		A B C B A E	T221
A A A A B C B	H544		A B C B A G	W2
A A A A B C C	S182		A B C B C B	B505
A A A A B C D	S1579		A B C Bb Ab G	B1332
A A A A G A	C73		A B C C D C	W86
A A A A G G E	M166		A B C C# D D#	G282
A A A A G G F	G67		A B C D B C	C397
A A A A G# A	B434		A B C D C B	S1092
A A A B A G	S1497		A B C D E E	B454g
A A A B B B	S1349		A B C D E F G A	S1074
A A A B G G	K83		A B C D E F G F	R219
A A A G F E	S654		A B C D E F G G	S462
A A A G G G	B1646		A B C D Eb D	R5
A A B A B C A	A69		A B C E F G	S779
A A B A B C D	D106		A B C G A E	B488
A A B B B A	R425		A B C G F G	S678
A A C A G F	S1098		A B D C C B	M761
A A C Ab Ab Eb	H791		A B D G F G	B1117h
A A D A B G	S832		A B E B A B	T296
A A E A Ab Ab	L227		A B E G D G	R278
A A E E F G	D216		A B F B A Ab	H809
A A F F B D	S596		A B F G A B C	B1740
A A G A G E	D237		A B F G A B D	L253
A A G E D E	D420		A B F# A Ab G	G352
A A G F E D C B	B1312		A B G A B B	B1185
A A G F E D C D	M906		A B G A D C	S1578
A A G G E E G	K22f		A B G B A B	H804
A Ab B Ab G A#	I 36		A B G C A F	E10
A Ab G B A G	S694		A B G C F E	T159
A B A B A B A	R137		A B G E F D	A21
A B A B A B D	L256		A B G G# A A	P280
A B A B A B F#	S1597		A Bb A A D F	H560
A B A B B A	B37		A Bb C Eb G C	S901
A B A B C D	T304		A C A C A E	R409
A B A B G C	H740		A C B A C B	H847
A B A D C B	D33		A C B A G C	B1094
A B A E A G#	D203		A C B C D E	K99
A B A E G A	D18		A C B G A C	D161
A B A G A C	S69		A C C A G F	G27
A B A G F E	D85		A C C D C D	M392
A B A G# A B	H486		A C D E E C	D223b
A B B A C C	S1506		A C D E F G	T305
A B B C D E	R428		A C D E G F#	I 57

Bb Bb C Bb Bb C	R195
Bb Bb C Bb G Bb	D72
Bb Bb C Db C Bb	F6
Bb Bb C Db Eb Db	F6
Bb C Bb F G F	C65
Bb C D D Eb D	M79
Bb C D Eb D C	F2
Bb C E D F E	S1393
Bb C F Bb Eb Bb	V38
Bb C F Eb D C	P222
Bb C G Ab Bb C	S1044
Bb C G C Bb G	S957
Bb G Bb G Bb Ab	T195
Bb G F Eb F G	V11
C A A B C G	H613
C A A C D F	R400
C A A F D A	B1287
C A Ab G F# F	D261e
C A B A G E	G159
C A B B C B	M182
C A B C A B	S1104
C A B C B A	K100
C A B C C G	S395
C A B C D E F E C	G12
C A B C D E F E E	T110
C A B C E G	W148
C A B C Eb D	B1201
C A B C G A	R226
C A B C G F	B1742
C A B E C A	D108
C A B G A F	H623
C A B G C A	G251
C A C A C A	D222
C A C A G E	T93
C A C D A A	I88
C A C D E C E	B1333
C A C E G A	C101
C A E F# E F#	M459
C A F D G B	B881
C A F E F D	W157
C A G A B G	H85
C A G A C A	S246
C A G A E C	R159
C A G B A G	S677
C A G C A G	C139
C A G C D A	V49
C A G C D E	C3
C A G C F G	B660a
C A G D E F	I41
C A G E B C	P253
C A G E C D E F	W75
C A G E D C	W42
C A G E D E	C103
C A G E G C	G213
C A G F E C C	S1418
C A G F E C G	W34
C A G F E D	R423
C A G F E F	G193
C A G F E G	S1542
C Ab G F Eb D	P175
C A G F# G C	S466
C A G F# G E	B604
C A G G A B	B1466
C A G G F E	S753
C A G G G G	A12
C A G# A C F	K115
C Ab B A C Ab	C447
C Ab Bb C Db F	E63
C Ab C Ab C Ab	S1508
C Ab C D C Ab	B1176
C Ab C G F Ab	B1433
C Ab F D C C	B454d
C Ab D Eb F C	L77
C Ab F G Eb F	B935
C Ab G B C C#	W85
C Ab G C B C	V63
C Ab G D D F	B1430
C Ab G D E C	S580
C Ab G Eb D G	S802
C Ab G Eb F D	V175
C Ab G F B A	H139
C Ab G F C Ab	M260
C Ab G F Eb Ab	C315
C Ab G F Eb D	B53
C Ab G F#	W85
C Ab G F# Ab B	S1535
C Ab G F# F# G	B1531
C Ab G F# G B	S605
C B A A A F#	H436
C B A A G A	S1354
C B A A G F	P46
C B A A G F#	W268
C B A B A G A	W129
C B A B A G C	G80
C B A B A G F	B474
C B A B C B A	D261d

C B A G F E F G A	M737
C B A G F E F G E	B390
C B A G F E G Bb	B1064
C B A G F E G Bb	B1062
C B A G F E G D	H15
C B A G F F E	B1486
C B A G F F F	H704
C B A G F G A	M88
C B A G F G Bb	H738
C B A G F G C	B1645
C B A G F# A	W256
C B A G F# F D	S1167
C B A G F# F E	W14
C B A G F# G A	M857
C B A G F# G B	C355
C B A G F# G C	A80
C B A G F# G E	S514
C B A G F# G F#	V39
C B A G G A A	L276
C B A G G A G	S1436
C B A G G E F	B1219
C B A G G E G	H431
C B A G G G A	T220
C B A G G G C	B963
C B A G G G G A	D347
C B A G G G G F	M560
C B A G G# A A	O9
C B A G G# A E	B776
C B A Gb Ab F	S268
C B A G# A B	T128
C B Ab B G G	B1135
C B Ab G C B	B656
C B Ab G F E	L186
C B A# B Bb A	F227
C B B A A G G A	T258
C B B A A G G F	B1013
C B B A B A	S1291
C B B A C B	A72
C B B B C C C E G	B799
C B B B C C C E G	B675
C B B Bb A Ab	T255
C B B Bb Bb A	R26
C B B Bb Bb Bbb	P189
C B B C B B	S404
C B B C C B	D135
C B B C C C	M158
C B B C G A	S1267
C B B G A B	C394

C B Bb A Ab Ab	V16
C B Bb A Ab C	R319
C B Bb A Ab G Bb	R246
C B Bb A Ab G C B	S1664
C B Bb A Ab G C B	S339
C B Bb A Ab G C B	B1230
C B Bb A Ab G C D	P93
C B Bb A E D	M222
C B Bb A F E	B641
C B Bb A G F	B107
C B Bb Ab G F	K45
C B Bb D Gb	D40
C B Bb Eb E F	H80
C B Bb F D F	T297
C B C A B A	F47
C B C A B C A	T210
C B C A B C D E	S438
C B C A B C D G	H56
C B C A B G A A	B1104
C B C A B G A F	G78α
C B C A C A	S571
C B C A C B	R64
C B C A C G	M70
C B C A F C#	W44
C B C A G A E	B1478
C B C A G A G	S1093
C B C A G E	G111
C B C A G F	B1023
C B C A G# A	B590
C B C B A B A G A	L264
C B C B A B A G A	C402
C B C B A B A G F	P198
C B C B A C	C398
C B C B A E	M136
C B C B A F#	K4
C B C B A G A C	C93
C B C B A G A F#	P314
C B C B A G A G F	A23
C B C B A G A G F	G155
C B C B A G A G G	H632
C B C B A G Eb	F80
C B C B A G F E D	T208
C B C B A G F E F	G73
C B C B A# B	T243
C B C B Bb A	C209
C B C B Bb B	R47
C B C B C A	M110

C C Bb G Bb C	V51
C C Bb G C Bb	M131
C C Bb G F G	C99
C C C A A A	C71
C C C A A A	W98
C C C A A C	S1231
C C C A C C	C98
C C C A G A	K22b
C C C Ab Ab Ab	B1336
C C C Ab F G	S618
C C C Ab G F#	P159
C C C B A B C C C#	S473
C C C B A B C C E	B670
C C C B A B C D	G176
C C C B A G A B	R225
C C C B A G A G	M989
C C C B A G F# G	S1629d
C C C B A G F# G	L133
C C C B A G G	G63
C C C B Ab G	R322
C C C B B A A A	B564
C C C B B A A G	H316
C C C B B A#	H733
C C C B B B A	M928
C C C B B B G	B1735
C C C B B Bb	T217
C C C B B C	V149
C C C B Bb Bb	S1590
C C C B C A	S93
C C C B C B	S1004
C C C B C C	D44
C C C B C D C E	S1430
C C C B C D C F	B365
C C C B C D D	M994
C C C B E E	S1265
C C C B F F	R429
C C C B G G	G300
C C C Bb A Ab	B1796
C C C Bb Ab Ab	M313
C C C Bb Ab G F Eb D	R102
C C C Bb Ab G F Eb Db	L204
C C C Bb C Bb	L149
C C C Bb Eb F	B1828
C C C C B A C	S400
C C C C B A G A	H673
C C C C B A G B	M367
C C C C B A G G	S1024
C C C C B A#	B1669

C C C C B B B	S1522
C C C C B B G	S1388
C C C C B Bb	H831
C C C C B C B	M538
C C C C B C C B	H799
C C C C B C C C	M641
C C C C B C D C B A	M968
C C C C B C D C B C	S1017
C C C C B C D C Bb	S854
C C C C B C D Eb	L242
C C C C B C D G Ab	T29
C C C C B C D G D	H12
C C C C B C E	M485
C C C C B D A	D55
C C C C B D C B	L46
C C C C B D C E D	M975
C C C C B D C E D	S665
C C C C B D C E E	T92
C C C C B F	M768
C C C C B G	M952
C C C C Bb A	S1668
C C C C Bb Bb Bb	G58
C C C C Bb Bb C	K84
C C C C Bb F	P293
C C C C C A A	B1186
C C C C C A B	S749
C C C C C A F	M917
C C C C C Ab	M402
C C C C C B A	C157
C C C C C B B	P141
C C C C C B C C	M894
C C C C C B C D	M968
C C C C C C A	H307
C C C C C C B B Ab	C370
C C C C C C B B Eb	B202
C C C C C C B C	M408
C C C C C C B D B	M578
C C C C C C B D C	C435
C C C C C C B G	V167
C C C C C C Bb	C407
C C C C C C C A	H55
C C C C C C C B B	S1310
C C C C C C C B C	T111k
C C C C C C C C A A	R204
C C C C C C C C A G	C439
C C C C C C C C Ab	W264
C C C C C C C C B A	S33
C8 B G#	T117

C E G G G C G	H515	C Eb D C B C D C D	R13
C E G G G G A B	S550	C Eb D C B C D C Eb	B216
C E G G G G A G	G57	C Eb D C B C G	B1415
C E G G G G C	T111c	C Eb D C Bb Ab Bb	L84
C E G G G G G	M858	C Eb D C Bb Ab G	V141
C E G G G G#	P321	C Eb D C Bb C	K13
C E Gb G Bb Cb	S266	C Eb D C C B	B216
C Eb Ab B Eb F#	S229	C Eb D C C C B C C	S1573
C Eb Ab F# B G	P212	C Eb D C C C B C G	H163
C Eb Ab G F D	B1556	C Eb D C C C D	H526
C Eb Ab G F# Eb	M496	C Eb D C C C Eb	H41
C Eb B B C G	R426	C Eb D C C Eb	F122
C Eb B C D Eb	V165a	C Eb D C C G	H152
C Eb B C D F	H349	C Eb D C D Bb Ab	E12
C Eb B C G C	S496	C Eb D C D Bb C	G78e
C Eb B D C Eb	T1	C Eb D C D C	S1521e
C Eb B G B C	H341	C Eb D C D F	C555
C Eb Bb C Bb Eb	B1203	C Eb D C D G	V57
C Eb Bb Eb G F	E43	C Eb D C Eb D D	S1179
C Eb C A A C	H118	C Eb D C Eb D G	G228
C Eb C B D C	B678	C Eb D C G A	T231
C Eb C B D G C	G143	C Eb D C G Ab	H386
C Eb C B D G G	B1034	C Eb D C G C Eb	V122
C Eb C D C Eb	M390	C Eb D C G C G	B82
C Eb C D Eb Ab	S14	C Eb D C G C G	V162
C Eb C D Eb D	S47	C Eb D C G D	B100
C Eb C D F C	B1174	C Eb D C G F Eb	F226
C Eb C Eb C Eb	D463	C Eb D C G F G	T75
C Eb C Eb C G	R409	C Eb D C G G	T75
C Eb C Eb D C	S792	C Eb D D C B	C533
C Eb C Eb F G	C491	C Eb D D C C	S562
C Eb C F C F#	B1179	C Eb D D C Eb	F140
C Eb C G C Bb	H172	C Eb D D D F	B400
C Eb C G C Eb	B93	C Eb D D Eb Gb	F191
C Eb C G C G Eb G Eb C	B178	C Eb D D F E	B122
C Eb C G C G Eb G Eb C	B218	C Eb D D G F	H79
C Eb C G Eb Ab	F132	C Eb D Eb C D	B94
C Eb C Gb Ab Bb	S1448	C Eb D Eb C Eb	B303
C Eb D A Ab B	B482	C Eb D Eb C G Ab	B539
C Eb D Ab G C	B173	C Eb D Eb C G D	B248
C Eb D B C D	T61	C Eb D Eb C G Eb	H769
C Eb D B G B	B812	C Eb D Eb D C C	S1358
C Eb D C Ab B	B1544	C Eb D Eb D C D C Eb	L99
C Eb D C Ab C	P114	C Eb D Eb D C D C G	W153
C Eb D C Ab G	G99	C Eb D Eb G C	M638
C Eb D C B A G C	C522	C Eb D F Eb G F Ab	S538
C Eb D C B A G G	B1711h	C Eb D F Eb G F Ab G Ab	P356
		C Eb D F Eb G F Ab G C	B364

C G D A C D	V3
C G D C D C	C111
C G D C G D	D63
C G D C G G	P78
C G D Eb Ab F	S287
C G D Eb D C	P325
C G D Eb F Eb D C D	I 22
C G D Eb F Eb D C G	C510
C G D F E G	D188
C G D G E B	F76b
C G D G E C	S903
C G D G E D	P67
C G D G E G	D184
C G E A G A	B986
C G E A G C	W265
C G E C A F	B334
C G E C A G D	H129
C G E C A G E	N21
C G E C C B A	H492
C G E C C B F	G221
C G E C C B G	B399
C G E C C C	M871
C G E C D E F E D C	S914
C G E C D E F E D D	W51
C G E C D E F E D G	W60
C G E C D G F	P63
C G E C D G G	D183
C G E C E G	M441
C G E C F C	B639
C G E C F F	M948
C G E C F# C	R418
C G E C G A B	I 70
C G E C G A F	H187
C G E C G C B	T114
C G E C G C E	B857
C G E C G C G F	H593
C G E C G C G G	H614
C G E C G E C D D	M529
C G E C G E C D Eb	S1595
C G E C G E C E	P64
C G E C G E C G E C	B699
C G E C G E C G E F	B1586
C G E C G E E C	D223c
C G E C G E E D	T118c
C G E C G E G	C151
C G E C G F E D C	M482
C G E C G F E D E	T118f
C G E C G F G	M886

C G E C G G	M523
C G E C# Bb Gb	H290
C G E D B A	H771
C G E D C B A	S225
C G E D C B D	M970
C G E D C B F	M984
C G E D C C B	G177
C G E D C C C	M610
C G E D C D D	B961
C G E D C D E	D388
C G E D C E	S261
C G E D C F	L309
C G E D C G C C D	H126
C G E D C G C C G	M76
C G E D C G E	M956
C G E D C G Eb	B1619
C G E D C G G	M815
C G E D E F	C160
C G E D E G C	B321
C G E D E G F	L100
C G E Db F E	S270
C G E E C G E	W234
C G E E C G G	M876
C G E E D A	W224
C G E E D G	M915
C G E E E D C C	H634
C G E E E D C G	B1271
C G E E E E E	W72
C G E E E E E	W82
C G E E E E F	R120
C G E E G G	B1337
C G E F A G C	M541
C G E F A G E	S546
C G E F D C G A	M786
C G E F D C G G	M771
C G E F D E	M885
C G E F F D	H291
C G E F G A	H54
C G E F G D	H127
C G E F G E D	G30
C G E F G E F	B36
C G E F G E G	R257
C G E F# G E	F79
C G E G B G	B341
C G E G C E C	M572
C G E G C E C#	W249
C G E G C E E	S337
C G E G C E G	M804

E D C D E F G G	S952	
E D C D E G A	D116	
E D C D E G E	B508	
E D C D E G F	B1647	
E D C D G A	S628	
E D C D G G	E70	
E D C E D C B	T87	
E D C E D C D C B	B999	
E D C E D C D C D	S1011	
E D C E D C E D	V110	
E D C E D C E F	K36	
E D C E D C F E D	W17	
E D C E D C F E Eb	G335	
E D C E D C G	T246	
E D C E D G	R262	
E D C E E D	B1835	
E D C E F C	R209	
E D C E G A B	F69	
E D C E G A G	S481	
E D C E G C	C264	
E D C F Ab G	V97	
E D C F B C	P160	
E D C F E D A	S620	
E D C F E D C A	H449	
E D C F E D C Ab	R1573	
E D C F E D C G	F128	
E D C F E D D	B1698	
E D C F E D G A	M697	
E D C F E D G B	T269	
E D C F E E	F169	
E D C F F E	C437	
E D C F G E	V120	
E D C F# G A	D261b	
E D C G A B	H243	
E D C G A Bb	L50	
E D C G A G	S163	
E D C G B A	C345	
E D C G C Bb	H311	
E D C G C D	P176	
E D C G C E	M604	
E D C G D E	B1594	
E D C G E C	W245	
E D C G E D C G E D	C312	
E D C G E D C G E D	S542	
E D C G E D E	B1565	
E D C G F E A A	H183	
E D C G F E A C	S664	

E D C G F E Bb	S1450
E D C G F E C	H616
E D C G F E D	M289
E D C G G A	B1750
E D C G G F	B1552
E D C G G G E	V81
E D C G G G E Eb	B1787
E D C# C# C# C#	S439
E D C# D E F	S996
E D D C C B B A A	C356
E D D C C B B A C	N12
E D D C C B D	S1447
E D D C C D D C	S1530
E D D C C D D G	B1387
E D D C C F	P35
E D D C E E	B1117f
E D D C G A	M248
E D D C G G	B1398
E D D D C C	D387
E D D D D E	T149
E D D E C A B	H502
E D D E F D	B1025
E D D F E E	R79
E D D F F E	I95
E D E A B C B	R41
E D E A B C C#	T278
E D E A D E	C140
E D E A E D	D218
E D E B A E	R163
E D E B C D	B1363
E D E C B C	S772
E D E C D B	B538
E D E C D E	S133
E D E C E B	P94
E D E C F D	B545
E D E C G G A	B435
E D E C G G C	C470
E D E D C B	M180
E D E D C D	S194
E D E D C G	B1414
E D E D E D C	D67
E D E D E D E	T118q
E D E D E F D	S702
E D E D E F E	B703
E D E D E F G	S413
E D E D E G E	I58
E D E D E G G	M91
E D E D F E	M100

E F F# G G F	B1640	E F G A G A G F E F	D10
E F F# G G F#	B92	E F G A G D	T136d
E F F# G G# A	P210	E F G A G E C	V136
E F G A A B	M82	E F G A G E D	R345
E F G A A D	B557	E F G A G E D#	T111k
E F G A A E	F198	E F G A G E F G A	G154
E F G A A G	I76	E F G A G E F G F	C185
E F G A B C B A G	C36	E F G A G E G	S151
E F G A B C B A G F	S868	E F G A G F E C	A79
E F G A B C B A G F	M757	E F G A G F E D C B	D305
E F G A B C C C#	B888	E F G A G F E D C E	S584a
E F G A B C C D C	F27	E F G A G F E D E	B862
E F G A B C C D E	B920	E F G A G F E D F	T62
E F G A B C D C	M723	E F G A G F E F	M419
E F G A B C D E E	G174	E F G A G F G C	B236
E F G A B C D E F F#	B743	E F G A G F G E	G62
E F G A B C D E F F#	S899	E F G A G F#	C242
E F G A B C D E F G	H864	E F G A G G	M151
E F G A B C D E G	T183	E F G Ab Bb C	B1761
E F G A B C D F	W183	E F G Ab G Ab	C49
E F G A B C E D	S257	E F G Ab G B	S1252
E F G A B C E E	S164	E F G Ab G F	D81
E F G A B C G A	M937	E F G B A D	S1617
E F G A B C G F E D	B549	E F G B A F	S1277
E F G A B C G F E D	R121	E F G B C A	S1428
E F G A B D	S1489	E F G Bb A D	B119
E F G A Bb Bb	F72	E F G C A C	S953
E F G A C A	V70	E F G C A G	H437
E F G A C B C	E58	E F G C B A	M264
E F G A C B G	H390	E F G C B B	B782
E F G A D C	D214	E F G C B C A	M6
E F G A D D	S680	E F G C B C C	B209
E F G A D E F G C C	B63	E F G C B C F	B813
E F G A D E F G C D	M522	E F G C B C G	E87
E F G A D E F G E	S613	E F G C B D	L175
E F G A E D	B63	E F G C C A	C441
E F G A E G	T186	E F G C C B	C511
E F G A F D	T101	E F G C C C A	S350
E F G A F G C	B222	E F G C C C B A F	G112
E F G A F G E	B788	E F G C C C B A G	L202
E F G A G A B A	R308	E F G C C C C	S157
E F G A G A B C B	H81	E F G C C C D	H19
E F G A G A B C D	L286	E F G C C E A	S1323
E F G A G A B C G	B749	E F G C C E D	H521
E F G A G A G A	S1101	E F G C D B	B183
E F G A G A G C	T33	E F G C D D	M784
E F G A G A G C	P73	E F G C D E A	S555
E F G A G A G F E D	R270	E F G C D E D	S1271

Notation	Ref	Notation	Ref
G C G G G G F G Ab Bb	K105	G D E C D E	C579
G C G G G G F G Ab C	G1	G D E D C B	C237
G C G G G G	P296	G D E E A C	E75
G C G G# A A	B1653	G D E F E D C	G26
G C G G# A E	B1384	G D E F E D G	H806
G C G# A D F	M279	G D E F F# G C	M234
G C G# E E D	B1096	G D E F F# G D	P18
G C# D E D C#	K57	G D E F G A	F91
G D A E D C	W158	G D E F G Ab	M8
G D A G C B	T133	G D E G C D	H35
G D Ab Ab C F	D351	G D E G D E	R298
G D B A B G	T136c	G D E G E G	P101
G D B C B A	S155	G D E G F E	P113α
G D B G D B	S1595	G D Eb B C D	M304
G D C	D63	G D Eb B C G	B982
G D C B A G	M676	G D Eb Bb A E	K60
G D C Bb A G	P89	G D Eb Bb Bbb Fb	K60
G D C D B C	S118	G D Eb Bb C Ab	M46
G D C D E D	C279	G D Eb C B C	H166
G D C D E E	B354	G D Eb C D B	C246
G D C D Eb D	R164	G D Eb C F# D	B1785
G D C Eb G D	S755	G D Eb D Eb C	T60
G D C G D C	B1208	G D Eb D F Ab	B1572
G D C G F A	T95	G D Eb Eb D Ab	L220
G D C# D C# D	T156	G D Eb F E F	S781
G D C# D D E	B1688	G D Eb F Eb C	B1480
G D D C D D#	B909	G D Eb F Eb D	S1128
G D D C Eb D	P240	G D Eb F Eb G	T226
G D D D C D C	N27	G D Eb F G F	R398
G D D D C D E	L38	G D Eb Fb Gb Eb	S870e
G D D D D E	S1494	G D Eb G Eb D	G16
G D D D D G	B735	G D F A C G	M25
G D D D E G	M298	G D F A E B	E23
G D D D G Bb	P138	G D F C D Eb B	R406
G D D E C D	B1158	G D F C D Eb F	T312
G D D E C E	M479	G D F C E D	W24
G D D E D C	O14	G D F E B D	S1319
G D D E G F#	N3	G D F Eb Ab C	T147
G D D Eb Eb Eb	L298	G D F Eb C Bb Ab	B1558
G D D Eb Eb F	B1595	G D F Eb D C Bb Ab Ab	D411
G D D F Eb D	K82	G D F Eb D C Bb Ab Bb	T272
G D D G D D	S1584	G D F Eb D C Bb Ab G	T272
G D D G E C	I67	G D F Eb D Eb	L297
G D D G E E	C436	G D G A B C	B650α
G D Db Ab G	H797	G D G A G D	L222
G D E B D Bb	R420	G D G C F# F	R150
G D E C A F	L299	G D G D C G	B1124
G D E C D B	T48	G D G D F G	T122α

G E E G E E	S1335
G E E G E F	M668
G E E G E G	B1509
G E E G F E E	S1366
G E E G F E F	H462
G E E G F E G	S1236
G E E G F G	H279
G E E G G A	S860
G E Eb D C G	P208
G E Eb F# F# A	S1669
G E F A D F	M490
G E F A G C	B1109
G E F A G E	D171
G E F A G F E D C	D453
G E F A G F E D C B	S568
G E F A G F E D G#	C88
G E F A G F E E	M434
G E F A G G	M612
G E F Ab G E	D118
G E F D B F#	B852
G E F D C E	M657
G E F D C G C	B937
G E F D C G E	H467
G E F D D D	C292
G E F D D E	M890
G E F D E C	T71
G E F D E D	H539
G E F D E G	S784
G E F D G E	Q5
G E F E A	C307
G E F E C B	B1756
G E F E C D	F77
G E F E D C D B	B260
G E F E D C D E	R349
G E F E D C G	S1564
G E F E D G E	C328
G E F E D G G	B1154
G E F E D# E	A51
G E F E E A	D306
G E F E F G A	B579
G E F E F G G	B1217
G E F F D E	S228
G E F F# A Ab	D139
G E F F# G E	S1152
G E F G A A B	F120
G E F G A A G	B1239
G E F G A B C	W26
G E F G A B D	M73

G E F G A C	E52
G E F G A D E C	B830
G E F G A D E F	H487
G E F G A F	M891
G E F G A G C	M394
G E F G A G G	G5
G E F G Ab E	I 48
G E F G B C	C275
G E F G C B A G F	H842
G E F G C B A G G	J19
G E F G C C B A	G144
G E F G C C B C	B679g
G E F G C C C	B289
G E F G C G	T118r
G E F G E C	B1002
G E F G E D	M341
G E F G E E	E34
G E F G E F	H348
G E F G E G	S1168
G E F G F E D E C	I 23
G E F G F E D E D	F56
G E F G F E D E F	M864
G E F G G A B	M652
G E F G G A Bb	B149
G E F G G A G	R72
G E F G G C	H305
G E F G G E A	W95
G E F G G E D	S61
G E F G G E F	V159
G E F G G F	G86
G E F G G G B	M466
G E F G G G C	M553
G E F# D# D# E	P124
G E F# G B A	G242
G E G	S564
G E G A B C	P288
G E G A D Ab	S851
G E G A D E F	T176
G E G A D E G	D23
G E G A E G	S1302
G E G A F A	W294
G E G B C C	S502
G E G Bb Ab G	B1446
G E G C A B	M81
G E G C B A G	C219
G E G C B A G#	S480
G E G C B C D D	H444
G E G C B C D E	A2

INDEX OF TITLES